P9-AFW-056

s

COMPASS AMERICAN GUIDES
An imprint of Fodor's Travel

YELLOWSTONE
and Grand Teton
National Parks

BY BRIAN KEVIN · PHOTOGRAPHY BY JEFF VANUGA

JACKSON HOLE

TETON RANGE

Jenny Lake

Jackson Lake

Yellowstone
Lake

Lake Village

ABSAROKA RANGE

Yellowstone
Falls

LAMAR VALLEY

Tower-Rooseve

17

1 Jackson
2 Teton Village
3 Jackson Hole Ski Area
4 South Teton
5 Teewinot Mountain
6 Grand Teton
7 Mount Moran
8 Traverse Peak
9 West Thumb Geyser Basin
10 Great Fountain Geyser
11 Grand Prismatic Spring
12 West Yellowstone and
West Entrance
13 Upper and Lower Falls
14 Norris Geyser Basin
15 Mammoth Hot Springs
16 Gardiner and
North Entrance
17 Tower-Roosevelt

PANORAMA VIEW OF
YELLOWSTONE AND JACKSON
HOLE, LOOKING SOUTH

PITCHSTONE PLATEAU

Shoshone Lake

Grant Village

9

Old Faithful

10

11

Madison

12

14

Norris

13

GALLATIN RANGE

Canyon Village

Mammoth Hot Springs

15

16

BERANN

Bison warm themselves
at a thermal pool in
Yellowstone National Park.

Aspen trees in Bridger–Teton National Forest. Since aspens share one root system, a whole stand of trees will turn colors simultaneously in fall.

COMPASS AMERICAN GUIDES: Yellowstone and Grand Teton National Parks

PUBLISHER: Amanda D'Acierno, *Senior Vice President*
EDITORIAL: Arabella Bowen, *Editor in Chief*; Linda Cabasin, *Editorial Director*
DESIGN: Tina Malaney, *Associate Art Director*; Chie Ushio, *Senior Designer*
PHOTOGRAPHY: Jennifer Arnow, *Senior Photo Editor*; Mary Robnett, *Photo Researcher*
MAPS: Rebecca Baer, *Senior Map Editor*; Mark Stroud (Moon Street Cartography), *Cartographer*
PRODUCTION: Evangelos Vasilakis, *Associate Managing Editor*;
Angela L. McLean, *Senior Production Manager*
SALES: Jacqueline Lebow, *Sales Director*
MARKETING & PUBLICITY: Heather Dalton, *Marketing Director*; Katherine Punia, *Publicity Director*
BUSINESS & OPERATIONS: Susan Livingston, *Vice President, Strategic Business Planning*; Sue Daulton,
Vice President, Operations
FODORS.COM: Megan Bell, *Executive Director, Revenue & Business Development*; Yasmin Marinaro, *Senior
Director, Marketing & Partnerships*

EDITOR: Luke Epplin
PRODUCTION EDITOR: Carrie Parker
DESIGNERS: Tigist Getachew, Nora Rosansky, Chie Ushio
ILLUSTRATIONS: William Wu

COVER PHOTO: Famous Old Faithful Geyser at Yellowstone National Park, Wyoming, U.S.A. by
Daniel A. Leifheit/Getty Images

Fourth Edition

ISBN 978-1-101-87969-6
ISSN 1943–0094

All details in this book are based on information supplied to us at press time. Always confirm information
when it matters, especially if you're making a detour to visit a specific place. Fodor's expressly disclaims
any liability, loss, or risk, personal or otherwise, that is incurred as a consequence of the use of any of the
contents of this book.

Special Sales
This book is available at special discounts for bulk purchases for sales promotions or premiums. For more
information, email specialmarkets@penguinrandomhouse.com.

Compass American Guides, 1745 Broadway, New York, NY 10019

PRINTED IN THE UNITED STATES OF AMERICA
10 9 8 7 6 5 4 3 2 1

A petroglyph left by Greater Yellowstone's earliest inhabitants. ▶ ▶

Dedicated to my parents, who

regularly unplugged the Nintendo

and loaded me into a camper.

Contents

INTRODUCTION **15**
How to Use This Book.. 18

BEST EXPERIENCES IN YELLOWSTONE AND GRAND TETON...**20**

GREATER YELLOWSTONE'S HISTORY **44**
Yellowstone's First Inhabitants................................... 46
The Mountain Men 47
Further Exploration and the Birth of the National Park......48
Early Administration and Army Years.........................51
A Modern Park...56

YELLOWSTONE'S LOWER LOOP **60**
Old Faithful Village..66
Lake Village..86
Grant Village and West Thumb.................................100
Madison and Norris...110

YELLOWSTONE'S UPPER LOOP..................................**134**
Mammoth Hot Springs 140
Tower-Roosevelt...156
Canyon Village 168

GRAND TETON NATIONAL PARK **192**
The Shaping of Grand Teton......................................198
Exploring the Park 203
Best Hiking Trails...212
On and in the Water 217
Other Activities 223
Where to Eat 227

GATEWAY TOWNS 230

    Jackson...232

    West Yellowstone...249

    Cody..253

    Gardiner 260

WHERE TO STAY 262

    Lodges, Hotels, and Inns...................................267

    Campgrounds 280

GEOLOGY, FLORA, AND FAUNA....................... 288

    Geology 294

    Flora..297

    Fauna 304

PRACTICAL INFORMATION 316

    Best Times to Visit 318

    Communications..319

    Festivals and Seasonal Events............................320

    Getting There..324

    Getting into the Parks..326

    Getting Around 327

    Licenses and Permits 330

    Online Resources 333

    Park Publications and Other Visitor Info 334

    Safety...335

INDEX 340

From the Publisher 351
About the Author and Photographer 352

SPOTLIGHTS
Geothermal Features 118
Winter in Yellowstone 176

SIDEBARS
The Flight of the Nez Percé 50
The Long Road to Grand Teton..58
Old Faithful...80
Junior Rangers..82
A Bad Dad Tale...94
Old Yeller Buses...99
Cascade Corner...100
People in the Parks: "Digger" Jerry George, Writer...........107
Yellowstone's Painter...153
Survivor: Yellowstone..154
Don't Tell Annapolis 156
Teddy in Yellowstone 160
A Smitten Trapper..165
Backcountry 101...167
People in the Parks: Linda Young, Ranger.........................172
Rockefeller Parkway...212
People in the Parks: "Black George" Simmons,
Volunteer Ranger 216
Not Your Average Park 221
Teton Science Schools..222
America's Alps 226

Bull Market 237
People in the Parks: Shane Moore, Wildlife Filmmaker 242
The Hebgen Lake Earthquake 251
Buffalo Bill Wrangling 259
The Father of Parkitechture 269
Mission Accomplished? 273
Leave No Trace 334
Recommended Books and Films 339

MAPS AND CHARTS
Panorama View of Yellowstone and Jackson Hole,
Looking South 2–3
Orientation to Yellowstone and
Grand Teton National Parks 19
Yellowstone National Park: Lower Loop 66–67
Around Old Faithful 70
Around Yellowstone Lake 87
Madison and Norris 111
Yellowstone National Park: Upper Loop 142–143
Mammoth Hot Springs 152
Tower–Roosevelt 158
Canyon Village 169
Grand Teton National Park and Jackson Hole 205
Jackson 236
West Yellowstone 249
Downtown Cody 253
Grand Teton National Park Campgrounds at a Glance 285
Yellowstone National Park Campgrounds
at a Glance 286–287

Steep Cone Geyser in the Lower Geyser Basin, Yellowstone National Park.

Introduction

When I was a kid, my parents once drove me two hours to the Milwaukee Public Museum to see an exhibit called *Dinamation Dinosaurs*. I, like any red-blooded American seven-year-old, was deep in the throes of my dinosaur phase. *Dinamation Dinosaurs* was one of those newly popular animatronic exhibits, an "edutainment" display where giant robot brontosaurs grazed herky-jerky behind a velvet rope, sending kids with stegosaurus backpacks into paleo-pleptic spasms of glee as a voiceover explained the finer points of herbivore digestion.

Exhibits like this blew my mind, and the minds of hundreds of thousands of other kids, because they *did something*. Why stare at a pile of bones when we could watch T-rexes the size of grain elevators swinging their tails, gnashing fiberglass teeth, and roaring ferocious, prerecorded roars? Children and adults alike fell for the moving parts. Museums and science centers quickly noticed this, and they've worked hard to incorporate everything from hands-on multimedia displays to Abe Lincoln androids.

So it's not surprising to anyone who has spent some time in Yellowstone National Park that occasionally a fellow visitor will sidle up to you at a hot spring, stare for a minute or two at the simmering water, and then ask, "Does this one *do anything*?"

It does, of course. When I hear this question, I'm tempted to answer, "Why yes! It simmers at something like 160 degrees Fahrenheit for 24 hours a day, 365 days a year. It circulates superheated water by convection through miles of subterranean fissures, dissolving and depositing ancient minerals along the way. It sustains entire colonies of microscopic bacteria— great, Technicolor mats of them—that thrive in temperatures no other organism on Earth can withstand."

I might want to answer this way, but I don't. I know that all the visitor really means is that he or she would like to see a geyser erupt. And that's understandable, because, let's face it, erupting geysers are incredible.

But I also don't answer this way because to do so would obscure a more important point: the wonders of Greater Yellowstone only amplify when you actively connect with them. This could mean lacing up your hiking boots and hitting some of the park's 1,500 miles of trail. It might mean trying to wrap your brain around Ma Nature's geothermal hijinks with some help from an interpretive guide. The Yellowstone eco-system has been quietly doing its thing for a few million years now. It's only when *you* do something to engage this landscape that you acquire the truest appreciation for the mountains, the hot springs, and the wildlife.

Yellowstone National Park is the country's original hands-on multimedia exhibit. It belches, thunders, and hisses. It shifts and quakes and burns. It teems with animals, from pikas to bison. When it was established in 1872, it introduced the world to the very concept of national parks, a model that Wallace Stegner famously hailed as "the best idea we ever had." Grand Teton joined the fold a few decades later, and together the two parks contain 4,000 square miles so chock-full of edutainment that a book like this one can only hope to scratch the surface.

I was well beyond my dinosaur phase when I first glimpsed Greater Yellowstone. As a college senior on summer break I hitchhiked into the park in the late 1990s, not expecting to see much more than a crowded tourist carnival and a handful of geysers. Instead I found an infinitely rich and varied landscape, one with more room to explore than a person could cover during a lifetime of summer breaks. I've since gone back to Yellowstone and Grand Teton national parks as a tourist, a backpacker, a seasonal employee, and an eager wannabe tour guide.

And each time I pass through the entrance gates I still feel giddy and awed, like a seven-year-old at a dinosaur exhibit, gaping my way through a surreal space of nature, history, and wonder.

Brian Kevin

HOW TO USE THIS BOOK

This guide tackles the national parks in three main chapters. Yellowstone is divided into the Lower Loop (the southern part of the park, starting at Old Faithful) and Upper Loop (the northern part of the park), defined by the figure eight of the main park roads. The Grand Teton National Park chapter follows.

Each park chapter is divided into regions corresponding to park villages. Sights and activities described in each section are found in or within a half-hour's drive of those villages. Because long driving distances often separate dining options in the parks, you'll most likely find yourself eating wherever you're staying or passing through, so listings for restaurants are also included in these village-based regional sections.

All three park chapters highlight a few favorite hikes. These are listed in "sweat order," beginning with gentler strolls and working up to longer, more challenging excursions. Trailheads are readily identifiable unless otherwise noted.

The next chapter digs into the gateway towns, such as Jackson, hitting the best sights, places to eat, and town-based activities.

Finding a place to stay is best done in advance, and your location will strongly influence your park experience. For this reason, reviews of hotels, lodges, and campgrounds are organized by village or town in a single, browsable "Where to Stay" chapter. Both restaurants and accommodations are listed, using the following price categories, in descending order from most to least expensive.

RESTAURANTS
(average cost of a main course at dinner or the equivalent)

$$$$=over $25	$$$=$16–$25	$$=$10–$15	$=under $10

LODGING AND CAMPING
(a single night's peak-season rate for a standard double room)

$$$$=over $175	$$$=$101–$175	$$=$50–$100	$=under $50

Throughout the chapters, my recommendations for the best sights, activities, or places to stay and eat are indicated with a ★ icon. In the "Best Experiences" chapter that starts this guide, you'll find an at-a-glance roundup of my personal favorites and those of the photographer, Jeff Vanuga.

ORIENTATION TO YELLOWSTONE AND GRAND TETON NATIONAL PARKS

0   20 Miles

0   30 Kilometers

MAMMOTH HOT SPRINGS
Colorful, terraced springs; rare year-round visitor services.

LAMAR VALLEY
Bison and elk and wolves, oh my! Terrific area for wildlife-watching.

NORRIS GEYSER BASIN
The park's hottest and most volatile thermal basin.

CANYON VILLAGE
Breathtaking waterfalls in a vast canyon.

OLD FAITHFUL
A geothermal wonderland. Yellowstone's main visitor area, with one of the world's most famous geysers.

YELLOWSTONE LAKE
The place to go for trout fishing and paddling. The action's on the north shore.

JENNY LAKE
This lake's known for the excellent surrounding hiking trails.

JACKSON LAKE
Glacial lake that's the boaters' favorite.

GRAND TETON
The namesake in the Teton range's dramatically sharp profile.

JACKSON HOLE
River valley with picturesque pioneer buildings, great wildlife-watching—and that famous ski resort.

Bozeman
Livingston
Gardiner / North Entrance
Cooke City
Northeast Entrance
MONTANA WYOMING
UPPER LOOP
Tower-Roosevelt
West Yellowstone
West Entrance
MONTANA WYOMING
Madison
LOWER LOOP
Lake Village
East Entrance
To Cody
Grant Village
YELLOWSTONE NATIONAL PARK
South Entrance
Ashton
JOHN D. ROCKEFELLER JR. MEMORIAL PARKWAY
Tetonia
Driggs
Moran Entrance
Moran Junction
Victor
IDAHO WYOMING
GRAND TETON NATIONAL PARK
Moose Entrance
Moose
WIND RIVER RANGE
Wilson
Jackson
Hoback Junction

GALLATIN RANGE
ABSAROKA RANGE
Snake River

191
89
212
20
14 16
20
89 191 287
32
33
33
89 191 26
22
26 287

S T

EXPERIENCES

Trust us, you can't see it all in one trip. At least not without spending months, if not years, in the Greater Yellowstone area and risking a serious grandeur overdose. Not only is there so much to see, there's an incredible amount to do. To help you home in on the most memorable options, we put together a list of favorite sights and adventures that we feel should shape your itinerary. These are the parks' can't-miss experiences, the places we take our own families and friends when they come out to visit. Let the following pages be a springboard as you head out to rack up some best experiences of your own.

—Brian Kevin, *author*
—Jeff Vanuga, *photographer*

BEST
Waterfall

Lower Falls, Yellowstone; *see p. 170*

"One of the ultimate
(and rare) panoramic
views is from
Artist Point on a
summer morning, when
the falls catch the light.
At sunset, head to
the magnificent,
dizzying **Brink** of the
Lower Falls overlook."

—*Jeff Vanuga*

You might spot a rainbow over the Lower Falls. ▶▶

BEST
Backpacking

Paintbrush Divide Trail, Grand Teton;
see p. 213

"Picking the 'best' trail for backpacking is like picking the 'best' breakfast food (they're all great!), but the Paintbrush Divide stands out for **amazing alpine scenery.** It's an aerobic hike— and you might cross snowfields . . .

Teton peaks seen from the Paintbrush Divide trail. ▷ ▷

... even in late summer—but there are few places in the park where the Tetons seem to envelop you like they do at the 10,500-foot divide. Count wildflower species on your way up and stop to lounge around the glassy lakes straddling the pass. You won't be alone up here, but it's still classic Teton backcountry."

—*Brian Kevin*

The Paintbrush Divide Trail passes String Lake.

INSIDER'S PICK

Black Canyon of the Yellowstone

"Spend at least three nights hiking the Black Canyon, a great area to spot wildlife. I met my first eyeball-to-eyeball grizzly here and I'll never forget it."
—*Brian Kevin; see p. 154*

BEST
Thermal Basin

Upper Geyser Basin, Yellowstone;
see p. 71

"I've been here so many
times it's almost ridiculous,
but there's always
something new to see.
Mornings are the
best time to come—
it's showtime!
As the sun lifts, the fog
rises and the geothermal
features emerge, steaming
and bubbling.

Old Faithful Geyser in the Upper Geyser Basin. ▶▶

In spring and fall, this atmospheric microclimate is even more dramatic. Beyond Old Faithful look for spectacular, long-lasting eruptions at the Great Fountain Geyser. If time is short, visit Clepsydra Geyser, which is constantly going off. In winter (my favorite visiting season), you'll see amazing frost formations. Remember to watch where you step."

—*Jeff Vanuga*

Morning Glory Pool in the Upper Geyser Basin.

INSIDER'S PICK

Monument Geyser Basin

"An occasional steam puff is all the activity you'll see at Monument, but the backcountry basin's tall, dormant cones are striking—like a silica sculpture garden." —*Brian Kevin;* *see p. 116*

BEST
Wildlife Watching

Lamar Valley, Yellowstone; *see p. 158*

"Hordes of habitual **wolf-watchers** can't be wrong—Lamar Valley is a broad, grassy mecca for herd animals and the predators and scavengers that follow them. Pull over around dawn or dusk to spot wolves skirting the bison and elk herds. **Bears and coyotes** often lope nearby, too, waiting to move in on a kill. Places like this are why you keep binoculars in the glove box."

—*Brian Kevin*

Lamar Valley is one of the best places to see wolves. ▶ ▶

33

BEST
Lodging

Old Faithful Inn, Yellowstone; see p. 267
Jenny Lake Lodge, Grand Teton; see p. 276

"I could walk into the
Old Faithful Inn every
morning and still go
slack-jawed at the sight
of the lobby, architect
Robert Reamer's seven-
story **tribute** to
wood, air, and shadow.
Absolutely unique."

—*Brian Kevin*

The main lobby of the Old Faithful Inn. ▶▶

"If you find yourself on the porch of the Jenny Lake Lodge one night, maybe admiring the peaks of the Cathedral Group following a five-course dinner, take a minute to breathe in and savor all that woodsy opulence. The all-inclusive lodge is one of the ritziest accommodations in any national park. No wonder you have to reserve at least a year in advance."

—*Brian Kevin*

◀◀ A sitting room in Jenny Lake Lodge.

◯ INSIDER'S PICK

Yellowstone Expeditions' winter yurt camp

"After a full day on skis, nothing relaxes you like falling into a down sleeping bag in your own cozy wilderness 'yurtlet.' Though an hour in the sauna yurt helps too." —*Brian Kevin;* *see p. 191*

BEST
Scenic Route

Teton Park Road, Grand Teton; *see p. 204*

"I imagine that every 30 seconds or so, a driver somewhere on Teton Park Road says, **'Wow.'** It only takes a couple of miles to see why. Out the window to the west, the Tetons leap up from the horizon so abruptly, they're like a **pop-up display,** and you can really see the glaciers and dikes that give the range its **personality.** Killer photo-ops at each of the roadside pullouts."

—*Brian Kevin*

Teton Park Road is the drive closest to the Teton range. ▶▶

BEST
Day Hikes

Mystic Falls Trail, Yellowstone; *see p. 84*
Hidden Falls, Grand Teton; *see p. 213*

see p. 84
see p. 213

"**A waterfall** at the end of a trail is like a big piece of cake at the end of a meal, and these two are among the parks' most alluring. Both hikes are flat and short, good for kids and beginning hikers. Plus you can extend them if you have extra time and energy—the climb to the Inspiration Point overlook above **Hidden Falls** is well worth the effort and much less crowded."

—Brian Kevin

A short ride on a Jenny Lake shuttle takes hikers to Inspiration Point. ▶▶

Best Panoramic Views

Mount Washburn, Yellowstone; *see p. 173*

"Climbing Mount Washburn is a great way to get a nearly 360-degree view of Yellowstone. From the summit, you'll see a mosaic of trees and meadows, with the Teton peaks in the distance. Expansive views like this are rare in Yellowstone. In June, look for bighorn sheep and their lambs; in fall, you'll hear bugling elk."

—Jeff Vanuga

Best Campground

Slough Creek, Yellowstone; *see p. 281*

"It's worth rolling into Slough Creek first thing in the morning to beat the fishermen to the campsites along the whispering creek. This campground may be the most tranquil place you can pitch a tent in Yellowstone and still be within a few steps of your car."

—Brian Kevin

Best History Lesson

Historic Yellow Bus Tours, Yellowstone; *see p. 99*

"Tour guides in these historic cabs are founts of Yellowstone knowledge. They're also all amateur comedians—laugh at their jokes and they'll tell you anything you want to know. Itineraries aren't always fixed, so just ask if there's something you want to see."

—Brian Kevin

Best Fishing

Madison River, Yellowstone; *see p. 117*

"Don't be put off by the glut of fishermen casting lines around Madison Junction—the river runs through the wildlife-rich Madison Valley for 14 miles, and every serious Yellowstone angler has his or her own favorite stretch. Get friendly with the guides in the West Yellowstone fly shops if you want a couple of pointers on where and what they're biting." —*Brian Kevin*

Best Places to Eat in the Parks

Lake Hotel Dining Room, Yellowstone; *see p. 99*
Dornan's Chuckwagon, Grand Teton; *see p. 227*

"I like to go to the Lake Dining Room after I've been backpacking, when I'm sick of trail mix and I'm ready for a little silver-spoon treatment—the service is superb. Dornan's isn't the only place in Greater Yellowstone to do the kid-pleasing chuckwagon thing, but nobody does it as authentically as Jackson Hole's original open-air dude diner." —*Brian Kevin*

Best Lodging in Town

A Teton Treehouse, Jackson Area; *see p. 279*

"I'm not usually a B&B sort of guy, but this inn among the pines has more heart than your usual doily-and-teacup nostalgia shack. I love how the building wraps around and through the trees so you can't glimpse the whole place at once. Owners Denny and Sally know the Tetons and Jackson Hole inside out, so quiz them over home-made breakfast." —*Brian Kevin*

Greater Yellowstone's History

The aurora borealis, or northern lights, glows
in the sky over Yellowstone National Park.

FIRST PEOPLES:
Roughly 8,000
B.C.E.

**FIRST MENTION ON
A MAP:** 1797

**ESTABLISHED AS
FIRST NATIONAL
PARK:** March 1,
1872

⊙→ YELLOWSTONE'S FIRST INHABITANTS

Eleven thousand years ago, retreating ice sheets from the waning Pinedale glaciation were leading a game of ecological follow-the-leader across the Yellowstone Plateau. In the glaciers' wake came vegetation, followed by birds and small mammals. Then larger game arrived on the scene, and bands of hungry humans weren't far behind. Archaeological evidence indicates that people were occupying greater Yellowstone roughly 10,000 years ago, once they found enough animals and plants there to sustain them.

Yellowstone's first peoples were nomadic hunter-gatherers, crisscrossing the landscape to take advantage of seasonal resources and favorable climates. Blood found on stone points and other tools suggests they had broad tastes in megafauna, hunting everything from bison to elk to big cats, while dispersed pieces of Yellowstone obsidian reveal their extensive migration and trade patterns.

Throughout the last millennia, several tribes, including the Blackfeet, the Crows, and Shoshone, used the Yellowstone area as a travel corridor or hunting grounds. One Shoshone band—the Tukudika, or Sheepeater—was the only group to call the Yellowstone high country home. A peaceable group of bighorn sheep hunters, the Sheepeaters were forcibly removed by the federal government to the

Wind River Reservation in Wyoming in the 1870s. Remnants of their wickiups, or temporary shelters, still stand throughout the park. (Look for groups of aspen poles arranged in a rough pyramid.) Despite ethnocentric pioneer claims that native people feared the park's thermal features, many tribes' oral traditions reveal a spiritual reverence for the geysers and hot springs.

⊙ THE MOUNTAIN MEN

A Missouri River tributary named "Rivière des Roches Jaunes" got its first ink on the map in 1797, labeled in the language of the French trappers then making inroads into the west. The "yellow stones" in question were probably the sandstone bluffs along the river's lower reaches in what are now eastern Montana and North Dakota—not, as often assumed, the colorful cliffs of the Grand Canyon of the Yellowstone.

Meriwether Lewis (left) and William Clark (right), painted from life by Charles Wilson Peale.

The expedition led by Captain Meriwether Lewis and First Lieutenant William Clark, called the Corps of Discovery, also glimpsed part of Yellowstone's wonders. Clark followed the northern half of the Yellowstone River in 1806 on the Corps of Discovery's return trip. His party came within 50 miles of Mammoth Hot Springs, and though he had heard rumors from the Shoshone of a volcanic area to the south, he pressed on to rendezvous with Lewis at the Missouri River.

One member of the Corps, a rugged Kentucky woodsman named John Colter, stayed behind in Yellowstone country. He wanted to make a go of it trapping beavers—a growth industry at the time, as the fashion scene back east demanded a steady supply of pelts. In the winter of 1807–08, Colter became the first person of European descent to make a recorded journey through Yellowstone, the Grand Tetons, and Jackson Hole. His old friend Clark published a map of Colter's route in 1814, the first to make mention of Yellowstone Lake and the "hot spring brimstone" of the thermal basins. One hot spring Colter visited near present-day Cody acquired the nickname "Colter's Hell," a label misapplied to Yellowstone off and on ever since.

Trappers told seemingly wild tales of petrified forests and Dante-esque landscapes where steam and boiling water exploded from the earth.

Colter is popularly known as the first of the mountain men, the hardscrabble society of trappers and traders who roamed beaver-rich basins in the northern Rockies throughout the first half of the 19th century. As they trapped on behalf of established fur companies, the routes and exploits of the mountain men helped to fill in the maps and fire up the imaginations of settlers in the western territories. Trappers told seemingly wild tales of petrified forests and Dante-esque landscapes where steam and boiling water exploded from the earth. Around today's Yellowstone, infamous trappers and storytellers like Jedidiah Smith, Jim Bridger, and William Sublette have had their names applied to everything from mountain ranges to restaurant desserts.

FURTHER EXPLORATION AND THE BIRTH OF THE NATIONAL PARK

In the mid-19th century, territorial skirmishes and the U.S. Civil War deflected interest from official exploration of Yellowstone, but the 1850s did see an influx of pickax-toting prospectors. Flush with optimism from the recent California gold rush, mining parties picked up where the mountain men left off after the decline of the Eastern fur market. They added new reports to the sensational descriptions that had newspapers comparing Yellowstone to California's newly famous

Yosemite region. The miners' gilded dreams didn't materialize, but their accounts inspired a few formal expeditions, notably the three-man Folsom-Cook-Peterson expedition in 1869. An eastern magazine published the Folsom party's detailed accounts of Mammoth Hot Springs, the Grand Canyon of the Yellowstone, and the Lower Geyser Basin, conferring some "establishment cred" that miners' and trappers' tales lacked.

Two expeditions in particular brought Yellowstone into the public eye. One was led in 1870 by Henry Washburn, surveyor general of the newly created Montana Territory. With 19 men and a military escort, the Washburn party took measurements of peaks and canyons, spotted and named Old Faithful, and brought back the first sketches of Yellowstone's natural wonders. In 1871 the director of the U.S. Geological Survey, Dr. Ferdinand Hayden, led 34 men on a scientific survey of the region; his group included landscape painter Thomas Moran and photographer William Jackson. The artists' efforts, com-

Dr. Ferdinand Hayden (above) led one of the earliest scientific expeditions to Yellowstone, traveling with a pack train (left).

bined with the detailed topographic work of Hayden's team, put to rest any doubt about the truth of earlier Yellowstone claims. The expedition produced the most detailed maps to date, and Hayden returned with a team a year later for a similar survey of the Grand Tetons and Jackson Hole.

The origin myth of Yellowstone National Park involves the members of the Washburn party camped along the Madison River on

THE FLIGHT OF THE NEZ PERCÉ

Yellowstone's darkest moment came in the late summer of 1877, when the park became the setting for a dramatic chapter in the tragic flight of the Nez Percé. Fleeing a cavalry division sent to force them onto a reservation, a band of 800 Nez Percé, including women and children, fled their traditional homeland in eastern Oregon and tried to make it across the border into Canada.

After several bloody battles and escapes in Idaho and Montana, the remaining refugees crossed into Yellowstone along the Madison River in late August. Almost immediately, they encountered a small tourist party camped in the Lower Geyser Basin. The tribe took them hostage, wounding several, and crossed the plateau to a ford of the Yellowstone River near Mud Volcano. Scout and warrior parties dispersed through the park, encountering other tourists and killing two at Mammoth and Otter Creek. The Nez Percé released the hostages before escaping the park, squeaking past the Army through a slot canyon along the Clark's Fork of the Yellowstone River.

In October, a remaining 380 people were cornered by the Army less than 40 miles from the Canadian border and forced into surrender. It was here, defeated, that the Nez Percé leader Chief Joseph made his famous statement, "From where the sun now sets, I will fight no more forever." Today, the Nez Percé National Historic Trail commemorates the tribe's route across four states. Though the exact route through Yellowstone is unknown, a wayside exhibit tells the story at Nez Percé Creek south of Fountain Flats Drive.

A Nez Percé man photographed in 1907 by Edward S. Curtis.

September 19, 1870, at the foot of what has since been dubbed National Park Mountain. As the story goes, the explorers debated whether and how they might stake claims to the amazing natural features they had witnessed before deciding that the whole region should instead be set aside as a national park.

Historians have since come to doubt the story, but it is true that, upon their return, members of both expeditions began speaking out in favor of government protection of Yellowstone. The Northern Pacific Railroad supported the plan, as it hoped to cash in on the potential tourist economy. The federal government had only recently ceded the Yosemite Valley to the state of California in 1864, on the condition that it be preserved for public use and recreation, so the concept of a national park wasn't too much of a stretch. Convinced by the entreaties of the explorers, the railroad lobby, and the artful images produced by Moran and Jackson, Congress passed the Yellowstone National Park Act on March 1, 1872. The world's first national park was to be "reserved and withdrawn from settlement, occupancy, or sale," held in common "for the benefit and enjoyment of the people."

⊛ EARLY ADMINISTRATION AND ARMY YEARS

Yellowstone National Park got off to a rough start. Congress hadn't actually allocated any funds for the park's management and administration, convinced by supporters' arguments that concessionaire fees could fund the fledgling park once the Northern Pacific Railroad arrived with tourists. The unenviable and unpaid task of managing this experiment went to Nathaniel Langford, a vocal proponent of the park concept and a veteran of both the Washburn and second Hayden expeditions. Still working full-time as a bank examiner in the territories, Langford visited the park only three times before he was replaced as superintendent in 1877.

Lacking any actual caretakers, Yellowstone's first 10 years were characterized by poaching, squatting, and profiteering. Congress began providing meager funding for a civilian administration in the early 1880s, but lawlessness in Yellowstone continued. It reached a tipping point in 1886 when, after a series of inept superintendents prompted Congress to revoke the funding, the U.S. Army was placed in charge of the park. In what was supposed to be a temporary stopgap, 50 soldiers marched into Yellowstone in August of that year.

Fort Yellowstone Cavalry—the U.S. Soldiers who guard the great National Park.   Copyright 1906 by Underwood & Underwood

A 1903 photograph shows U.S. Army cavalry parading near a young Fort Yellowstone at Mammoth Hot Springs. Such soldiers helped form the role of the modern park ranger.

The Army ended up running Yellowstone for thirty years, until the National Park Service was founded in 1916.

Yellowstone's Army years represented a sea change in park management. Poachers were pursued and punished, vandalism was discouraged, and shady park entrepreneurs had a military body to answer to. The era also saw the construction of the park's Grand Loop Road and many of its soaring hotels. For the soldiers staffing Yellowstone, patrolling the two-million-acre wilderness required fortitude and long hours on the back of a horse. Because the Army initially lacked legal authority to do much more than expel a criminal from the park, punishments for vandals or poachers were creative. In some cases, soldiers would march the apprehended miscreant all the way across the park to the southern boundary, informing the offender he could pick up his confiscated posessions from Army headquarters—80 miles away, at the north entrance.

Being equal parts law enforcement, game warden, and tour guide was an awkward post for some soldiers, and desertion rates were high at first. But as the Army matured into its administrative role, Yellowstone's soldiers helped to establish the template for the modern park ranger. Their ability to adapt to a more civilian-like role helped smooth the transition when the National Park Service took over Yellowstone in 1916.

Early motorists drive past the Shoshone Dam toward Yellowstone.

On following pages: (top left) at Sapphire Pool; (bottom left) looking sharp while descending by rope into the Grand Canyon of the Yellowstone; (top right) wading in the Great Fountain Geyser; (bottom right) the first known boat on Yellowstone Lake, circa 1871.

⊙ A MODERN PARK

In 1882 the Northern Pacific railroad finally reached Livingston, Montana, and rail travel became a central element of the Yellowstone experience. By 1908 the gateway towns of Gardiner, West Yellowstone, and Cody all had train depots. The railroad companies, led by the Northern Pacific, poured money into the expanding park hotels and concessions. Visitors arrived by rail by the tens of thousands, and by the 1920s and '30s, by the hundreds of thousands. Typical Yellowstone tourists in the early 20th century were well-heeled Easterners out to play the dude. Clad in light suits, golf skirts, and linen dusters, they saw the park via stagecoach tours and stayed in lodges, while more adventurous and less affluent tourists bunked in elaborate tent camps.

Cars came to Yellowstone in 1915 and forever changed the national park experience. As Yellowstone grew increasingly autocentric, the two rings of stagecoach routes known as the Grand Loop Road became entrenched as the central means of seeing the park. The rise of the automobile and an increasingly prosperous nation kept visitation stats climbing, reaching a fever pitch in the years following World War II. Park visitation doubled from prewar numbers, surpassing a million annual visitors in 1948. Marginalized by auto traffic, the rail-

A bear cub "holdup." Lax regulations in the park's postwar era encouraged wildlife to beg for food.

YELLOWSTONE AND GRAND TETON NATIONAL PARKS

roads abandoned Gardiner, West Yellowstone, and Cody one by one. When the modern incarnation of Grand Teton National Park was established in 1950, the two linked parks became the classic American summer vacation. Visitor numbers doubled again by the mid-1960s, and today around three million people visit Yellowstone each year.

With more park visitors came more congestion on the roads, more foot traffic near the park's major attractions, and a larger commercial circus in the towns adjoining the park. The modern environmental ethic evolved—and indeed, is still evolving—in this atmosphere. Harmful wildlife practices, like the tradition allowing bears to feed in public view at park dumps, began to be phased out during the 1950s and '60s. Gradually, NPS moved toward a policy that sought to balance visitor-service demands with the needs of Yellowstone's unique ecology. Visitor education on ecological issues became a bigger priority. The growing strength of the new environmental ethic emerged in the late 1960s, when biologists initiated the first quiet calls for the reintroduction of wolves (see the Geology, Flora, and Fauna chapter).

The sweeping fires of 1988 dramatically illuminated the complex ecological relationships at work inside Yellowstone. The previous NPS policy of fire suppression had already been reformed to allow for controlled burns, but Yellowstone was long overdue for a big blaze. During the very dry summer, the accumulated fuel built up during years of misguided fire policy fed more than a dozen large and small forest fires. Despite fire crews' heroic efforts at control, the fires scorched over a third of the park before being extinguished by damp weather in the fall. You can see the fires' fascinating ecological effects today in acres of eerily beautiful "ghost forests," where new plant and animal species have gained a foothold among the maze of blackened poles.

The park's administration and advocates continue to address ecological issues of enormous complexity, everything from fire management to trout management to snowmobile management—all while debating how much "management" any given element of the Yellowstone ecosystem should receive. What characterizes the intricate decision-making processes in Yellowstone now is the tightrope effort to balance the visitor experience and the demands of conservation biology. For instance, when the park adopted a catch-and-release policy for all native game fish in 2001, that move was accompanied by a new emphasis on fish-watching as a guest activity. The search for balance in Yellowstone is perpetual.

THE LONG ROAD TO GRAND TETON

While the campaign to establish Yellowstone National Park succeeded inside of two years, the genesis of Grand Teton National Park was a strung-out affair, jampacked with power struggles and political intrigue. From its inception, the National Park Service had its eye on Jackson Hole at the Tetons, but skeptical ranchers, hunters, and homesteaders actively resisted the loss of grazing lands and the threat of commercialization. Locals got antsy, however, when the state proposed a dam on scenic Jenny Lake, and their grudging support led the way to the "first" Grand Teton National Park in 1928.

The 1928 park included only the mountains themselves and a handful of lakes in their shadow, leaving out the lion's share of Jackson Hole. Enter billionaire tycoon and philanthropist John D. Rockefeller Jr., whose visits to the valley in the 1920s convinced him of the need for federal protection. With support from the NPS, Rockefeller's Snake River Land Company spent two decades buying up Jackson Hole—

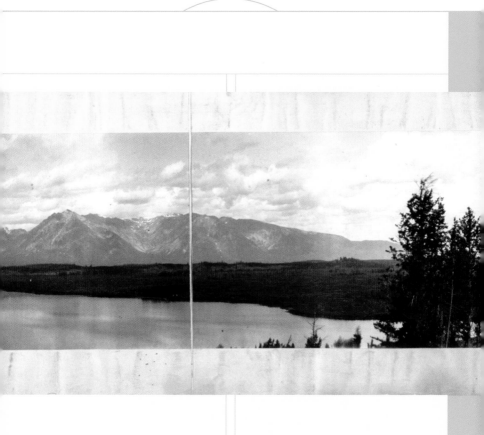

32,000 acres of it—as insurance against ranchers and developers. His repeated attempts to "gift" the land to the NPS were rebuffed by Wyoming's congressional delegation, which feared the loss of tax revenues if the valley became federal land. In 1942, a fed-up Rockefeller threatened to sell his holdings if the government wouldn't take them. This prompted President Franklin Roosevelt to establish Jackson Hole National Monument by executive order—an end-run around Congress.

Reactions from angry locals included a protest run of 500 cattle across the new monument. But dissent quieted down during World War II, and in the postwar boom, the locals heard the cash registers ringing around Yellowstone. In 1950, popular support finally led to the merging of park and monument, creating the Grand Teton National Park we know today.

A Teton panorama, with Jackson Lake in the foreground.

Yellowstone's Lower Loop

The aptly named Beauty Pool in the Upper Geyser Basin.

An evening wind buffets Castle Geyser in the Upper Geyser Basin.

Clepsydra Geyser erupting
in the Lower Geyser Basin.

OLD FAITHFUL

AMOUNT OF WATER IN AN ERUPTION:
3,700 to 8,400 gallons

AVERAGE INTERVAL: 90 minutes or so

⌖ OLD FAITHFUL VILLAGE

See the Yellowstone National Park: Lower Loop and Around Old Faithful maps.

More than any other natural features in the park, the surreal thermal basins along the Firehole River are responsible for Yellowstone's earliest and most enduring nickname, "Wonderland." The area's explosive fountains and kaleidoscopic springs make wide-eyed Alices out of even the savviest geyser-gazers. Veteran hydrogeologists and field-tripping third graders all break into dumbstruck grins when Old Faithful sends its 150-foot column of water hissing into the sky.

It's always been this way. After the genteel explorers of Henry Washburn's expedition first saw Giantess Geyser erupt in 1870, Washburn wrote, "Our usually staid and sober companions threw up their hats and shouted with ecstasy at the sight."

The Upper Geyser Basin around the Old Faithful village contains a full one-fifth of the world's geysers, with more than 200 spouters crammed into less than two square miles. This corner of the park is a global geyser clearinghouse, because it has a rare combination of an underground heat source, sufficient water, and the right plumbing system. (*See* Spotlight on Geothermal Features *and* the Geology, Flora, and Fauna chapter.) The conditions to create a geyser field like this one occur in only a handful of locations worldwide.

Exactly what Yellowstone's native groups made of these thermal wonders has been the subject of curiosity and misunderstanding since the arrival of the first fur trappers. Only recently have researchers and anthropologists begun to learn some of the stories passed on through various oral traditions. One of the most evocative tales comes from the Kiowas of Oklahoma, whose ancestral lands bordered the upper Yellowstone River. The tribe tells of a Kiowan hero led by the creator spirit, Doh Ki, across a bleak volcanic landscape in search of a homeland for his people. The tribe followed the hero through the land of steam and boiling

★ Inspiring Geyser ★

Morning Glory Pool inspired the popular children's book *Hedgie Blasts Off!*, in which a hedgehog goes to another planet to unclog a geyser clogged by space tourists' debris.

water, eventually reaching the cave known today as Dragon's Mouth. Doh Ki tested the hero by promising to give him the surrounding lands if he leapt into the bubbling spring. When the hero met the challenge, he was plucked from the scalding water to find a lush, bountiful land around him—today's Yellowstone National Park.

The early tourist trade at Old Faithful erupted with the same suddenness and force as its spouting geysers. No sooner had Yellowstone received its first federal appropriation in 1878 than a rough-and-tumble road was pushed through to the Upper Geyser Basin. Guided tours reached the basins shortly thereafter, followed by temporary camps; by 1882 the Northern Pacific Railroad was surveying the region for a possible rail line.

By 1885, Old Faithful had its first hotel, a flimsy pine structure that even Yellowstone's assistant superintendent decried as "a shack and a disgrace to the park." But such hasty development gradually tapered off, and except for a few missteps over the years (like a naval searchlight placed atop the hotel to light the geysers at night), hospitality facilities at Old Faithful were designed with an eye to the long term. The Old Faithful Inn and the Basin Store are among the oldest park structures still in use.

Observation Point is a good place to watch Old Faithful erupt from a distance.

"At the appointed hour
[at Old Faithful]... a rush, and that
glittering column
of diamonds rose...."
–Rudyard Kipling

The village today is the main tourist zone, with several places to eat and stay, two gas stations, two general stores, and a state-of-the-art visitor center unveiled in the summer of 2010. Robert Reamer's 1903 Old Faithful Inn is the crown jewel of national park lodging, looming above the geyser basin like a feudal castle. In the summer, some 25,000 visitors pass through the Old Faithful area each day, and lumbering snowcoaches from West Yellowstone and Mammoth make the rounds in winter. It's important to stay on boardwalks and trails, both for safety's sake and to protect the fragile landscape. But don't be too turned off by the crowds—the basins and backcountry in the Old Faithful region have plenty of grandeur to go around.

OLD FAITHFUL VISITOR EDUCATION CENTER

TEL:
307/344-2751

THE GEYSER BASINS

Not all of Yellowstone's geysers can be as faithful as you-know-who; prediction is an inexact science. Geysers' complex underground plumbing is affected by earthquakes and other subterranean hijinks that geologists are only beginning to understand. It's a dynamic system, where some spouters spring to life and others fall dormant with little or no warning. Upcoming predicted eruption times are sometimes posted in the basins, and the **Old Faithful Visitor Education Center** (307/344–2751) posts times for the powerhouses Old Faithful, Riverside, Daisy, Grand, Castle, and Great Fountain. The center also offers a schedule of guided geyser walks, from 10-minute strolls to half-day hikes.

Plan a half-day at the very least to walk the boardwalks of the **Upper Geyser Basin.** (It really takes two or three days at Old Faithful to see eruptions from each of the major geysers. At any given time, though, you're almost guaranteed to see some sort of geyser action.) ★**OLD FAITHFUL** is easy to pick out—it's surrounded by a huge boardwalk and a few hundred people. Across the Firehole River is **Geyser Hill,** a treasure trove of geysers large and small. Among the standouts is **Beehive Geyser,** a squat cone with enormous jets of up to 190 feet. Beehive settles in and out of periods of regularity, but you can usually count on at least one show a day during the summer. There's an indicator vent in front of the cone—when it starts steaming a full geyser blast is not far behind. **Giantess Geyser** is another prominent resident of the hill, and though she usually averages just a few magnificent eruptions per year, the roar of steam during these can be heard up to a mile away.

Grand Geyser erupts in a series of beautiful and violent spurts, capturing rainbows in its spray.

From Geyser Hill the boardwalk follows the Firehole River to the northwest, then loops back along a paved trail, with a few spurs branching off along the way. There's a viewing platform set up at **Grand Geyser,** and inevitably there's a small crowd waiting to see 200-foot bursts from the world's largest predictable geyser. Roughly every eight to nine hours, Grand erupts in a series of beautiful and violent spurts. Farther up the boardwalk, the massive cone of **Giant Geyser** looks like a surfacing whale in a sea of sinter. (The sinter, or silica deposit, has a coarse texture like tree bark.) It's the world's second-largest geyser when it erupts, with a spray that can reach 250 feet and last for an hour. Since the Hebgen Lake Earthquake in 1959, Giant has "on years" and "off years." There were only six eruptions between 1963 and 1987, more than 50 in 2007 alone, and a long dormant period that began in 2010.

YELLOWSTONE AND GRAND TETON NATIONAL PARKS

(Top left) A rare Giant Geyser eruption; (bottom left) colorful Morning Glory Pool; (this page) Riverside Geyser, on the bank of the Firehole River.

Excelsior Geyser discharges more than 4,000 gallons of boiling water into the Firehole River every minute. When active, it was the largest geyser in the world.

74

Farther along the paved trail, **Riverside Geyser** sends a 70-foot arc of water out over the Firehole River every six to seven hours, making it one of the basin's most predictable geysers, as well as one of its most beautiful. **Morning Glory Pool** is worth the walk to the pavement's end, as its concentric circles of brilliant orange and aqua signal the bacterial life that thrives in the superheated water. In the past, visitors have inconsiderately tossed coins and other items into the spring, affecting its temperature, color, and water circulation. Heading back toward the village along the paved trail, you'll pass **Castle Geyser** near a bridge over the river. Castle's whopping 12-foot cone is evidence of at least 5,000 years of continual activity, and the name bestowed by the Washburn party perfectly captures its imperial stature. It erupts two or three times a day with intervals from four to 15 hours.

You can drive to **Black Sand Basin,** a half-mile north of the Old Faithful exit, though the walking trail from the Upper Basin winds its way there as well. This is a quick stop, with thermal features more subtle than in the neighboring basins. The most alluring feature at Black Sand is not a geyser at all but **Emerald Pool,** a broad hot spring that gets its dreamy translucent greenness from cyanobacteria living on the crater walls.

Biscuit Basin (Grand Loop Rd., 2 miles north of Old Faithful) demonstrates the paradox of naming sights in such a volatile landscape. The basin was named for a cluster of funny biscuit-shaped geyserite formations that flanked the crystal-blue **Sapphire Pool.** But the major 1959 earthquake tweaked Sapphire's internal plumbing, and the once placid pool exploded with 125-foot eruptions that demolished the namesake biscuits. Today Sapphire Pool gurgles and boils but is a dormant spring once more.

Midway Geyser Basin (Grand Loop Rd., 10 miles south of Madison Junction) is the more pedestrian name for what park visitor Rudyard Kipling called "Hell's Half-Acre" in 1889. ★**GRAND PRISMATIC SPRING** is the main draw; it's the world's third-largest hot spring at more than 370 feet across. The pool's vivid red and orange colors drizzle down its runoff channels, but from the boardwalk you can glimpse only a portion of these psychedelic tentacles. For the full picture, follow a faint, unofficial "social" trail up the 250-foot **Midway Bluff,** across the highway and a quarter-mile south. There are also good photo ops along the Fairy Falls Trail (*see below*). Lest you start thinking of geysers as just cute little underground fountains, witness the massive crater around **Excelsior Geyser,** evidence of its cataclysmic eruptions before going dormant in the 1880s.

Thank the little guys:
        heat-loving microorganisms
(bacteria and algae) tint the

Grand Prismatic Spring

with a rainbow of colors.

It's like dropping a
boulder into a kiddie
pool. Great Fountain
Geyser's eruptions
can be almost as wide
as they are tall.

OLD FAITHFUL

Before Old Faithful became the world's first celebrity geyser, it was just another spouter in the Upper Geyser Basin, waiting for its big break. But this particular geyser is separated from other major features by a good 400 yards, so its unshared underground plumbing system allows for relative predictability. Members of the Washburn party noticed that consistency in 1870, and though earthquakes in 1959 and 1983 affected Old Faithful's intervals, the name the Washburn party thought up is still accurate.

Old Faithful erupts every 60 to 90 minutes, depending on the previous eruption's length. The closest viewpoint is the surrounding semicircular boardwalk. Another popular place to watch is the Inn balcony just above the carriage porch, where you can relax in a deck chair facing the geyser. There's also a seldom-mentioned second-floor vantage point that fits a few people, where the old Inn joins the east wing. For a great photo, head up Geyser Hill and stand near the Sponge and Pump geysers; you'll get the landmark Inn in the foreground. A slightly taxing half-mile walk to Observation Point puts Old Faithful's 100- to 180-foot plume against a backdrop of wooded hills.

A crowd gathers for the most popular show in Yellowstone National Park.

So many rushed visitors opt to bypass the one-way, three-mile **Firehole Lake Drive** (Grand Loop Rd., 9 miles south of Madison Junction) that you can sometimes take in its thermal wonders in relative solitude. The big dog in this southern unit of the **Lower Geyser Basin** is **Great Fountain Geyser**, which erupts in a series of angled, 100-foot bursts every nine to 11 hours (predicted at the Old Faithful Visitor Center). Even between eruptions, pools of water on the fountain's vast, tiered sinter platform are a gorgeous sight. It was here in 1869 that the Cook–Folsom party became the first "respectable" (non–Native American, non–mountain man) group to witness a Yellowstone geyser eruption. It's also worth pulling over to examine the peaceful simmering pool of **Firehole Lake and White Dome Geyser**, an erratic splasher with a 20-foot cone that looks like a pile of lumpy oatmeal.

The wide, watery explosions of **Fountain Geyser** every half-hour or so are the main attraction at **Fountain Paint Pots** (Grand Loop Rd., 8 miles south of Madison Junction), along with near-perpetual 20- to 40-foot bursts from **Clepsydra Geyser**. The namesake mud pots are the most interesting feature, though, blurping and gurgling as muddy bubbles burst, flinging flecks of confetti-like clay in all directions. Iron in the mud oxidizes at differing rates, giving some mud clumps a pinker hue than others.

Mud pots pop and gurgle in Pocket Basin.

Fountain Flat Drive (Grand Loop Rd., 6 miles south of Madison Junction) marks the northern edge of the Lower Basin. This old service road remains open to cars for about a mile, almost as far as **Ojo Caliente Hot Spring**. The deep-blue "hot eye" gives off great clouds of

JUNIOR RANGERS

A rigorous course (wink) of scientific study is all that stands between your 5- to 12-year-old and the elite status (and patch!) of a Junior Ranger. Grab a program guide from any park visitor center, then get to work completing worksheet activities, hiking a trail, and participating in a ranger-guided education program at one of the villages. (See the park newspaper for ranger-program schedules.) If one patch isn't enough, a similar Young Scientist program at the Old Faithful and Canyon visitor centers issues kids a $5 toolkit, complete with a magnifying glass and infrared thermometer for field research.

steam and discharges about a hundred gallons of water per minute into the Firehole River. Geysers and springs cluster along the riverbanks. Though a number of fishermen's trails skirt the banks, it's best to follow someone who knows where they're going through this dangerous area.

NEARBY SIGHTS

The Park Service opened the **Old Faithful Visitor Education Center** (307/344–2751) in the summer of 2010, and the stunning facility is second only to the geyser itself as a hub of activity. You can watch the famous eruptions from behind the center's floor-to-ceiling windows. Rangers give information about backcountry trips, and the Yellowstone Association runs one of the park's nicest bookstores. The center has very cool, hands-on exhibits explaining the inner workings of the park's many thermal features, and a special kids' exhibit is arranged around a giant, see-through model of a geyser's underground plumbing.

An Army lieutenant with the Washburn party in 1870 observed of the 150-foot **Kepler Cascades** (Grand Loop Rd., 2.5 miles south of Old Faithful), "[t]hese pretty little falls, if located on an eastern stream, would be celebrated in history and song; here amid objects so grand…they were passed without a halt." Halt at the roadside pull-out for a good photo opportunity, or pick your way down to a wooden bridge at the foot of the falls to feel a bit of its cool spray.

BEST HIKING TRAILS

The **Fairy Falls Trail** through Midway Geyser Basin leads you to four striking sights in an easy, very flat 6.5-mile round-trip. Start a mile south of the Midway Basin lot, at the south end of the gravel Fountain Freight Road. Right away you cross a historic steel bridge, then it's a mile along the abandoned road grade to the junction with the trail. As you pass Grand Prismatic Spring to the east, get a photo-perfect view by scrambling up the hill to your left. Leaving the gravel, the trail goes through forests hit hard by the 1988 fires. You'll hear splashing

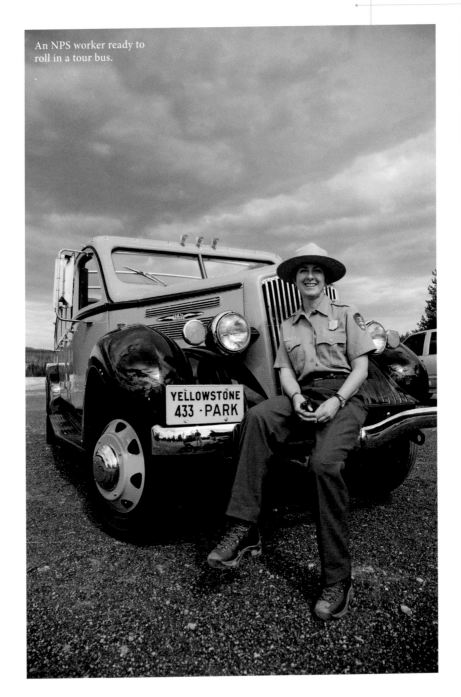

An NPS worker ready to roll in a tour bus.

YELLOWSTONE
433 · PARK

from the 197-foot falls before you see it, a delicate-looking ribbon that tumbles into a perfect swimming pool. Less than a mile ahead is the last wonder, **Imperial Geyser,** a broad blue pool that's been active throughout the 2000s.

It's just a one-mile, flat hike to the sublime namesake of the ★**MYSTIC FALLS TRAIL,** where young pines frame a tiered, 70-foot cascade as steam rises from the Little Firehole River. The whole scene, boxed in by sloping rock walls, has the feel of a secluded nook—which it can be during spring and fall, though this is a popular hike during peak season, especially with families. Shake some of the crowd by completing the whole three-mile loop, past the falls and up some moderately taxing switchbacks to an overlook at almost 8,000 feet. The loop ends back at the trailhead on the far side of Biscuit Basin, and views of steam rising from the Upper Basin are worth the effort.

An overnight hike to the **Shoshone Geyser Basin** is an opportunity to experience a boardwalk-free, backcountry thermal area without having to go off-trail. This mostly flat, nine-mile hike begins along the paved route to **Lone Star Geyser,** at the trailhead just south of the Kepler Cascades. A well-defined trail follows the upper Firehole River through unburned lodgepole, rising only mildly across the Continental Divide, then descending along quiet Shoshone Creek to the basin. The trail winds through some of the basin's remote, hundred-plus thermal features—if you choose to explore off-trail, use caution and common sense. You'll hear the waves of Shoshone Lake from inside your tent at nearby shoreline campsites.

OTHER ACTIVITIES

Cycling is a top activity around Old Faithful; you'll have more options here then anywhere else in the park. The **Bear Den** (307/545–4825) gift and gear shop at the Old Faithful Snow Lodge rents mountain bikes throughout the summer.

From Old Faithful village the paved trail through the Upper Geyser Basin meets an abandoned service road near Daisy Geyser that runs 1.5 miles to Biscuit Basin. North of the village, the Fountain Freight Road picks up where Fountain Flat Drive ends. This four-mile stretch of gravel, which once had the Monopoly-esque handle of National Park Drive, now leads bikers through elk-frequented meadows in the Lower and Middle Geyser basins.

Another good bet is the 2.5-mile ride to Lone Star Geyser. Yellowstone's Army administration built the stagecoach road to this geyser in the early 1890s, and the flat, paved, two-mile route wasn't closed to auto traffic until 1971. The geyser's isolation, consistent three-hour eruption intervals, and tanklike 11-foot cone make it one of the most enjoyable geysers to visit.

WHERE TO EAT

Geyser Grill. Funky decor gives the Geyser Grill more character than Yellowstone's other fast-food options. The room's dividing wall is shaped like a mountain, and stuffed-animal voyageurs peer over the edge of a canoe hung from the ceiling. Collect your basic burgers and breakfast sandwiches on a cafeteria tray. The first-come, first-served seating gets jam-packed during the summer, but you can always pull up some concrete on the shaded porch. *Old Faithful Snow Lodge; 307/344–7311 or 866/439–7375.* **$**

Obsidian Dining Room. A long row of east-facing windows lets in natural light during breakfast and lunch here, while candelabra shaped like pine trees glow in the evening. Rotating comfort-food specials might include goulash or lamb stew. Vegetarians can opt for polenta fritters or linguini in peanut sauce—improvements on the typical pasta-or-veggie-burger choices. The Firehole Lounge, separated from the dining room by a two-sided fireplace, serves creative appetizers and might be the only room in the park going for a sleek, contemporary look instead of the usual woodsy decor. *Old Faithful Snow Lodge; 307/344-7311 or 866/439-7375.* **$$$-$$$$**

Old Faithful Basin Store. This historic building was park entrepreneur Charles Hamilton's first commercial venture way back in 1897, and the ornate, knotty-pine facade still reads "Hamilton Store." You'll find the best budget breakfast in the village in the small cafeteria. Thick pancakes and buttery French toast are a steal at around $9. Burgers, salads, and sandwiches make up the lunch menu, and if you eat on the porch, they come with an excellent view of Geyser Hill. *Old Faithful, northwest of Inn; 307/545-7282.* **$**

Old Faithful Inn Dining Room. A massive, two-story, volcanic stone fireplace strikingly anchors this historic dining room. Original timber ceiling beams, hickory chairs, and copper chandeliers all recall the days when meals were served with silver and china, though there's no need to dress for dinner today. Buffets are at the heart of every meal, with a few sandwiches added to the lunch menu and a handful of additional entrées at night. The classic Old Faithful dinner is farm-raised bison, carved onto your plate at the buffet table. After dinner, have a cocktail at the leather-topped tables in the adjacent and equally historic Bear Pit Lounge. *Old Faithful Inn; 307/344-7311 or 866/439-7375.* **$$$-$$$$**

Old Faithful Lodge Cafeteria and Bake Shop. The cafeteria itself is a drab, fluorescent-lit cluster of lunch and dinner stations serving pizzas, pastas, and the like, but the dining space is a grand hall of pine and stone dating back to the 1920s. Settle into a woven-cane chair by the massive windows and drink in a superb view of Old Faithful. Breakfast isn't served in the cafeteria, but there's an espresso cart, and the cinnamon rolls at the tiny bakery can get you through a morning of geyser-gazing. *Old Faithful, east end of village; 307/344-7311 or 866/439-7375.* **$-$$**

 ## LAKE VILLAGE

See the Around Yellowstone Lake map.

For a while there, during the first half of the 19th century, it seemed like **Yellowstone Lake** was the one thing everybody could agree on. Early accounts from Yellowstone's mountain men, miners, and mapmakers disagreed about the directions of rivers and the sources of the implausible-sounding hot springs. But they all agreed on the lake. Trapper Jim Bridger exaggerated its size as 60 miles across, and early government cartographers wrongly drew it in the shape of an oval, but the wide expanse of Yellowstone Lake has always been a landmark to explorers.

On first glance, Yellowstone Lake seems pale and placid and permanent, a steadfast body in a landscape celebrated for unpredictability. It's an act, though. Not only is the 136-square-mile lake prone to rough water and sudden storms, but on the scale of geologic time it's perhaps the park's most dynamic feature. It once extended all the way into Hayden Valley, some 10 miles north, and geologists once suspected that it originally discharged to the south, joining the Snake River and, eventually, the Pacific Ocean. Scientists doubt that today, and the lake drains north, via the Yellowstone River, eventually reaching the Atlantic via the Missouri and Mississippi. After the last Ice Age, ice dams broke at the mouth of the lake, releasing catastrophic floods that carved the deep Yellowstone Canyon. Since the mid-1990s, scientists have monitored rising underwater magma domes in the lake's northern reaches, features that are slowly "tipping" the lake, enlarging beaches on the north shore, and flooding formerly dry areas to the south.

"No other lake in North America
of equal area lies so high as
the Yellowstone,
or gives birth to so noble a river."
– *John Muir*

The bison herds in Hayden Valley are most impressive from mid-July to August, when burly males try to out-macho one another by locking horns and kicking up dust.

Hayden Valley's Crater Hills Geyser is a rare sight, as it's off-trail in grizzly-bear habitat.

A BAD DAD TALE

"There is one story—totally uncon-firmed—of a father trying to place his young daughter on a bison's back. It is said that the father was injured. I like to think he was beaten savagely by onlook-ers, but that probably didn't happen. . . ."

—Tim Cahill, *Lost in My Own Backyard: A Walk in Yellowstone National Park,* 2004

These days, the lake's north shore has all the action, with the historic **Lake Village,** the bustling marina at Bridge Bay, and the gaggles of sightseers at Fishing Bridge and its visitor center. Summer visitors to Lake Yellowstone should expect heavy traffic and plan to stop frequently at the many lake overlooks between West Thumb and Bridge Bay. By contrast, the land south of the lake is some of the park's most remote country, where a long backpacking trip brings you as far from a paved road as you can get in the continental United States.

NEARBY SIGHTS

The thermal grotto at **Mud Volcano** (Canyon–Lake Rd., 6 miles north of Fishing Bridge) is dwarfed by those sur-rounding Old Faithful, but its springs and fumaroles have as much character as any of the park's thermal features. The sharp smell of sulfur hits you hard as you approach the basin's namesake. Mud Gey-ser was once a powerful 30-foot cone, but sometime before 1872 a particularly vicious eruption blew the cone away, leaving only a muddy, gurgling crater.

Along the same boardwalk is **Dragon's Mouth Spring,** a cave that audibly roars as seething waters crash against its cavern walls. Farther up the hill, the mesmerizing **Churning Cauldron** stews at an average temperature of 164 degrees Fahrenheit, sloshing and steaming as if a monster might emerge at any minute. **Sour Lake** spreads out behind the basin's boardwalks. The bluish pool looks innocent enough, but a submerged forest of dead trees attests to a pH level somewhere in the neighborhood of battery acid. Set aside at least an hour to see and smell everything in this area.

Just north of Mud Volcano, the landscape opens up into a treeless plain once drowned beneath the swollen waters of glacial Yellowstone Lake. **Hayden Valley** is one of the park's finest spots for wildlife-watching in any season; in summer it's a hangout for grizzlies, elk, wolves, and especially bison. The herds are most impressive from mid-July to August, when bison from throughout the park congregate in the valley for the rut, or breeding season, burly males trying to out-macho one another by locking horns and kicking up dust. The Yellowstone River meanders through the grassland; here you might spot pelicans and cranes, as well as a few families of river otters. Dusk and dawn are the best times for viewing, though the roadside pull-offs stay full throughout the day. Don't expect to pass through Hayden Valley in a hurry—if the bison aren't causing traffic jams then the people watching them are.

At **Fishing Bridge** (East Entrance Rd., .5 mile south of Grand Loop Junction) the Yellowstone River leaves the lake to wind north toward Canyon. The current log-and-concrete bridge, with pedestrian walkways, went up in the late 1930s. Critical cutthroat spawning grounds made this a popular place to wet a line for decades, and ironically, it's also why the area was closed to fishing in 1973. Grizzlies love trout almost as much as fishermen, though, and you may spot a bruin or two from the bridge in early summer. The **Fishing Bridge Visitor Center** (307/344–2450) is an impressive gabled hut made of hewn logs and boulders the size of easy chairs. Inside is a circus of taxidermy, one of the few places you're likely to see a legally mounted bald eagle or trumpeter swan.

You can find some great souvenir bargains on the second floor of the **Fishing Bridge General Store** (East Entrance Rd. at Fishing Bridge; 307/242–7200), a "sale loft" of discounted grizzly-bear sweatshirts, Old Faithful Inn collectible plates, and other Yellowstone keepsakes. The only lodging at Fishing Bridge is an RV park, but services include a gas station and general store, and the area stays packed all summer with folks arriving and departing via the East Entrance.

> **FISHING BRIDGE VISITOR CENTER**
> ----------------------------
> **TEL:**
> 307/344–2450
> ----------------------------

Best Hiking Trails

The flat 1.5-mile hike to ★NATURAL BRIDGE is probably the best short hike in the park in terms of the sweat-to-scenery ratio. From the trailhead at Bridge Bay marina, a short jaunt through a pine forest reveals a 50-foot arch reminiscent of Southwestern sandstone formations. A few gentle switchbacks lead to the top of the bluff, but hikers should stay off the fragile formation. A hare-brained plan for a stagecoach route over the arch failed in the late 1870s, but cars accessed Natural Bridge until 1991 on what's now a separate bike trail. Because of frequent bear activity, the area is off-limits in the spring.

Pack a picnic before setting out for the forested hilltop known as **Elephant Back.** The lake overlook on top is a perfect site for an outdoor family lunch, and you'll probably be hungry after gaining 800

Hiking near the
Mud Volcano in
winter.

feet in two miles. The lollipop loop is four miles start to finish, beginning on the north side of the road a half-mile east of Lake Village Junction. You'll see spruce and fir trees in the woods along the way, boldly defying the tyranny of the dominant lodgepole pine. If you can get to the summit by sunrise, you'll see the lake spread out like a dark blanket before the orange-tinted Absarokas.

The Yellowstone River cuts a lush, green passageway as it squiggles through the jagged Absaroka Mountains in the southeast corner of the park. Trappers nicknamed this easily navigable route the Thorofare. A trip along the 33-mile **Thorofare Trail** requires at least a weeklong commitment. It's a true classic among backcountry adventures. The route follows the lake's eastern edge and runs past a chain of 10,000-foot peaks to the park's southern boundary—and from there it's a grueling hike out via the South Boundary Trail or the Bridger-Teton National Forest. But the West's most unspoiled country is its own reward, promising unsurpassed solitude, abundant wildlife sightings, and a dozen campsites with jaw-dropping panoramic views.

Other Activities

Bridge Bay has come a long way since explorer David Folsom described the idyllic inlet in 1869 as "a beautiful little lake…fashioned by the practised hand of nature, that man had not desecrated." It's still wooded and scenic, but tourism has the upper hand now. The natural bay was dredged in the early 1960s to construct the **Bridge Bay Marina** (Grand Loop Rd., 2 miles south of Lake Village; 307/344–7311 or 866/439–7375). The area stays packed with recreational boaters, fisherman, and strolling families from the adjacent campground. Among the boats docked at Bridge Bay is the *Lake Queen II*, a 44-foot tour boat that makes hour-long interpretive trips around Stevenson Island. These cruises leave five to seven times a day between mid-June and mid-September.

Eighteen-foot outboards are available for hourly rental at Bridge Bay, and you can get a humble rowboat for a couple hours or an overnight trip. Guided sightseeing trips run from $180 for two hours on a 22-foot cabin cruiser.

Chartered **fishing trips** (866/439–7375) include guide, tackle, and fishcleaning. The gorgeous native cutthroat trout is catch-and-release only, but if you're trolling deeper water, you're likely to pull in one of the many invasive lake trout. Illegally introduced sometime in the 1980s, the larger fish devour the cutthroats, and their rapid colonization of the lake spells ecological disaster, since cutthroats are an important food source for raptors and grizzlies. The only rules governing lake trout are that you must kill and report any you catch.

Paddling along the shore of Lake Yellowstone can be one of the wildest and most scenic experiences in the park. Outfitters offering day trips and guided, multiday tours include Jackson's **Geyser Kayak Tours** (307/413–6177). Overnight, four-night, and six-night trips run from $445 to $1,295 per person, and they include a boat shuttle for you and your kayak to the south end of Yellowstone Lake, plus nightly gourmet dinners prepped by the outfitter's chatty guides. If you want to explore without a guide, you'll need your own boat or a rental from outside the park.

Many paddlers set out along the undeveloped eastern shore from the **Sedge Bay Boat Launch** (East Entrance Rd., 8 miles southeast of Fishing Bridge), heading toward one of four backcountry campsites within a leisurely three-hour paddle. The lake's south and southeastern arms are thick with waterfowl and see very little motorized traffic—in fact, the lower reaches of each are closed to motors altogether. The most expedient route to these stunning and silent shores is via the **lake shuttle,** which drops off and/or picks up you and your boat at an agreed-upon location. Call the Bridge Bay Marina direct (307/242–3893) to set up a shuttle.

Yellowstone Lake stays icy cold throughout the year, and the threat of hypothermia is a serious one. Sudden winds can make for abruptly choppy conditions, particularly on the eastern shore. Kayaks offer a bit more stability than most canoes, but both craft should stick to the shore—open-water crossings can be very dangerous.

On the outside looking in at the Lake Hotel sunroom and lounge.

WHERE TO EAT

Fishing Bridge General Store. With pancakes, French toast, and omelets, the cheap breakfast menu at Fishing Bridge beats out the other general stores' pre-packaged morning offerings. The snack bar doesn't have much seating, but you can make lunch and dinner alfresco at the picnic area across the road. *East Entrance Rd., at Fishing Bridge; 307/242-7200.* $

Lake General Store. The cheap breakfast and lunch items won't win any culinary accolades, but you can get in and out of this location relatively quickly after an egg-and-cheese biscuit or a wrap. The counter is tiny and the seating sparse, but the cedar-framed, octagonal store dates back to 1922, and it's worth a visit just to check out the kooky architecture. *Lake Village; 307/242-7563.* $

Lake Hotel Deli. Recently expanded, this deli offers inexpensive sandwiches and sweets from late morning through late evening. Cheese sandwiches and PB&Js make this a great spot to feed the kids for cheap. Take your meal around the corner to the elegant sunroom to feel like you're having a more polished meal than you paid for. *Lake Village; 307/344-7311 or 866/439-7375.* $

★LAKE HOTEL DINING ROOM. Sunlight spills from huge windows into this vast, open room. Lake's dining room has a deserved reputation for the best food in the park, particularly at dinner. You might start out with a shared plate of rich lobster ravioli before tucking into Montana-raised tenderloin with rosemary-cabernet sauce. The sandwiches at lunch are a cut above, with choices like a hand-carved corned-beef reuben and artisan cheeses. (The breakfast buffet, though, doesn't stand out.) *Lake Village; 307/344-7311 or 866/439-7375.* $$$-$$$$

Lake Lodge Cafeteria. This warm, wood-beamed space hasn't changed much since it was built in 1920. The place gets packed at mealtimes, particularly breakfast and dinner, when families from the

OLD YELLER BUSES

The yolk-yellow antique touring buses spotted along Yellowstone's roads date back to the 1930s. Whole fleets were retired in the 1960s, but in 2007 eight of the classic vehicles were restored and returned to service. The buses' nicknames reflect how they spent the second half of the 20th century. "Monty," for instance, was owned by a Vermont collector, while "Hollywood" starred (bizarrely) in *Big Trouble in Little China*. For info on getting on board, *see* the Practical Information chapter.

neighboring cabins pour in for eggs and bacon or a plate of pasta or fish. In the main lodge room there's a popular bar next to a hulking stone fireplace. The wide porch overlooking the lake, complete with rocking chairs, is easily the best spot in Yellowstone to unwind with a cocktail. *Lake Village; 307/344–7311 or 866/439–7375.* **$–$$**

⊙→ GRANT VILLAGE AND WEST THUMB

See the Yellowstone National Park: Lower Loop map.

Southwest Yellowstone remains something of an undiscovered country to most visitors. Though the area lacks an easily accessible "name" attraction like Old Faithful or the Grand Canyon, the sheer number of natural wonders—from waterfalls to hot springs to massive backcountry lakes—rivals any other region of the park. It wasn't until almost 40 years after Yellowstone became a national park that the southwest corner finally got its own ranger station, and the wet and wooded landscape remains remote and roadless still today.

The flooded volcanic basin known as the West Thumb of Yellowstone Lake is named for the lake's vague resemblance to an upside-down hand. **Grant Village** is on its south shore. In some respects the black sheep of the Yellowstone hospitality family, the village was established in the 1960s by the NPS's controversial Mission 66 program (*see* the Where to Stay chapter), which sought to modernize and "green" Yellowstone's visitor facilities, but sometimes did ecological damage of its own. Grant Village, for instance, was the result of relocating facilities from the environmentally fragile West Thumb and Fishing Bridge areas, but the village was constructed in prime grizzly habitat. Because of this clash, the campground is closed during the trout-spawning season in May and early June when bears come to feed.

CASCADE CORNER

Hidden within the forested acres of Yellowstone's wild southwestern corner are more than a hundred known waterfalls, earning the area its nickname. Known more formally as the Bechler region, after its most prominent river, Cascade Corner is hemmed in by two plateaus, and the abundant creeks and streams pouring off the plateaus' sloped edges create chains of stunning ivory falls. This country is remote yet extremely popular with backpackers; it's a great place to spot moose. Because backcountry hot springs empty into a lot of the streams, secret soaking spots are almost as tempting to hikers as the waterfalls.

The dated facilities at Grant lack the rustic-historical vibe of much of the rest of the park, but it has an off-the-beaten-path feel that attracts many dedicated explorers. It's also the best launching pad for day trips into the Tetons. Paddlers line up at the boat launch to explore the bay's bluff-lined coast, and on the wind you can smell the blue-green tartness of the lake.

WEST THUMB GEYSER BASIN

The West Thumb is actually a caldera within a caldera. A volcanic explosion here 150,000 years ago caused the land to collapse in on itself, and the hole filled with water to become the West Thumb of Yellowstone Lake. The thermal basin here has always been known more for its beauty than its action, and in the high water of spring and early summer many of the features are actually submerged, giving them a cool, sunken-treasure look. West Thumb is also a rare opportunity to see all four varieties of thermal features within just a few steps of one another.

The **West Thumb Visitor Information Station** (no phone) is a squat 1925 log cabin, worth a peek in the winter when it's a cozy warming hut. The building is a bookstore in the summer, and it's usually crowded. You'll find a posted schedule of guided ranger programs; call the nearby Grant Visitor Center (307/344–2650) for more information.

Check out an example of mud pots at the **Thumb Paint Pots,** which have grown increasingly soupy in the past 40 years. During low-water periods they can still spit their semi-solid clay far enough to form funky, gloppy mud cones. On the other side of the geyser basin is the dark emerald trench of **Abyss Pool.** At 53 feet, it's the deepest hot spring known in Yellowstone. Though unpredictable, **Surging Spring** is the most entertaining West Thumb feature to watch when it's active. The light blue pool looks innocent, but every five or 10 minutes it gurgles up and floods the lake with some 2,400 gallons of water. Meanwhile, the fumaroles on the west end of the boardwalk hiss angrily as they release ribbons of steam.

On the lake side of the boardwalk, **Lakeshore Geyser** and **Fishing Cone** are the most visually arresting formations at West Thumb. Their two cones peek up from the water like one-eyed, geyserite sea monsters. When the water level is low, Lakeshore can very rarely erupt to 25 feet. Fishing Cone is dormant and acts as a hot spring. Yellowstone's early visitors bragged of catching fish while standing on it, then turning around and boiling their catch in the spring. Damage

Visitors brave the February cold to explore the West Thumb Geyser Basin.

The vent of Blue Funnel Spring in West Thumb Geyser Basin seems to shift as you walk past the pool—an optical illusion at work.

to the cone suggests this was indeed attempted, and needless to say fishing is no longer permitted from Fishing Cone.

Technically, this is the only frontcountry geyser basin where you don't have to stay on the boardwalk—but that's just because you have the option of paddling. **O.A.R.S.** (800/346–6277) leads three trips daily in summer from Grant Village, including a stunning sunrise trip that offers your best bet for wildlife sightings. The half-day ★**WEST THUMB KAYAK TRIPS** take you past the main basin and farther up the shore to a cluster of springs called the Lake Shore Group, accessible only by water. Gliding past the cones and springs at eye level offers a completely different perspective and a truly unique view of thermal features. Only paddlers see the swirls and eddies that mark hydrothermal vents hidden in the lake bottom.

NEARBY SIGHTS

Architecturally, the **Grant Village Visitor Center** (307/344–2650) is the least interesting of the park's interpretive facilities. It does house an excellent display on the 1988 forest fires, though, reminding visitors it's a miracle that Grant Village still exists. The Shoshone fire in 1988 completely surrounded Grant, forcing two evacuations and coming within 100 feet of several buildings. In summer, rangers host a nightly kids' program on the center's back porch, discussing wildlife and geography with some hands-on props.

Mama porcupine nuzzling Junior and the migratory mountain bluebird, Yellowstone's harbinger of spring.

It's a two-mile round-trip stroll to the **Lake Overlook** across the road from the West Thumb Geyser Basin. The route is so gentle it can't even be called a hike. A scant gain of 200 feet (easier if you take the loop clockwise) leads through a patchwork of unburned spruce and fir stands alternating with new lodgepole growth—evidence of the 1988 fires. The overlook itself offers views across the choppy waters of the West Thumb, with the Absaroka Mountains looming distantly to the southeast.

Ten miles south of Grant, the 30-foot **Lewis Falls** makes for a good photo op; the Lewis River pours in a fat cascade off the lip of the erosion-resistant caldera and cuts into the softer rock below. From here, the Lewis heads south toward the Snake River, carving out the 350-foot deep Lewis Canyon on the east side of the South Entrance Road. The pullout for the falls' overlook is small and gets very crowded with folks on foot, so drive with caution.

PEOPLE IN THE PARKS:
"DIGGER" JERRY GEORGE, WRITER

"DIGGER" JERRY GEORGE is a trained high-altitude ecologist. For several years he was a *San Francisco Chronicle* columnist, filing dispatches from wild places across the country—particularly Yellowstone, where he spent three years as a de facto "embedded reporter."

Brian Kevin: So you lived *inside* the park?

Jerry George: I essentially was the baggage—it was my wife who had the reason to live in the park, teaching elementary school [for children of employees] at Mammoth.

BK: What other work goes on in the park behind the scenes, that visitors usually don't see?

JG: I'm blown away by what Xanterra [the park concessionaire] accomplishes. In seven weeks they go from having no hotels open to all hotels open. They go from no employees to nearly 5,000 trained employees. How does Xanterra accomplish that?

BK: Your columns are often about the unique natural details you observe. What can visitors do in order to start noticing the types of things an ecologist notices?

JG: When I was a photojournalist in Vietnam, I was viewing and defining the world in terms of what made a "good shot." And I failed to see anything outside of that "good shot." You have to learn *not* to look for specific things—that's like looking through a camera. If you let yourself fall into that trap, you don't notice the things that ultimately may be the real message.

BK: Given all your park experience, what makes Yellowstone stand out?

JG: All life in Yellowstone has been extinguished five times in the last two million years—maybe six. And look at what it is today. Yellowstone does more to renew our faith in the ability of the planet to persevere than any other place.

It's humbling. And yet, the humbling that Yellowstone does is not a debilitating humbling. It's actually an empowering humbling. It leaves you feeling comfortable that it's not all on your shoulders. In fact, it doesn't give a damn about your shoulders at all. And that's a healthy thing for people to realize.

Best Hiking Trails

Moose Falls, near Yellowstone's south entrance, is great for a dip in summer.

The flat, easy **Riddle Lake Trail** is all the more special for being closed half the year. From spring until July 15 the area is off-limits for bear management, but the rest of the year the 2.5-mile route leads through a quiet, partially burned forest and over the Continental Divide. Because there's almost zero elevation gain, it's likely the easiest crossing of the divide you'll ever attempt. (It's a big favorite for families.) The lake seemed like a "riddle" to early explorers because it was thought to have straddled the divide, draining in two directions. Alas, it's just north, and it drains directly into Yellowstone Lake via the snarkily named Solution Creek. Watch for moose in the marshes, as well as a variety of waterfowl. Find the trailhead two miles south of Grant on the east side of the South Entrance Road.

The **Heart Lake Trail** allows for trips of various lengths, but a hike to the shoreline campsites about eight miles in is one of the best short backpacking trips in the park. Along the way, hikers cross wildflower meadows, smell sulfur from fumaroles and hot springs along Witch Creek, and maybe glimpse an active geyser. Five idyllic campsites line a vast, blue stretch of Heart Lake, in the shadow of 10,308-foot Mount Sheridan. A strenuous three-mile climb leads to a lookout shelter and sweeping views of the Yellowstone Plateau and the Tetons. On cold mornings, steam pours from the Heart Lake Geyser Basin like a science project gone awry, making for a spooky hike out. Head out from the trailhead five miles south of Grant on the east side of the South Entrance Road.

The second-highest falls in the park, ★UNION FALLS is a magnificent, thunderous cascade where Mountain Ash Creek pours in a dramatic pyramid over a 265-foot rock wall. You'll feel the spray even from the overlook, some hundred yards away. The falls is at the end of a moderately strenuous eight-mile hike through the unburned forests of the Cascade Corner district. It's a tough day hike, but two backcountry sites along bubbling Mountain Ash Creek allow for overnight trips. You can also take a dip in a naturally warmed swimming hole a half-mile below the namesake falls. Find the trailhead just outside the park's southern boundary on Grassy Lake Road, 10 miles west of Flagg Ranch.

OTHER ACTIVITIES

The interconnected Shoshone and Lewis lakes dominate the southwest quadrant of Yellowstone. You can set out to hike their shorelines from trailheads along the South Entrance Road or the Grand Loop Road near Old Faithful, but you can only get out on the water via the **Lewis Lake boat launch**, 8.5 miles south of Grant.

Motorized boaters are restricted to Lewis Lake. Lined with silent, sandy beaches, Lewis has hot springs off the northwest shore, offering ideal soaking spots where the warm waters drizzle into the lake. **Geyser Kayak Tours** (307/413–6177) offers three- and four-night paddling excursions with beachside campsites and knockout campfire meals. There are no boat rentals offered, though, so bring your own craft if you're not going out with a guide.

Stretching across 8,000 acres, Shoshone Lake is the largest backcountry lake in the continental United States, an inland sea at 7,800 feet that keeps its ice until mid-June. Shoshone is a paddler's dream, surrounded by gorgeous campsites and teeming with wildlife, from abundant brown trout below the surface to impossibly large, white pelicans skimming it. The only access is via Lewis Lake downstream, by paddling up the shaded Lewis Channel, which may require wading and pulling your boat. Because of the effort involved, a trip to Shoshone is at least an overnight affair.

Like Yellowstone Lake, both Shoshone and Lewis lakes are prone to high winds and aggressive waves in the afternoon. Neither gets particularly warm, and turning over a canoe or kayak can spell disaster. Avoid open-water crossings.

Not two miles inside the park's south entrance, a small pullout allows a glimpse at 30-foot **Moose Falls.** The frothy little falls is pretty to look at but more renowned among park staff as a top-notch swimming hole. Thermals upstream keep temperatures warmish, and the pool below the falls is large and deep enough for a gaggle of swimmers. The truly bold can take a 20-foot plunge from a notch just to the left of the falls.

WHERE TO EAT

Grant Village Dining Room. The focal point of this long, open room is a wall of windows facing the lake—unfortunately, the pine trees outside obscure the view. The daily three squares are familiar fare, but a standout bison meatloaf puts a Western spin on a comfort-food fave. Vegetarians should expect slim pickings. (Reservations are required for dinner.) *Grant Village; 307/344–7311 or 866/439–7375.* **$$$–$$$$**

Grant Village Grill. The lines are often long, but they move quickly in this small fast-food stand inside the general store. Almost everything is in sandwich form: breakfast croissants, cheeseburgers, chicken sandwiches. This is the fastest place in the village to get a milk shake or root-beer float, and it has the most seating of any of the snack shops. *Grant Village General Store; 307/242–7266.* **$**

Lake House Restaurant. You can do only breakfast and dinner at the Lake House. The breakfast buffet is nearly identical to the one at Grant's table-service counterpart and at a slightly lower price. Dinner is a build-your-own pasta bar with some appetizers, and you can also grab a local Bozone Amber Ale and stroll on the shoreline deck overlooking the retired marina. Lake views are unobstructed here, and three of the four walls are all windows. *Grant Village; 307/344–7311 or 866/439–7375.* **$**

⊙→ MADISON AND NORRIS

See the Madison and Norris map.

After the earth heaved during Yellowstone's last major volcanic event, it collapsed in on itself, leaving a crater so large it's difficult even to recognize it without an aerial view. But the rim of the Yellowstone caldera is clearly visible between Madison and Norris junctions, a gray ridge of jagged cliffs that parallels the road west of Gibbon Falls. This proximity of the caldera's rim characterizes the rough-hewn landscapes

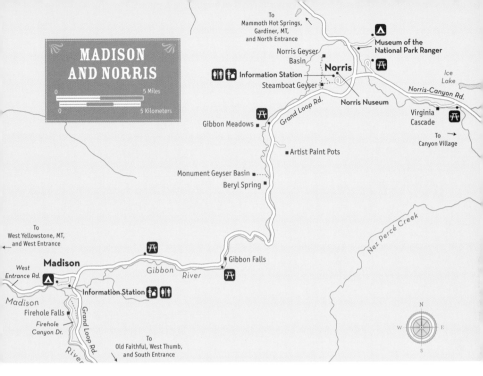

surrounding Norris and Madison, and the scenery gets a boost from the nearby Gallatin Range and the tumbling Gibbon and Madison rivers.

Norris borrows its name from Yellowstone's second superintendent, Philetus Norris, a transplanted Easterner known to patrol the park dressed head-to-toe in buckskins. He built the first road to the Norris geyser basins in 1878, and the area has been an important crossroads since.

Today Norris and Madison both host hordes of campers in the summer, though neither offers the same breadth of services as the larger villages. You won't find gas stations, groceries, or dining facilities, but there are more picnic sites surrounding Norris and Madison than just about anywhere else in the park. Otherwise, each junction has a few basic amenities, like bathrooms and pay phones.

NORRIS GEYSER BASIN

The hottest and most volatile thermal basin in the park sits at the intersection of three fault lines. Those cracks in the earth allow energy from Yellowstone's underground magma pool to heat the groundwater more easily. They also make for a network of geysers and hot springs that's constantly changing in response to geologic disturbances. On the surface, the colorful mats of heat-loving microorganisms swell and fade with changes in water temperature and acidity. More than any other basin in the park, Norris is in constant flux.

Two miles of trails and boardwalks weave through Norris's Porcelain Basin and Back Basin. Staying on the boardwalks in thermal areas is always important, but even more so in Norris, where water temperatures over 200 degrees Fahrenheit and extremely low pH levels pose an even greater threat. Located between the two basins, the **Norris Museum** (307/344–2812) has a detailed geology exhibit and a Yellowstone Association bookstore. Schedule a couple of hours to thoroughly explore the one-of-a-kind Norris basin.

Starting out in the Porcelain Basin behind the museum, the first feature you'll encounter is **Black Growler Steam Vent.** A cluster of hissing holes in a barren hillside, Black Growler emits a thick tower of steam that occasionally switches from one hole to another—nobody knows why. The three sporadically active geysers named **Constant, Whirligig,** and **Pinwheel** often support some of the basin's most colorful thermal mats. Stripes of jade, rust, and traffic-cone orange stretch out along the basin floor.

MADISON
INFORMATION
STATION

TEL:
307/344–2876

On the museum's south side, the sprawling Back Basin is a buffet of thermals spread out over a modestly forested plain. **Emerald Spring** is a boiling pool tinted an exquisite green by sulfur deposits. Farther along the boardwalk, colorful **Cistern Springs** is constantly overflowing. Its waters are heavy with silica, and formations below the water line look like barnacle-crusted remains of ancient shipwrecks. In the basin's southeast corner, **Echinus Geyser** is the world's largest acidic geyser, with a pH similar to that of vinegar. Pebbles around this geyser have a prickly-looking coat of sinter. Echinus's once-frequent eruptions have been rare and erratic since the late 1990s, a case study in the perplexing changes that sometimes sweep through Norris.

The real thermal rock star at Norris is **Steamboat Geyser.** Seeing the world's tallest active geyser erupt is a little bit like seeing a total eclipse, only rarer and utterly unpredictable. Steamboat can go years without a major eruption, but when it does, water sprays 300 feet into the air, and the steam plume might double that. The steam phase following an eruption lasts hours, and the roar can be heard for miles. Steamboat sometimes has mini-eruptions of 10 to 40 feet, and its gnarled cone is worth examining even in dormancy.

Nearby Sights

Formerly a soldier station for Army troops, the **Museum of the National Park Ranger** (Mammoth–Norris Rd., 1 mile north of Norris Junction, 307/344-7353) traces the evolution of the park's guardians. Display cases hold an array of early park uniforms and tools, and a short film examines the rangers' complex roles as both tour guides and law enforcement. The museum is staffed by retired rangers and NPS employees, and when business is slow they're happy to relax on the back porch and chat about park secrets and lore. Take advantage.

A three-mile scenic cut-off hugs a wooded cliff to lead past the 60-foot **Virginia Cascade** (Norris–Canyon Rd., 1.5 miles east of Norris Junction). It's tough to catch a glimpse as you drive by—there's no established pull-out and the trees obscure the view—but the white veil of the falls stands out against the piney backdrop. Try to imagine the first Norris–Canyon Road, which arrived at the foot of the falls before climbing out of the canyon along the steep cliffs; it must've been sheer terror for stagecoach drivers.

The meadows along the Madison River are wildlife hot spots, and at the picnic area next to the **Madison Amphitheater** (Grand Loop Rd., .2 mile south of Madison Junction, no phone) you're almost certain to share your lunch hour with a cluster of grazing elk, especially in fall. The amphitheater faces National Park Mountain, and legend says the Washburn party camped in this meadow when they first proposed national park status in 1870. Check inside the adjacent historic **Madison Information Station** (307/344-2876) for schedules of astronomy programs, concerts, and other summer events at the amphitheater.

Unquestionably the giggliest attraction in all of Yellowstone, the **Artist Paint Pots** (Norris–Madison Rd., 4 miles south of Norris Junction) are a group of heated, chowderlike mud pools that bubble and spurt in continuous, extra-noisy, flatulent outbursts. Explorer Nathaniel Langford compared the texture of the bubbling glop to "the consistency of thick paint" and complained of "a villainous smell" with each burst bubble. The best pots at Artist are at the top of the hilly, mile-long boardwalk loop. These fling mud as high as 15 feet.

It's a quick stop to admire the beautiful **Gibbon Falls** (Norris–Madison Rd., 5 miles east of Madison Junction), which you can't miss from the road. Here the Gibbon River slides in smooth diagonal ribbons 84 feet down a shelf created by the caldera rim. The river and falls were named for an Army colonel who explored the park in 1872, so don't believe the tale—often repeated by

Fly-fishing on the
Firehole River.

mischievous park employees and guides—that the Asian lesser ape was once native to Yellowstone.

Describing **Beryl Spring** (Norris–Madison Rd., 5 miles east of Norris Junction) in the 1921 edition of his *Haynes Guide*, Yellowstone's first guidebook writer, F. Jay Haynes, cautioned, "The violent boiling of its surface, together with the hiss of escaping steam, causes some nervous apprehension to the feelings of the traveler." Though the spring is named for the gemstone with which it shares its aquamarine color, Beryl hovers around 200 degrees Fahrenheit, and it's recognized as much for its massive steam discharge as for its color. There's a small viewing boardwalk next to the road.

BEST HIKING TRAIL

It's a wickedly steep climb to ★MONUMENT GEYSER BASIN, but it's nonetheless Yellowstone's easiest backcountry thermal basin to reach. If you have any itch to explore a thermal area without the distractions of crowds, cars, and boardwalks, the trail to Monument Basin is a must-hike.

The trail begins on the west side of the road a half-mile north of Beryl Spring, and gently follows the Gibbon River for the first three-quarters of a mile. Look for trumpeter swans in fall and winter, plus steam from mid-river thermals. The trail doubles back suddenly to ascend the adjacent hill, a gain of more than 600 feet in less than a mile, with views of the Gibbon Canyon and wide, grassy Gibbon Meadows. You'll smell the thick sulfur aroma before reaching the basin. In addition to fumaroles and hot

springs, long-dormant geysers at Monument have formed beautiful and alien sinter cones, tall gray cylinders that seem to reach
up from the ground like deathly fingers. Remember to stick to the
trail and keep your distance from the features.

Bison and elk jams are common near Gibbon Meadow.

OTHER ACTIVITIES

Not far from Madison Junction you can track down a rare NPS-
acknowledged **swimming hole.** The one-way Firehole Canyon Drive
leaves the Grand Loop Road a half-mile south of Madison, shadowing
the Firehole River as it runs between 700-foot rock walls. The 40-foot
Firehole Falls is pretty enough for a photo op, but the real action along
the two-mile cutoff is upstream from the falls. Here the avowedly anti-
swimming NPS has given in to the popularity of a long-utilized swimming hole and has installed changing stations, parking, and a stairway.
The unstaffed swimming area is rocky, but a great place to stop on a
warm day. The current is slow, so it's relatively safe for kids.

Along the West Entrance Road, the Madison River is a meadow
stream, a 23-mile stretch full of weedy pools hiding fat rainbow and
brown trout. It's a terrific place for **fly-fishing** in early summer and
fall. (Avoid midsummer, when high temperatures from the Firehole
tributary send the fish away.) Dry fly-fishing is especially popular on
the Madison, and no fewer than five outfitters in West Yellowstone
are permitted to guide trips. With elk crowding the banks and the
mountain views, few trout streams are more picturesque.

Spotlight on ✶
GEOTHERMAL FEATURES

Windows into the earth: it's a frequently repeated metaphor for the geothermal wonders that make the Yellowstone landscape so exceptional. More than half the world's thermal features are found in Yellowstone National Park, including some 10,000 hot springs, mud pots, and fumaroles, plus 300 or so active geysers. You'd need to search two or three other continents for as many geysers as you can see during a single afternoon around Old Faithful. If these geothermal features are the earth's windows, then Yellowstone is like its sun porch, a place unlike any other spot on the globe, where you can peek in on the effects of extreme pressure and heat that are usually hidden deep within our planet.

◄◄ Castle Geyser erupts in its steam phase.

HOW DO GEYSERS WORK?

GEYSERS

A few main ingredients make geysers possible: abundant water, a heat source, a certain kind of plumbing system, and rock hard enough to withstand some serious pressure. The layout of any one geyser's underground plumbing is a mystery, but we know that below each vent is a system of fissures and chambers, with constrictions here and there that prevent hot water from rising to the surface. As the underground water heats up, these constrictions and the cooler surface water "cap" the whole system, keeping it from boiling over and ratcheting up the underground pressure. When a few steam bubbles eventually fight their way through the constrictions, the result is like uncapping a shaken-up soda bottle, when the released pressure causes the soda to spray.

GEYSER FAQs

Old Faithful's surface water temperature? 204° F before eruption.

Hottest geyser basin? Norris, with water 1,000 feet below ground at 450° F.

Tallest geyser? Steamboat at Norris, more than 350 feet.

Strangest geyser name? "Deleted Teakettle" at Upper Geyser Basin.

Word origin? From *geysir*, Iceland's earliest known geyser.

Beehive Geyser has an indicator vent in front of its cone. When the vent steams, an eruption is on the way.

Monument Geyser Basin

Norris Geyser Basin

Lower Geyser Basin

Upper Geyser Basin

West Thumb Geyser Basin

YELLOWSTONE NATIONAL PARK

① RECHARGE STAGE

Groundwater accumulates in plumbing and is heated by magma chamber. Some hot water flashes to steam and bubbles try to rise toward surface.

② PRELIMINARY ERUPTION STAGE

Pressure builds as steam bubbles clog at constriction. High pressure raises the boiling point, preventing superheated water from becoming steam.

③ ERUPTION STAGE

Bubbles squeeze through constriction, displacing surface water and relieving pressure. Boiling point drops. Trapped water flashes to steam, forcing water out of chambers and causing chain reaction.

④ RECOVERY STAGE

Eruption ends when chambers are emptied or temperature falls below boiling. Chambers begin to refill with groundwater and process begins again.

A **cone geyser** like Lone Star Geyser has a spout-like formation around its vent, formed by silica particles deposited during eruptions.

A **fountain geyser** like Daisy Geyser erupts from a vent submerged in a hot-spring-like pool. Eruptions tend to be smaller and more sporadic.

Not every thermal basin in Yellowstone has a boardwalk and a parking lot. Dozens of geyser and hot spring groups bubble away in the backcountry, miles from the nearest road. Reaching them may be as easy as following a day-hike trail or as tough as backpacking off trail with a map and compass. Standing alone next to a steaming hot spring, in untouched country, is a truly wild and sublime experience. It can also be very dangerous, as no signs or guard rails warn about unstable ground. Backcountry basin seekers should consult rangers before heading out and always use extreme caution. My favorite remote thermals include the hissing Witch Creek fumaroles near the Heart Lake Trail and the scrappy spouters along the Seven Mile Hole Trail.

Lone Star Geyser is fairly easy to reach, at the end of a former roadway.

No trail reaches the Gibbon Hill Geyser Group, though steam can be seen from the road south of Norris on cool days.

HOW DO HOT SPRINGS WORK?

A crust of mineral deposits around the Doublet Pool hot spring.

A thermal pool in the Rabbit Creek Thermal Area.

Essentially, what keeps a hot spring from becoming a geyser is a lack of constriction in its underground plumbing. Like their more explosive cousins, hot springs consist of water that seeps into the earth, only to simmer its way back up through fissures after it's heated by magma. Unlike in constricted geysers, water in a hot spring can circulate by convection. Rising hot water displaces cooling surface water, which then sinks underground to be heated by the magma chamber and eventually rise again. Thus the whole soup keeps itself at a gurgly equilibrium. As it rises, superheated water dissolves some subterranean minerals, depositing them at the surface to form the sculptural terraces that surround many hot springs.

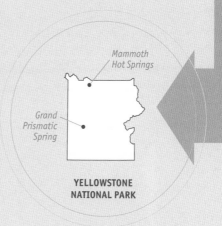

Mammoth
Hot Springs

Grand
Prismatic
Spring

**YELLOWSTONE
NATIONAL PARK**

The Inner Workings of Hot Springs

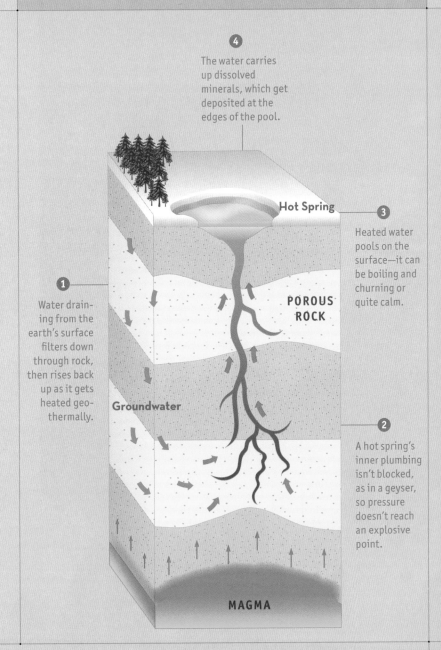

4 The water carries up dissolved minerals, which get deposited at the edges of the pool.

Hot Spring

3 Heated water pools on the surface—it can be boiling and churning or quite calm.

POROUS ROCK

1 Water draining from the earth's surface filters down through rock, then rises back up as it gets heated geothermally.

Groundwater

2 A hot spring's inner plumbing isn't blocked, as in a geyser, so pressure doesn't reach an explosive point.

MAGMA

The vivid colors that characterize hot springs and their terraces can be attributed alternately to minerals like sulfur and iron or to thermophiles. Thermophiles are microorganisms that thrive in extremely high temperatures. Blooming in thick bacterial mats, they convert light to energy, like plants, and their bright photosynthetic pigments help give hot springs their rainbow hues. Scientists suppose only a small percentage of Yellowstone's thermophiles have been identified. Still, these microbes have had a big impact on science. In 1965, a microorganism called *Thermus aquaticus*, or Taq, was discovered in the Lower Geyser Basin. From it, scientists extracted an enzyme that revolutionized molecular biology, ultimately making possible both DNA fingerprinting and the mapping of the human genome. NASA is among those performing research in the park today, studying thermophiles to gain insight on extraterrestrial life.

The Giant: Grand Prismatic Spring, Yellowstone's largest and deepest hot spring.

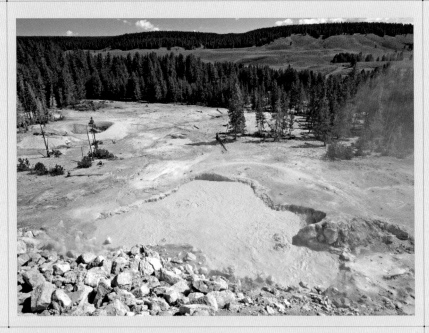

The Stank Bomb: Sulfur Cauldron, one of Yellowstone's most acidic springs.

The Life of the Party: Punch Bowl Spring.

The Perpetual Spouter: Firehole Spring.

WHAT'S THAT SMELL?

Most people think it smells like rotten eggs, though I've also heard "burnt gunpowder" and "paper mill smokestack." Whatever simile you settle on, there's no question that hot springs and other thermal features stink to high heaven. This sulfur smell occurs when a spring's superheated water dissolves trace amounts of sulfates found in the porous rock below. The sulfates bond with hydrogen in the water to form the stinky chemical hydrogen sulfide, which bubbles up to the surface. In high concentration, hydrogen sulfide can actually kill you, but the small amounts released by thermals can only kill your appetite. It's because hydrogen sulfide is often present in volcanic areas that we associate brimstone (or sulfur) with the underworld.

At the Mammoth Hot Springs terraces, sulfur is dissolved from the mineral gypsum.

Sulfur and other chemicals contribute to springs' acidity, leading to dead vegetation as here at Mammoth.

WHAT ARE MUD POTS?

MUD POT FAQs

Source of "paint pots" nickname? Iron and other metals tinting the mud red and orange.

Where's the biggest cluster of mud pots? Pocket Basin in Lower Geyser Basin.

How big was Mud Volcano before it exploded in 1872? 30 feet tall by 30 feet wide.

Original name of West Thumb Paint Pots? Mud Puffs.

Might as well say it up front: Mud pots are great because their thick, bursting bubbles can sound like a chorus of rude noises or "greetings from the interior." That's why the few places they're found in Yellowstone are usually surrounded by gaggles of giggling visitors with video cameras rolling. A mud pot is basically just a hot spring where a low water table results in a bubbling broth of water and clay. Hydrogen sulfide also helps to keep mud pots muddy, breaking down chemically (with help from thermophiles) in order to form rock-dissolving sulfuric acid. As heat and gasses escape from below, bubbles in the muck swell and pop, flinging mud chunks onto the banks to form gloppy clay mounds. The mud's thickness varies as the water table changes with the seasons.

The Fountain Paint Pots, mid-gurgle.

Artist Paint Pots

Lower Geyser Basin

West Thumb Paint Pots

YELLOWSTONE NATIONAL PARK

131

WHAT ARE FUMAROLES?

Take away the water from a hot spring and you're left with a fumarole. Often called steam vents, these noisy thermals occur when available water boils away before reaching the surface. All that escapes the vent is heat, vapor, and the whisper-roar of a giant, menacing teakettle. Fumaroles are often found on hills and scarps. The gases expelled from fumaroles might include carbon dioxide, sulfur dioxide, and hydrogen sulfide. Some features, like Red Spouter in the Lower Geyser Basin, can exhibit different behaviors depending on the seasonal water table, so what's a fumarole today could be a hot spring in a few months.

FUMAROLE FAQs

Word origin? From Latin *fumus* for "smoke."

Also known as? Solfataras, from *sulpha terra*, Latin for "land of sulfur."

Yellowstone's hottest fumarole? Black Growler at Norris, up to 280°F.

How many fumaroles are in Yellowstone? Around 4,000.

Roaring Mountain fumarole.

Lower Geyser Basin

YELLOWSTONE NATIONAL PARK

TIPS ON EXPLORING

SAFETY TIPS

Don't leave trails or boardwalks in the frontcountry basins.

Stay at least 10 feet away from backcountry thermals.

Keep extra distance in winter in case of unstable snow shelves.

Never (ever!) bathe or soak in a geyser, hot spring, or mud pot.

Never bring pets into thermal areas.

Don't throw or dip any objects into thermal features.

Leave the area if you feel sick or dizzy—it could be overexposure to thermal gases.

Keep an eye on kids and be sure they understand the danger.

LEARN MORE

Geyser Observation and Study Association: www.geyserstudy.org.

The Geysers of Yellowstone by T. Scott Bryan.

Windows into the Earth by Robert B. Smith and Lee Siegel.

Microbial Life resources from Carleton College's Science Education Resource Center: serc.carleton.edu/microbelife.

PHOTO TIPS

Set your alarm clock: generally, the best light for shooting the geothermal features is early in the morning. (You'll avoid the thickest crowds then, too.) The runner-up time is the late afternoon.

Breezy days are good for photographing geysers, since the steam will be blown away from the jetting water. But avoid standing down wind or your view can be clouded with steam.

If you get water from a thermal feature on your lens, be sure to dry it off quickly. The water has a high mineral content and can mark your lens.

Taking in the view at Grand Prismatic Spring.

Yellowstone's
Upper Loop

Mammoth Terraces

Travertine terraces like this one at Mammoth's Canary Spring can grow by as much as two feet per year.

Superheated water pours over the ledges and tiers of Canary Spring.

MAMMOTH HOT SPRINGS

WATER TEMPERATURE:
130 to 168°F

ROCK FORMED:
Travertine

RATE OF TRAVERTINE ACCUMULATION:
Two tons a day

 # MAMMOTH HOT SPRINGS

See the Yellowstone National Park: Upper Loop and Mammoth Hot Springs maps.

A bull elk strides like a general across the lawn of the former cavalry barracks, his bugle call echoing the reveille that once proclaimed sunrise and sunset at Fort Yellowstone. His harem grazes silently among stately stone buildings, where the ghosts of soldiers and settlers mingle with wide-eyed park visitors and rangers directing traffic. Just yards away, the landscape takes on the color and contours of a burnt marshmallow, an otherworldly hillside with pale turquoise pools and rivulets of super-heated water coursing across sculpted travertine terraces. Find the right spot at Mammoth Hot Springs and you can take in this entire panorama with one sustained gaze.

Because the northern reaches of the park lie beyond the rim of the Yellowstone caldera, the region's geological footprint differs from much of the rest of the park. In the absence of the rhyolitic lava flows that helped form most of central and southern Yellowstone, great subterranean limestone deposits still exist in the Mammoth area, and these help to give the hot springs terraces their unique color and character. What's more, the region's nonrhyolitic soil supports a wider variety of plant life, and although much of the low, dry northern range is dominated by sagebrush steppe, stands of aspen and fir can be found in the forested areas, interspersed with the ubiquitous lodgepole pine.

The remnants of Sheepeater wickiups in the forests east of Mammoth evoke the tribe's presence in the area before the arrival of Euro-American explorers. In the mid-1800s, the Shoshone and Bannock tribes began tracing hunting migrations over the Gallatin Range and across the Yellowstone Plateau, forced east by rapidly dwindling buffalo herds in their ancestral territories west of the Continental Divide. Mammoth Hot Springs was an important stop on what has become known as the Bannock Trail, and it's easy to imagine great hunting parties descending from nearby Snow Pass to rest at the sacred springs.

The hot springs were also known to Western fur trappers by the early 19th century, and primitive maps based on their tales identify the spot as "Boiling Spring White Sulphur Banks" and "Sulphur Mountain." By the time the Hayden expedition gave Mammoth Hot Springs a name that stuck, savvy settlers and Montana miners were already using the springs for their supposed therapeutic value. In fact, when the Hayden party arrived at the hot springs in 1871, expecting to find themselves more or less alone in the still largely unexplored territory, they were surprised to discover a small community of blissed-out soakers lounging in a semi-permanent camp at the base of the springs.

A bull elk crosses a meadow near Mammoth.

Mammoth Hot Springs has the honor of having housed the first tourist accommodation in Yellowstone, a reportedly squalid hotel and bathhouse built in 1871 by a pair of businessmen from nearby Bozeman. Attempts to cash in on Yellowstone's thermal features continued after the national park was established in 1872. The glut of unauthorized commercial activity—along with widespread poaching and vandalism—helped prompt Yellowstone's beleaguered civilian administrators to relinquish control of the park to the U.S. Army in 1886.

Mammoth was an easy choice for the Army's Yellowstone headquarters due to its low elevation and relatively mild winters, as well as its proximity to frontier towns to the north. Today, you can glimpse the Army's legacy at Mammoth in the imposing sandstone structures that make up the Fort Yellowstone Historic District. The buildings continue to serve as Yellowstone's administrative heart, and Mammoth is the only village with a few year-round services, including a post office, a health clinic, and a general store. These services, along with those mild winters, make Mammoth the base camp of choice for Yellowstone's cold-weather adventurers.

The Springs

The chalky tiers at Mammoth Hot Springs stand out visually among Yellowstone's many thermal areas, but they were formed in much the same way. Though the springs lie more than 20 miles outside of the Yellowstone Caldera, a fault line stretching north from the **Norris Geyser Basin** channels hot water into the porous rock layers below, and water from this scalding subterranean river ascends to the surface via an underground maze of fissures and cracks. Along the way, the water bonds with carbon dioxide, and the resulting acidic solution dissolves minerals as it rises. When the water reaches the surface, a portion of these minerals are deposited, forming the alien terraces and cones of Yellowstone's thermal areas.

Substantial underground layers of sedimentary limestone set Mammoth apart. In contrast to the silica-producing rhyolite found elsewhere in the park, dissolved limestone recrystalizes at the surface to form a gray-white mineral called travertine, and this is the rock that makes up Mammoth's hot springs terraces. Thousands of years of accumulated travertine have given the place its unique look, a

YELLOWSTONE NATIONAL PARK: UPPER LOOP

landscape somewhere between an ice palace and an ashtray. Scattered like paint spills across this terrain are the telltale polychrome of thermophiles, the heat-loving bacteria whose algaelike colonies tint the pools as well as their perimeters.

The fickle shifting of the earth continues to affect conditions at Mammoth Hot Springs, and a radiant spring that's furiously churning today might be dry and colorless next month. Check in with rangers at the **Albright Visitor Center** (*see* Nearby Sights, *below*) for updates on recent conditions and schedules of ranger-led programs and tours.

The Mammoth Hot Springs are divided into a Lower and an Upper Terrace. The Lower Terrace is the more compelling of the two, traversed by a winding boardwalk that takes you past a number of fascinating springs. At a good clip, you could stroll the whole thing in an hour, but it's best to take your time. The Upper Terrace is a paved, two-mile road open to cars and foot traffic (but not trailers, buses, or motor homes). You could spare yourself some sneaker tread by taking the car, but you'll be in and out every 500 feet to peer at the springs, so walk if at all possible.

ALBRIGHT VISITOR CENTER

LOCATION: Off the Grand Loop Road, near the Mammoth Hotel

TEL: 307/344-2263

Start your Mammoth exploration on the Lower Terrace boardwalk at **Liberty Cap,** a dormant, 37-foot cone that stands like a sentry at the base of the Lower Terrace. During its presumably long period of activity, the pressure below the spring allowed water to reach unusual heights, gradually adding layers to the mineral pillar. Liberty Cap is named for the tapered Phrygian caps that symbolized freedom during the French Revolution—there's one on the seal of the U.S. Senate, too, but it looks more like a hipster beanie. Across the street, **Opal Terrace,** at the base of Capital Hill, is a popular lounging spot for the local elk herds and an equally popular photo op.

Before setting out on the boardwalk, head just north of Liberty Cap and walk west along the path that leads to the Beaver Ponds trailhead. Here you can glimpse **Hymen Terrace,** sometimes overlooked because it's a few steps off the beaten path—and because it goes unmentioned in the park's Mammoth Hot Springs guide pamphlet. The diamond pattern along the terrace's edge takes on some of Mammoth's most vibrant colors when the thermophiles are in full bloom, and during high water periods the water cascades evenly over the honeycombed edges like a Champagne pyramid.

The Albright Visitor Center holds historical exhibits, along with a bookstore.

The travertine formations of the famed **Minerva Terrace** could be a scale model of a grand cliff-dwelling civilization, its miniature bluffs and escarpments rendered in alabaster and ash. Minerva has cycled through periods of activity and inactivity in the park's recent history, and you'll notice raised boardwalks in some areas nearby, constructed to accommodate rapidly advancing travertine deposits during a particularly active stretch in the early 1990s.

Spend some time examining **Canary Spring,** which makes up much of the broad plateau of the Lower Terrace. Areas in and around the pool retain the sulfur-yellow tinge that earned the spring its name, though brilliant ochre and aqua shades figure into Canary's spectrum as well. Follow the boardwalk to the spring's southeast edge to check out some menacing travertine stalactites where the water spills over a series of tiers.

Nearby Sights

You're literally taking a step into Yellowstone's past when you walk into the **Albright Visitor Center** (off the Grand Loop Rd., just east of Mammoth Hotel; 307/344-2263), as the building once served as a Fort Yellowstone officers' quarters. Along with a bookstore, the center has a first-floor exhibit dedicated to the wildlife of the park's north-

A former Fort Yellowstone officers' quarters now houses park staff.

ern reaches, and a downstairs exhibit tracing the human presence in Yellowstone, complete with a sketchbook by the artist Thomas Moran, who accompanied the Hayden survey on its first park expedition in 1871. If you want to learn more about the red-roofed, double-chimneyed buildings lining the streets at Mammoth, rangers lead daily tours of the rest of **Historic Fort Yellowstone** throughout the summer. One fascinating (and creepy) historic site that doesn't make the tour is the **Kite Hill Cemetery,** where early park employees, settlers, and soldiers lie beneath 19th-century headstones and several dilapidated cairns. You won't find the cemetery on the park map, but rangers can tell you what to look for on the hill behind the Mammoth Hotel.

Drive four miles west along the Mammoth–Tower Road to visit two of the

Thousands of years of accumulated travertine have given the place its unique look, a landscape somewhere between an ice palace and an ashtray.

park's most accessible and impressive waterfalls. You'll find **Undine Falls** at a marked roadside pull-out, a messy, gorgeous falls where Lava Creek pours 60 feet into a canyon. For a different perspective, drive another quarter mile up the road and park at the Lava Creek Picnic Area just past the bridge. Hike the quarter mile back along the Lava Creek Trail to view the falls from the north rim of the Canyon. Just up the road from the picnic area you'll find the trailhead to **Wraith Falls.** An easy half-mile hike with three gentle switchbacks leads to an overlook where you can see Lava Creek slither down a broad, angled rock face. Wraith Falls is less a thundering cataclysm than a wide brook gone diagonal, and in low water it actually splits into two parallel streams that fall separately and reconnect at the base.

A park visitor eloquently described **the Hoodoos** in 1922 as "a wrecked mountain where giants once played." Not to be confused with the eroded volcanic rocks of Hoodoo Basin in the eastern Absarokas, the Hoodoos south of Mammoth are not true geologic hoodoos, but a collection of travertine boulders wrenched by glaciation and earthquakes from nearby **Terrace Mountain.** There's an extremely short scenic drive 3.5 miles south of Mammoth along the road to Norris, but to walk through the Badlands-esque boulder field, you'll want to hike north a short 1.5 miles along the Howard Eaton Trail, beginning on the west side of the road at the Glen Creek trailhead.

Obsidian was one of the most widely traded minerals among native peoples in early America, and if the smooth volcanic glass set the pre-Columbian gold standard, then Yellowstone was its Fort Knox. Obsidian samples from Yellowstone have been found as far away as Ontario and Ohio, and much of it was likely quarried at the **Obsidian Cliff,** 11 miles south of Mammoth on the Mammoth-Norris Road. Unfortunately, you can't visit the cliffs, as the park service was forced to close the cliffside trails in 1996 after years of tourists breaking off and pocketing rock fragments. You can still glimpse a few obsidian deposits on the east side of the road—be sure to leave them as you find them!

Bright lichens and mosses
stand out like paint splashes
on the ebony rock of Obsidian Cliff.

Sometimes it spits: a hot spring exhibiting geyserlike behavior at the Upper Terrace of Mammoth Hot Springs.

Best Hiking Trails

The **Beaver Ponds Trail** that begins and ends at Mammoth is a gently rolling five-mile loop that leads through a Douglas fir forest and sage-brush meadows sprinkled with wildflowers and aspen stands. Though the marshy ponds that lend their name to the trail are less than spectacular, the solitude is a definite plus for those seeking a break from the bustling Mammoth village. Vistas along the way offer bird's-eye views of the hot springs terraces and the knifelike ridge of Mount Everts. Pick up the trail just south of Liberty Cap along Clematis Creek; it'll deposit you just up the road, behind the Mammoth Hotel.

Haul your hiking boots, mountain bike, or skis to the Bunsen Peak trailhead just south of the cliff-hugging Golden Gate bridge. If it's the vertical you crave, you'll gain 1,300 feet in just over two miles on the **Bunsen Peak Trail** on your way to the domed summit. Take in the views of craggy Electric Peak to the northwest and Mammoth Hot Springs to the north. For a slightly less rugged trip, hike the abandoned **Bunsen Peak Road,** a six-mile unpaved route that curves halfway around the base of the mountain. This route is popular with

YELLOWSTONE'S PAINTER

When Ferdinand Hayden's survey party set out for Yellowstone in 1871, they brought with them a young, informally trained artist from back East, Thomas Moran. Moran had previously done some magazine illustrations of Yellowstone based on explorer Nathaniel Langford's descriptions, but he had no wilderness experience. He went clutching watercolors and a sketchbook and riding with a pillow on his saddle.

Moran proved to be an essential member of the expedition. Throughout the trip, he worked furiously at watercolor studies of features like Mammoth Hot Springs and the Grand Canyon of the Yellowstone. Lat-er that year, Hayden and Langford armed themselves with Moran's work when they lobbied Congress to create Yellowstone National Park. He eventually used his sketches to paint larger, richer oil paintings, including a rendition of the canyon that is now hanging at the Smithsonian.

Moran evolved into a genuine Western adventurer, accompanying John Wesley Powell on a Grand Canyon expedition in 1873 and later exploring the Colorado Rockies with Hayden. Upon his death in 1926, he was considered one of the West's greatest landscape painters.

(far left) The Devil's Slide, Yellowstone, *1871, by Thomas Moran; (center) a photo of the artist; (below)* Grand Canyon of the Yellowstone, *1872, by Moran.*

SURVIVOR: YELLOWSTONE

Yellowstone's first recorded survival story is also its most epic. Halfway into the Washburn party's 1870 Yellowstone expedition, Truman Everts fell behind. Knowing him to be a competent woodsman, his pals kept moving. Then Everts's horse bolted, leaving him on foot and without supplies. He wandered for a month, eating thistles and sleeping near hot springs for warmth. When searchers found him, he weighed 50 pounds, was frostbitten, and half-mad (having crawled halfway across Yellowstone without food or fire). The long, steep mountain east of Mammoth bears his name.

skiers in the winter, and it's one of the few places in the park open to mountain bikers. Because the road snakes back to the Upper Terrace Drive, it's best to make this an out-and-back trip or combine it with the Bunsen Peak Trail to form a 7.2-mile loop. Where the two trails meet, the 1.4-mile **Osprey Falls Trail** descends into Sheepeater Canyon to reach Osprey Falls. The Gardner River dives 150 feet into the gorge here, and the misty nook at the foot of the falls feels like a secret hideout—just you, the falls, and maybe a couple of bighorn sheep peering down from the rim.

For a longer excursion—and some of the most classic and diverse scenery in the American West—the ★BLACK CANYON OF THE YELLOWSTONE is an unparalleled hiking experience. The trail follows the Yellowstone River 18.5 miles through the park's northern range, a remote and largely flat trail that's got a little of everything: mountain views, excellent fishing, a grand suspension bridge, the thundering Knowles Falls, and likely run-ins with elk, pronghorns, and even bears. What's more, if you start your hike at the Hellroaring Trailhead four miles west of Tower Junction, you'll lose more than a thousand feet in elevation and end up in the border town of Gardiner, where you can treat yourself to a huckleberry milk shake.

East of Mammoth, the landscape is dominated by the stunning peaks of the Gallatin Range, and a vast network of long-distance trails provides true alpine junkies entrance to this mountain wilderness. If you came to Yellowstone in search of serious backcountry adventure, few routes pose the challenge, or offer the jagged, high-country beauty, of the 40-mile **Gallatin Skyline Trail**. Well-conditioned and well-prepared hikers can graze the sky as they ascend and descend multiple mountain passes, topping out near 10,000 feet above sea level at the lordly Big Horn Peak.

Other Activities

You won't find ★BOILING RIVER on your park map, but that doesn't mean it won't be crowded when you get there. This spot where nearby hot springs pour into the Gardner River lures soakers from mid-summer onward. The rare park-sanctioned frontcountry soak is found a half-mile upstream from the parking area near the sign marking the 45th parallel along the North Entrance Road. Naturists should seek their baths elsewhere, as this is a strictly family-friendly area.

Mountain biking on Old Gardiner Road, the former stagecoach route between Mammoth and Gardiner, will keep your adrenaline level well within street-legal limits, but you'll have good views of Sepulcher Mountain and perhaps an elk herd nonchalantly following your progress. Auto traffic is only allowed to drive north on the gravel road, and though bikers have two-way privileges, it's a five-mile uphill trip from Gardiner to Mammoth.

In winter, check out a free pair of skates from the front desk at the Mammoth Hotel and hit the ice at the **Mammoth Hot Springs ice rink** out back. Holiday tunes trumpet from a PA and a fire roars on the edge of the rink—BYO chestnuts. Winter is also a great time to explore the hot springs of the Upper Terrace, as groomers condi-

Horseback riders silhouetted by the sunset.

DON'T TELL ANNAPOLIS

An elaborate wooden map of the United States hangs on the north wall of the **Map Room**, just off the lobby in the Mammoth Hot Springs Hotel. Architect Robert Reamer designed the map during his renovation of the hotel in 1906, and its rich, mosaiclike appearance comes from the 16 different varieties of wood used to craft it. The hired woodworker's skill is evident in the precise cut of the map's 2,544 pieces, but so is his imperfect grasp of geography—Baltimore is wrongly identified as the capital of Maryland.

tion the easy loop for snowshoes. Check www.yellowstonenationalparklodges.com in winter for grooming status.

WHERE TO EAT

Mammoth Hot Springs Hotel Dining Room. The green-and-burgundy art deco interior of Mammoth's main restaurant is almost enough to keep you from gazing out the large windows at the graceful hump of Capitol Hill. Ignore the menu headings taken from the bad-chain-restaurant playbook (no dessert list should ever come with the title "Perfect Endings"), because the kitchen can impress at dinner, especially with regional fish and a few authentic Italian pasta options. You can make reservations only in the off season, so in summer you should get here early for a table. Breakfast and lunch choices are less exciting. *Mammoth Hot Springs; 307/344–7311 or 866/439–7375.* **$$$–$$$$**

Mammoth Terrace Grill. The counter-service grill that adjoins the dining room at Mammoth is your basic fast food–style budget option, good for a quick bite or for the moment when a greasy burger craving gets the best of you. They also scoop a mean ice cream cone. *Mammoth Hot Springs; 307/344–7311 or 866/439–7375.* **$**

TOWER-ROOSEVELT *See the Yellowstone National Park: Upper Loop and Tower-Roosevelt maps.*

It's fitting that the northeast corner of Yellowstone hosts the Old West–themed Roosevelt Lodge, since in many ways, this region of the park embodies the qualities we attribute to the Western frontier. It's rugged and picturesque, home to robust trout streams and framed by the hackly skyline of the Absaroka Range. It's also comparatively empty, attracting just a fraction of the visitors who make the pilgrim-

Lamar Valley is one of the most reliable places in the park to **spot bison year-round.**

age to Old Faithful or Canyon. Many come just to glimpse the regal Tower Falls, leaving the rest of the region as lonesome as a cowboy campfire ballad. Roosevelt itself is a midsized village, with the lodge, a general store, and a gas station, but not much else.

Yellowstone's northeast corner has long been something of a hinterland, far enough from the park's first nerve centers at Mammoth, Norris, and Old Faithful that early administrators had trouble fending off squatters. Early exploration of Lamar Valley and the Absarokas fell to the miners and prospectors searching for gold there in the mid-1800s. When they discovered it in 1870, Lamar Valley became an important supply route to the burgeoning, rough-and-tumble mining town of Cooke City, then known by the charming moniker "Shoo-Fly."

The frosted face of a bison is one of the park's most iconic images.

LAMAR VALLEY

Low elevation makes Lamar an important wintering range for bison and elk, and in the spring, wildlife watchers line up to see the herds' frolicking new arrivals. The valley is one of the most reliable places

TEDDY IN YELLOWSTONE

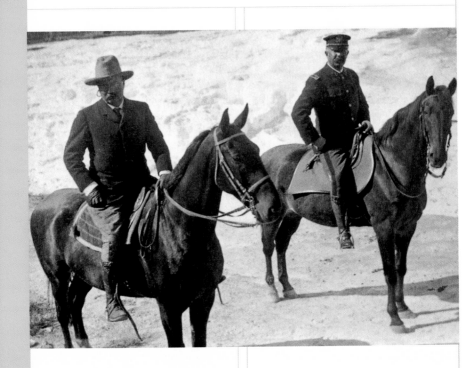

As cofounder of the conservationist Boone and Crockett Club, Theodore "Teddy" Roosevelt was an active advocate for Yellowstone throughout his political career. Among other things, he used his influence as President to help end the practice of exterminating cougars in the park. Roosevelt's visit in 1903 prompted Yellowstone's first bona fide media circus. One reporter even attempted to get a scoop on the President's visit by stalking his party through the backcountry, but cavalry rangers discovered him and gave him the boot. Years later, in his autobiography, Roosevelt would recall his wildlife encounters on that trip, writing, "In Yellowstone, the animals seem always to behave as one wishes them to!"

Theodore Roosevelt (left, with the wide-brimmed hat) at Mammoth Hot Springs in 1903.

in the park to spot bison year-round. It's the site of the Rose Creek Buffalo Ranch, where the park managed a semi-domesticated herd from 1907 to 1952, and which today serves as the campus for the non-profit Yellowstone Institute.

The valley is also home to several competing wolf packs. It's the former territory of Yellowstone's famous Druid Peak Pack, once the world's largest and the park's most frequently glimpsed, though in recent years the Druids have collapsed due to disease and competition from other packs. The Yellowstone Institute (406/848–2400) offers multiday wolf-watching trips, including some lodging and meal packages. The 30-mile route through Lamar Valley is breathtaking; unescorted wildlife watchers should take advantage of its frequent pullouts.

NEARBY SIGHTS

Viewed from across a yawning canyon and surrounded on all sides by menacing, 100-foot stone sentinels, **Tower Fall** comes at you like something out of *Lord of the Rings*. The 132-foot cascade just south of Tower Junction, where the Northeast Entrance Road meets the Grand Loop, would be impressive even without the massive eroded rock columns that inspired its name. A paved trail leads 200 feet down from the lookout to the floor of the Grand Canyon. (From down there you'll have a good view of the imposing canyon walls, but you can't glimpse the fall.) The Yellowstone General Store at Tower Fall draws a crowd, as it's one of few places for groceries and supplies in the northeast corner of the park.

A mile north of Tower Fall is the small and usually crowded parking lot for the **Calcite Springs Overlook.** A short boardwalk loop leads to views of **The Narrows** section of the Grand Canyon, where rapidly cooling lava from an ancient volcanic flow formed the columnar basalt formations that give the far canyon wall the look of a medieval fortress.

Fifty million years ago, in the aftermath of one of Yellowstone's powerful volcanic eruptions, mud and ash swallowed the tree that now sits 1.5 miles west of Tower Junction. Silica particles clogged air pockets in the tree's bark, trunk, and root systems, hardening and preserving the tree in remarkable detail. Just over a century ago, this **Petrified Tree** was put behind a big iron cage—a move that seems unnecessary until you learn there were once *two* petrified trees at this site. Vandals carried away all evidence of the second in the early 1900s. Though the fence prevents close inspection of the remaining fossilized trunk, you can clearly admire the gnarled and knotty

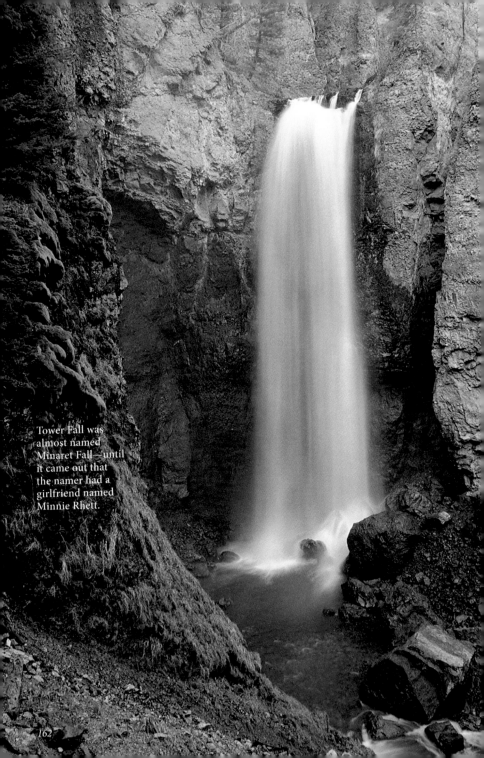

Tower Fall was almost named Minaret Fall—until it came out that the namer had a girlfriend named Minnie Rhett.

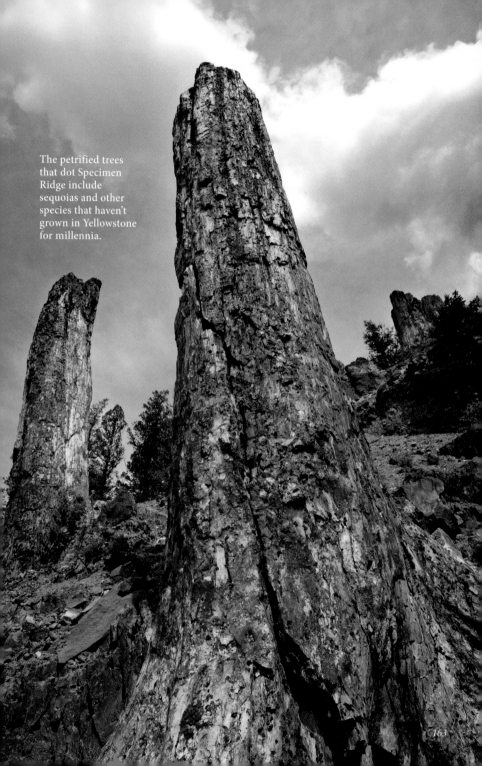

The petrified trees that dot Specimen Ridge include sequoias and other species that haven't grown in Yellowstone for millennia.

163

texture of the preserved bark. This roadside attraction is just one of hundreds of petrified specimens scattered throughout the park's northeast corner. (For a much closer look at Yellowstone's petrified trees, and a much tougher trip, *see* Best Hiking Trails, *below*.)

Best Hiking Trails

Few Yellowstone hikes as gentle as the **Yellowstone River Picnic Area Trail** offer as much solitude or such an abundance of spectacular scenery. This 3.7-mile loop begins at the picnic area trailhead one mile east of Tower Junction and starts by ascending a mellow 200 feet up a sagebrush hillside to the rim of the Grand Canyon. And that's it for elevation gain. The rest of this two-hour amble is a lovely series of canyon overlooks, wildflower explosions in late spring and summer, and Absaroka mountain vistas. Glacial erratic boulders strewn around the trail make fine playgrounds for troupes of yellow-bellied marmots, so keep an ear cocked for their high-pitched chirps and whistles.

Tough out the first 1.5 miles of the **Pebble Creek Trail,** a steep 900-foot climb beginning across the road from the Warm Creek Picnic Area, just west of the Northeast Entrance. The ensuing 10.5 miles more than compensate, descending gradually through lupine-perfumed meadows (and a handful of agreeably brisk stream crossings). Colonies of marmots chum it up with you at picturesque backcountry campsite 3P1, perfectly situated on the creek banks beneath the imposing flat-top of 10,404-foot Barronette Peak. The trail winds up at Pebble Creek Campground, an eight-mile shuttle from the trailhead.

Yellowstone's through-the-roof wow factor comes in part because its most astonishing features are all relatively easy to access. Not so in the case of the ★**PETRIFIED FOREST,** a cathedral-like plot of millennia-defying trunks that's something of a hidden Yellowstone gem. This astonishing frozen grove can be reached only after a grueling climb in a remote section of the park. Mountain man and world-class exaggerator Jim Bridger once famously recalled a visit, describing a land of "peetrified trees a-growing with peetrified birds on 'em a-singing peetrified songs."

A SMITTEN TRAPPER

"I almost wished I could spend the remainder of my days in a place like this, where happiness and contentment seemed to reign in wild romantic splendor, surrounded by majestic battlements which seemed to support the heavens. . . ."

—Trapper Osborne Russell, writing in his journal after first seeing Lamar Valley in 1835

Blobs of lava hardened to form the columnar basalt cliffs that line sections of the Grand Canyon of the Yellowstone.

You may not spot any calcified birds, but on this silent hillside you'll find dozens of cold stone trees standing within a still-living forest. Begin at the unmarked trailhead just west of the Lamar River Bridge on the Northeast Entrance Road. An old service road leads through 300 feet of sagebrush flat to a trail on the right. The out-and-back trail immediately begins climbing a steep forested hill, and it only stops climbing 1.5 miles and 1,200 feet later, where an immense petrified redwood stump welcomes you to the fossil forest. On the well-defined network of social trails clinging to the slopes below, fossilized wood chips littering the ground are almost indistinguishable from the rocks, and you can peer down into the Lamar Valley at entire constellations of bison.

OTHER ACTIVITIES

The Old West is new again at Roosevelt, and the **Roosevelt Corral** (307/344–7311 or 866/439–7375) just east of the lodge is a hopping equine headquarters in the summer. One-hour horseback rides lead pack trains north through the sagebrush flats of Pleasant Valley, where the toothlike ridge of Hellroaring Mountain rises behind Garnet Hill's gentler forested bump. If you sign up for the two-hour option, you'll hear a chorus of croaks while detouring around marshy Lost Lake.

Stagecoach and horseback rides are popular activities at Roosevelt Lodge.

Feeling saddle-shy? Daily **stagecoach rides** take guests on an hour-long trip in replicas of what once passed for mass transit in Yellowstone. The bright yellow coaches are covered, the benches padded, and the high, spare scenery is spaghetti-western perfect.

Each of these horse-powered trips can be combined with the immensely popular ★**OLD WEST DINNER COOKOUT** (307/344–7311 or 866/439–7375), a family-friendly cowboy grubfest served three miles north of the village beneath a canvas awning in a high-country meadow. This is ranch-hand chow—thick ribeyes and cornbread—and the sound of forks scraping tin plates is accompanied by a crooning cowboy balladeer. The cookout site was once the grounds of the Pleasant Valley Hotel and saloon, a rough-and-tumble and only quasi-legal establishment opened by longtime park squatter "Uncle" John Yancey in 1884. Much of the property burned to the ground in 1906, but your wranglers can spin a few tales about the backcountry hotelier known to brag that his whiskey glasses had never seen a drop of water. Last-minute seats on the stagecoach are usually available, but trail rides to the rain-or-shine cookout should be booked months in advance.

"'Twas but a slough," is how one prospecting scout wrote off the shallow, meandering waters of **Slough Creek** in 1867. His party sought gold, but today the river is filled with anglers seeking the fat and wily trout that have made it a world-famous cutthroat stream. Slough Creek Road provides access to the creek six miles east of Tower Junction, off the Northeast Entrance Road, and the river-following trail at Slough Creek Campground extends another 11 miles to the park boundary. The trail is actually a wagon road providing nonmotorized access to a guest ranch north of the park, so foot travel is easy. In fact, access is so easy and the **fishing** so good that hordes of fly fisherman must compete for space in the prime months of July and August. Midsummer mosquitoes and deerflies make a wade in Slough Creek torturous, but the lurking 22-inch trout are a powerful lure.

WHERE TO EAT

Roosevelt Lodge Dining Room. Just because you're pausing to eat is no reason to get out from among Yellowstone's towering pines. The bark-and-all trunks serving as pillars in the Roosevelt Dining Room complement the organic feel of the room's hardwood floor and fieldstone fireplace. The menu has a slight south-of-the-border flair, with entrées like pork carnitas and shrimp tacos, but the bulk of the menu is cowboy chow, like smoky-sweet barbecue, fried chicken, and knockout baked beans so loaded with beef and bacon they eat like a meal. *Roosevelt Village at Tower Junction; 307/344–7311 or 866/439–7375.* **$$–$$$**

BACKCOUNTRY 101

The cluster of cabins sitting in the sagebrush halfway up Lamar Valley is the humble field campus of the Yellowstone Institute. The Institute is the educational arm of the nonprofit Yellowstone Association, which funds a variety of park endeavors with privately raised donations and proceeds from its bookstores throughout the park.

The breadth of courses offered by the Institute during any given season is almost dizzying. In summer, dozens of different Field Seminars ($150–$1,500) bring guests together with biologists, historians, and other experts for one- to four-day classes at either the Lamar campus, park lodges, or a new field campus just outside Gardiner. Topics range from waterfowl migration to native history to sculpting, while a smaller catalog in winter might include first aid and tracking classes. Lodging & Learning Programs ($790–$2,100) offer lodge stays combined with more active days spent delving into wildlife and geography topics. Dedicated wilderness students might consider customizable backpacking trips, on which small groups, led by both wilderness guides and interpretive specialists, trek through some of the park's far-flung regions. Rates vary by group size and itinerary.

⊙ CANYON VILLAGE

See the Yellowstone National Park: Upper Loop and Canyon Village maps.

It's a long way down.... Peering over the brink of the Lower Falls.

Following his first glimpse of the vast Grand Canyon of the Yellowstone in 1869, early Yellowstone explorer David Folsom wrote, "Language is inadequate to convey a just conception of the awful grandeur and sublimity of this masterpiece of nature's handiwork." Folsom's "awful grandeur" still permeates the canyon—it echoes as river-roar off thousand-foot cliffs tinged with ochre and henna, it rides the same spiraling air currents that cradle a wing-wet osprey, and it shimmers in the backsplash mists that obscure the base of the Lower Falls like a silver-sequined skirt.

Canyon is the second most-visited area of the park, behind Old Faithful, and its history as a tourist destination is as colorful as the rocks lining the V-shaped slopes. A plot just upstream from the Upper Falls hosted one of the park's first "tent hotels" beginning in 1883. In the 1890s, park administrators and concession companies considered installing a massive elevator to transport guests from the lip of the canyon to the base of the Lower Falls—a proposal that was blessedly abandoned. The first Canyon Hotel was erected in 1891, and parts of that structure were incorporated 20 years later into the "new" Canyon Hotel, a grand Prairie-style lodge designed by unofficial park architect

Robert Reamer. Few demolitions in the park have prompted as much bitter controversy as when the popular but structurally unsound Canyon Hotel was razed in 1959. Its replacement, today's Canyon Village, is a squat, bustling, and almost suburban spread with a full range of visitor services.

Fifteen miles upstream from the canyon is the mouth of Yellowstone Lake, where ice dams once repressed the flow of the Yellowstone River during the last glacial period. As the ice age waned, the dams gave way, releasing torrents of water that flooded and charged downriver toward the current-day canyon area. The rock in this region is volcanic rhyolite, deposited by a lava flow about 480,000 years ago. The area is also hydrothermally active, and the heat and gases from the thermal basins soften and weaken the rhyolite, making it particularly susceptible to erosion. When the furious waters released by the ice dams struck this hydrothermally enfeebled rock, they carved out the massive canyon we recognize today.

The canyon remains an active hydrothermal basin—you can spot steam plumes and geyser spouts here and there from the rim—and it continues to be slowly eroded by the Yellowstone River. Oxidized iron lends the cliff faces their burnt orange, red, and yellow tones. The canyon extends for 20 miles, descending 1,200 feet at its deepest and ranging from 1,500 to 4,000 feet across.

THE FALLS

The Upper and Lower Falls of the Yellowstone River mark the edge of the region's hydrothermal activity. Where normally erosion-resistant rhyolite from the Canyon lava flow meets up with softer, hydrothermally altered rock, the river has carved the two massive falls that rank among Yellowstone's most recognizable landmarks. The 308-foot **Lower Falls** is the taller of the two, and easily the most photographed. Though spectacular in any season, the water volume is at its highest in the spring. You have a choice of observation points along the North Rim and South Rim drives. Bring binoculars to glimpse osprey nests in the adjacent cliffs and active geysers at the foot of the falls.

Gravity seems to tug a bit more insistently here, as you watch more than 37,000 gallons of water careen into the canyon each second.

The first observation point you reach along the one-way North Rim Drive is the **Brink of the Lower Falls,** where you can experience the singular rush that comes from breathtaking scenery cut with impending doom. The easily tired and vertigo-prone might avoid the 600-foot descent (in less than a mile) that takes you within spitting distance of the falls' lip. Gravity seems to tug more insistently here, as you watch more than 37,000 gallons of water careen into the canyon each second.

★RED ROCK POINT, a half-mile east, may be the best place to glimpse the Lower Falls. It's a long walk down on a series of paved switchbacks, but from the lower vantage point, the canyon seems to open up around you. You'll feel like you're in an encompassing bowl rather than a crevasse. Plus, the steep walk deters many folks from making the trip, so you can be all alone here, when the other lookouts are packed. You'll be closer to the rushing water and looking up at its dizzying height.

Farther along, **Grandview Point** and **Lookout Point** are much roomier and similarly picturesque. Each of these has a bit of a scenic drawback, though. Grandview lacks a view of the falls, and Lookout's canyon view is less stellar than that at Inspiration Point.

The final observation point is **Inspiration Point,** a mile southeast of Canyon Junction. The 15- by 15-foot concrete slab is surrounded

The classic view of the Lower Falls of the Yellowstone River. At 308 feet, the waterfall is twice the height of Niagara.

PEOPLE IN THE PARKS: LINDA YOUNG, RANGER

Now Yellowstone's chief of resource education, Young spent 30-plus years working in the park, including stints as a seasonal interpreter and a curator.

Brian Kevin: In the visitor education centers, how do you balance the need for thorough information about complex scientific concepts with the need to explain those ideas to people like me?

Linda Young: We know first of all that when people come to the park, they want to be *in* the park, so we don't develop visitor centers to replace the real experience. You design exhibits to focus in on one or two key ideas. You use a lot of visuals, maybe some kind of verbal presentation, since people learn differently.

BK: Love the Yellowstone podcasts on iTunes. Is Yellowstone going digital?

LY: It's important to be able to explore the park from a distance. Live streaming webcams at Old Faithful Geyser—we're so excited by that. Some people leave their browser open all day to watch the geysers. We're also experimenting with some live-streaming ranger programs.

BK: Bad news—Monday will be the next cataclysmic eruption of the Yellowstone volcano. How do you spend your last few days in the park?

LY: Pulled over in the middle of Hayden Valley in the summertime where there are vast herds of bison. Watching them rolling and dusting themselves or wading through the river—it's just sort of mesmerizing, I think.

by chain-link fence at the end of a short flight of concrete stairs. The view is fantastic, as you can see the Lower Falls peeking from behind a bend in the canyon. Being trapped in a concrete box with 25 other sightseers, however, is less than inspiring. You might seek this inspiration in the evening when it's less crowded.

On South Rim Drive, off Canyon–Lake Road, two points give particularly awesome views of the Lower Falls. **Uncle Tom's Trail** (.5 mile off Canyon–Lake Rd.) takes you down 500 feet, inside the deafening roar and dampening spray at the foot of the falls. The paved grades and 300-plus stairs beat the early-20th-century alternative, though, when tourists reached the lookout via rope ladder. ★**ARTIST POINT** (end of South Rim Drive) draws crowds for its easy accessibility and its jawdropping view of the canyon and falls. This perspective prompted the artist Thomas Moran to famously declare the area "beyond the reach of human art." He gave it his best shot, though, and the resulting oil painting hangs prominently at the Smithsonian Museum.

The **Upper Falls** suffers from a serious inferiority complex. If it were located anywhere other than Yellowstone, the majestic 109-foot falls would draw busloads of tourists. As it happens, you might find yourself alone at either of the Upper Falls overlooks, free to contemplate the cascade that explorer Captain John Barlow described in 1871 as "the embodiment of beauty." Get the long view at the **Upper Falls Viewpoint** on the south rim (South Rim Dr., just east of Chittenden Bridge) or the extreme close-up at the **Brink of the**

Upper Falls (just off Canyon–Lake Rd., .5 mile south of Canyon Junction) on the north rim.

The canyon overlooks are accessible sans car via the three-mile **North Rim Trail** and the 1.75-mile **South Rim Trail.** These two flat trails parallel the roads and are partially paved. You can hop onto them at several points, but an easy place to access either one is at Chittendon Bridge. Only from the North Rim Trail can you glimpse the hush-hush "third falls." **Crystal Falls** dives 129 feet in an elegant triple cascade about halfway between the two "brink" overlooks. On the trail just above the falls is a fascinating spot where Cascade Creek plunges in and out of a small cave. Cautious and sure-footed hikers can shimmy about 20 yards down a barely visible spur trail for a closer look.

Nearby Sights

The hands-on multimedia exhibits at the ★CANYON VISITOR EDUCATION CENTER (307/242–2550) do the work of piles of textbooks to catch you up on Yellowstone's complex geologic story. You can easily spend a half-hour just exploring the massive, three-dimensional park relief map, which lights up to illustrate fault lines, glacial routes, and a timeline of the Yellowstone supervolcano's major lava flows. If the cataclysm of a Yellowstone eruption doesn't trip you out, you might try ogling one of the world's largest lava lamps or spinning (yes, spinning) the 9,000-pound granite globe. This is one of the parks' most engaging visitor centers.

CANYON VISITOR
EDUCATION
CENTER
- - - - - - - - - - - - -
TEL:
307/242–2550

A glacial erratic boulder along the road to Inspiration Point marks the trailhead for the aptly named Glacial Boulder Trail, along which you can spot the **Silver Cord Cascade** on the south rim. Over the course of a leisurely and largely flat mile, you pass several eye-popping canyon vistas, but none compares to the graceful thread of water pouring 800 feet into the canyon from Ribbon Lake. Though it's actually a series of several separate falls, Silver Cord was likely the inspiration for tall tales among Yellowstone explorers of 1,000-foot waterfalls along the canyon rim.

Best Hiking Trails

Three different routes reach the summit of ★MOUNT WASHBURN, the 10,243-foot remnant of a mountain range that once stretched 40 miles across the Yellowstone plateau to the Red Mountains near the park's southern boundary. When those mountains literally blew up during Yellowstone's last great volcanic event 600,000 years ago, the result was the 1,500-square-foot Yellowstone caldera—and the killer panoramic views that bring thousands of visitors up Mount Washburn each year. The most popular and least strenuous route begins at **Dunraven Pass,** five miles north of Canyon Junction. The three-mile former stagecoach route gains 1,400 feet as it ascends Washburn's south face, passing through the park's most spectacular and diverse wildflower meadows that peak in June and July. Watch for bighorn sheep, and be sure to take advantage of the telescope in the fire-lookout cabin at the summit.

The campsite cluster at **Sevenmile Hole** represents one of just two opportunities to camp inside the Grand Canyon of the Yellowstone. (The other is far to the north at Agate Creek, where the canyon is neither as steep nor as deep.) It isn't a seven-mile descent into the canyon, though it may feel like it on the way up; the site is actually about seven river-miles downstream from the Lower Falls. Follow the Glacial Boulder Trail from the Inspiration Point road two miles to the Sevenmile Hole Trail, then descend three steep miles into the canyon. The hike up is worth it for a close-up look at the multicolored canyon walls and several backcountry thermal features.

You can walk with the swagger of a genuine wilderness adventurer after a trip along the **Wapiti Lake Trail.** The route begins on the south end of the South Rim Drive, just east of Chittenden Bridge, and ascends gently for 14 miles before steeply dropping off to meet Wapiti Lake at mile 16. But the real adventure begins at mile 15, where well-conditioned backpackers with solid route-finding skills can follow Broad Creek off-trail toward the rainbow-tinged hills and pools of Josephs Coat Hot Springs, five miles downstream near backcountry campsite 4B1. This is a treacherous route, thickly wooded and pocked with unmarked thermal features. The springs themselves are glimpsed by only a handful of people each year—a reminder that the essence of Yellowstone remains thorny and wild.

OTHER ACTIVITIES

Five miles north of Dunraven Pass, the gravel **Chittenden Road** provides a route to the summit of Mount Washburn open to **cycling.** Granted, it takes a semi-masochistic cyclist to appreciate the view and the admittedly fun three-mile descent after the punishing incline of the approach.

If you feel like you're running into the **Howard Eaton Trail** every time you turn around, you're not imagining things. The park's longest trail once meandered its way to nearly all of the villages, though today much of it is unmaintained or off-limits as habitat. The stretch just west of Canyon is good for **backpacking;** it's got shoreline campsites surrounding four high-country lakes. This area is popular for **fly-fishing** and **birding,** too. Marshy Grebe Lake has rainbow and increasingly rare grayling trout, plus whole councils of waterfowl and raptors. You can access the Eaton trail from several trailheads along the Norris-Canyon and Canyon-Tower roads.

The **Canyon Corral** (Canyon–Lake Rd., 1 mile south of Canyon Junction) leads one- and two-hour **horseback trips** along nearby Cascade Creek. The longer trip takes a route along the shallow but scenic Cascade Canyon, and the views are worth a saddlesore bottom. Make reservations at the Canyon Lodge or through the Xanterra reservation hotline (307/344–7311 or 866/439–7375).

Where to Eat

Canyon Lodge Dining Room. Some parts of the distinctly 1950s-style Canyon development have aged better than others, and where the dated cabins and hokey retro gift shop are village shortcomings, Canyon's lounge and dining room have a Rat Pack-ish vibe. In the lounge, you can sip a huckleberry martini beneath giant, asterisk-shaped light fixtures as embers crackle in the stone fireplace. The dining room's specialty burgers are a good bet at lunch or dinner; try the superb, smokey-sweet salmon burger made with sustainably raised fish. *Canyon Village; 307/344–7311 or 866/439–7375.* **$$–$$$**

  Canyon Lodge Cafeteria and Deli. The crowds at Canyon move fluidly and quickly through this clean, bright room. Think egg dishes for breakfast, sandwiches for lunch, and dinner entrées like those in the dining room: chicken, fish, a pasta bar. It's counterservice only at both the caf and the neighboring deli. *Canyon Village; 307/344–7311 or 866/439–7375.* **$–$$**

  Canyon Soda Fountain. Just because you're not cooking over a fire pit doesn't mean you can't have a little camp with your meal. The 1950s-style diner inside Canyon's Yellowstone General Store takes the village's Eisenhower-era look and runs with it, serving up burgers and diner-style breakfasts in a room full of neon, swivel stools, and broad Formica countertops. Sure, it's all a little hokey, but the paper-hat-wearing waitstaff serves up the best root-beer float in the park. If Richie Cunningham and the Fonz came to Yellowstone, this is where they'd stop. *Canyon Village; 307/242–7377.* **$**

Spotlight on
WINTER IN YELLOWSTONE

The best reason for a visit to the Yellowstone region between December and March is the opportunity to experience the parks without crowds. There are many intense, unique sensory and sightseeing pleasures, too. The first thing that strikes you about winter here is the quiet. The gargantuan snowpack—as many as 200 inches annually at low elevation—seems to muffle the sounds of bison foraging in the geyser basins and of hot springs simmering. Wildlife migrates into the valleys, meaning elk and bison herds are easier to spot. If you're ready to work up a sweat on a pair of skis or snowshoes, you'll be rewarded with alpenglow in the Gallatin, Teton, and Absaroka ranges that's at its most luminous in winter. In the solitude and silence of Greater Yellowstone's "secret season," even an easy boardwalk stroll feels like an exhilarating journey.

◄◄ Moose Falls, an easy-to-reach spot near Yellowstone's South Entrance.

It's amazing to see how wind and cold make Greater Yellowstone even more otherworldly. The thermal basins look like factories, as steam pours from geysers, hot springs, and fumaroles. Plants cling to life around the thermals, where heat leaves patches of open ground and melts the snowdrifts into bizarre, Seussian shapes. Cold temperatures send mud pots into slow motion, their bubbles gradually swelling and popping. Heavy coats of snow disguise the familiar faces of the Teton peaks. Smaller waterfalls freeze solid, while giants like Yellowstone's Lower Falls freeze partially, with water cascading over icicles as big as grain silos. Despite its size, Yellowstone Lake ices over completely, becoming a great white snowscape that groans as the ice beneath it shifts.

Air bubbles trapped in lake ice.

As surface ice on frozen lakes changes temperature, it cracks and thrusts up ice slabs called pressure ridges.

Lower
Falls

Old Faithful

Yellowstone
Lake

**YELLOWSTONE
NATIONAL PARK**

A hot spring pool in the West Thumb Geyser Basin remains unfrozen in winter.

Steam from the hot springs smothers snowy boardwalks at West Thumb.

WILDLIFE SPOTTING

As a rule, animals in Yellowstone and Grand Teton head *down* when the thermometer falls. Herbivores like elk and bison head to the warmer, less snowy valleys to find vegetation; predators like wolves and cougars follow them. As a result, you're more likely to see these animals in the frontcountry in winter than in other seasons, and they're often easier to spot against the white backdrop. Some bison journey west from their rutting grounds in Hayden Valley to forage in the geyser basins. Others move to Lamar Valley and other low areas north of Yellowstone. Elk congregate in a massive herd at the National Elk Refuge outside of Jackson. Keep one eye on the ground as you explore—the snow makes it easy to pick out animal tracks.

Heat-seeking bison in the Lower Geyser Basin.

A looker of a cow elk stops snowcoach traffic in Yellowstone.

The red fox *(top left)* hunts small rodents in winter by listening for them beneath the snow. Its most endearing habit is its pounce, when it dives headfirst into a snowdrift to come up with a wriggling snack. If you're lucky, you might spot the tracks of the elusive, rare lynx *(upper right)*. It's easier to spy the lookalike bobcat. Resourceful otters *(left)* take advantage of thermal ice-melt in the rivers to fish and avoid predators.

GET OUT IN THE COLD

Since motorized travel is limited in Greater Yellowstone during winter, you'll have the greatest range of exploration if you're traveling under your own steam. But in Yellowstone, you can also travel by snowcoach. These coaches have tracks instead of tires to navigate the park's snowed-in roads and are used for both tours and general transportation. The old-school variety, called Bombardiers, are squat, sputtery little things with snug interiors often dominated by the sound and smell of the engine. Newer models are often no more than conversion vans all Frankensteined up with giant skis and tank treads—a more comfortable, if less authentic, ride. Snowcoaches carry passengers in groups of a dozen or so, with drivers acting as chatty guides. Keep your camera handy as you trundle along in these slow-going behemoths.

AERIAL TRAM

Powderhounds cheered when Jackson Hole Mountain Resort unveiled its bigger, faster "Big Red Box" in 2008. The Jackson Hole Aerial Tram traverses the largest vertical rise in North America, ascending by cable 4,139 feet to the summit of Rendezvous Peak—with breathtaking alpine views along the way. It's used by both skiers and sightseers. *See* the Gateway Towns chapter for more info.

One of Xanterra's Bombardier snowcoaches unloads in front of Old Faithful Snow Lodge.

Jackson Hole
Aerial Tram

**GRAND TETON
NATIONAL PARK**

Swooshing through the snow behind a team of sled dogs, you can barely hear their excited panting over the sound of the wind in your ears. Jackson is a mushing capital, home to multiple Iditarod veterans. Though dogsledding isn't permitted in the parks, **Jackson Hole Iditarod Sled Dog Tours** (800/554–7388) and **Continental Divide Dog Sled Adventures** (307/222–0421) lead trips in the nearby national forests.

Snowmobiling in Greater Yellowstone remains popular, if controversial. There are plenty of designated routes in the national forests, but the parks have been embroiled in court battles over snowmobiling inside their borders. (Opponents cite the snowmobiles' noise and pollution.) At this writing, Yellowstone allows a regulated number of guided and nonguided snowmobiles, with strict emission and permit requirements. In Grand Teton National Park, snowmobiles are allowed only on Jackson Lake to provide access to ice fishermen. Here, a sledder roars along the hills at Togwotee Pass, east of Grand Teton.

Cross-country skiing is the best way to see the parks in the secret season. You'll see the landscape on a more intimate scale, a sense reinforced by the closeness of the winter weather. Snowed-under roads and paved trails make ideal routes for beginner skiers, with the chance of encounters like this one between skiers and bison in the Upper Geyser Basin. Yellowstone is also a backcountry skier's Shangri-La. In Grand Teton, the relatively flat floor of Jackson Hole makes for easy skiing with breathtaking views.

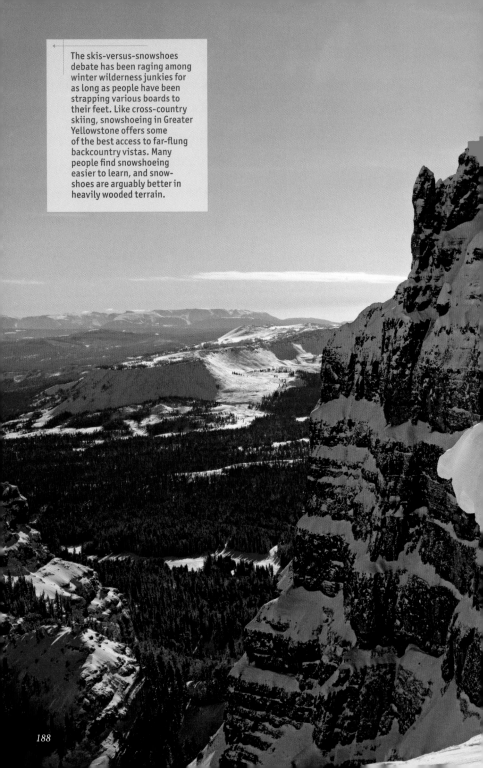

The skis-versus-snowshoes debate has been raging among winter wilderness junkies for as long as people have been strapping various boards to their feet. Like cross-country skiing, snowshoeing in Greater Yellowstone offers some of the best access to far-flung backcountry vistas. Many people find snowshoeing easier to learn, and snow-shoes are arguably better in heavily wooded terrain.

WINTERTIME TIPS

SAFETY FIRST. Admittedly, official safety checklists can be a bit overbearing. But in these winter extremes, there's no messing around. The parks' newspapers and the NPS website publish exhaustive gear guides and safety tips. Follow them to the letter.

PACK SUNSCREEN. It's 10°F and overcast—why bother with sunscreen? Because UV rays don't take winter vacation, so slather on the SPF. (I learned the hard way by getting a debilitating sunburn while skiing in Yellowstone.)

WARMING TREND. Most structures are shuttered up throughout winter, but Yellowstone maintains a few warming huts with drinks and snacks. Find them at Canyon, Fishing Bridge, Indian Creek, Madison, Mammoth, Old Faithful, and West Thumb. In Grand Teton, the Dornan's complex in Moose keeps some concessions open year-round.

GIVE YOURSELF SOME WIGGLE ROOM. Winter travel to and from Yellowstone and Grand Teton is complex. The closest airports to Yellowstone are more than an hour away, road conditions are volatile, and snowcoach schedules are capricious. Don't time your travels to the hour. Instead, bookend in-park excursions with nights in the gateway towns.

TOTAL PACKAGE. The easiest and most budget-friendly way to stay in Yellowstone's two winter lodges (Mammoth Hotel and Old Faithful Snow Lodge) is to book a single package with **Xanterra** (866/439–7375; www.yellowstonenationalparklodges.com) or the **Yellowstone Institute** (406/848–2400; www.yellowstoneassociation.org). This takes less time and money than separately booking lodging, meals, activities, and snowcoaches.

Hitting the powder.

Yurt Camp

Yellowstone River

**YELLOWSTONE
NATIONAL PARK**

Deep in Yellowstone National Park, outfitter **Yellowstone Expeditions** (406/646–9333; www.yellowstoneexpeditions. com) erects a temporary skiers' community each winter. Yurt Camp is where to find Yellow-stone's most intense winter experience, skiing your brains out and relaxing in the yurts themselves, cozy wood-and-canvas structures that serve as the camp's cooking, dining, and social areas. The excellent guides lead flexible daily trips, and beginners are welcome.

Grand Teton National Park

Mount Moran reflected in the Snake River at Oxbow Bend—one of the most popular spots in the park for landscape photography.

In summer, entire
meadows of Grand
Teton National
Park explode with
silvery-blue lupines.

195

Mountain climbers ascending Grand Teton, looking down at the Middle Teton Glacier.

GRAND TETON

ELEVATION:
13,770 feet

PART OF: The Cathedral Group, along with Mt. Owen and Teewinot

FASTEST ASCENT/ DESCENT: 3 hours, 6 minutes, set by Bryce Thatcher in 1983

Sunrise over Jackson Hole.

◉→ THE SHAPING OF GRAND TETON

Seven thousand feet above the sagebrush flats of Jackson Hole, protruding like a cufflink from a hunk of wind-battered granite, a tiny disk of scuffed aluminum marks the summit of Grand Teton. It was placed there in 1968, anchored into the rock at 13,770 feet by members of the U.S. Geological Survey. In the space where most USGS summit markers note an elevation, Grand Teton's marker is left blank, a reminder, perhaps, that the mystique of Wyoming's second tallest peak comes not from its height, but from the dramatic profile it cuts across the sky. To touch the summit of Grand Teton is a singular feat, but it is equally transcendent to be touched *by* the mountain—by its angles, its authority, and the long shadow it casts over Grand Teton National Park.

The Grand, as it's known, and the similarly impressive peaks surrounding it form the Teton Range, the youngest mountains in the Rockies. The mountains themselves abut the park's western border, with the broad valley of Jackson Hole filling in the rest of the park's 310,000 acres. (It's less than one-seventh the size of Yellowstone.)

Unlike the volcanically formed Absarokas that dominate Yellowstone's eastern skyline, the abrupt rise of the Tetons is the result of earthquake activity. The Teton fault formed this way about 13 million years ago, a crack in the Earth running north to south along

Elk grazing with a
Teton range backdrop.

Sunset over Grand
Teton and the rest
of the Teton range.

the mountains' eastern front. During millions of years of tremendous earthquakes—some prompted by energy from the hotspot—the plate on the east side of the fault slid deeper into the earth, displacing chunks of subcrustal material that then wedged beneath the western plate, forcing it upward. We have this tectonic movement to thank for great views of the Tetons' sharp eastern face; there are no foothills to block the panorama. Over time, the mountains' highest sedimentary layers eroded away, exposing rock types usually hidden deep within the earth. As a result, though the Tetons are the youngest mountains in the Rockies, they're comprised of some of the oldest rocks. The glacial millennia gave the mountains their nips and tucks, carving valleys, chiseling rock faces, and leaving behind the park's signature glacial lakes, each one reflecting the surrounding peaks.

The indigenous groups that hunted and foraged in the Jackson Hole region, notably the Shoshone and Bannock tribes, had fine Dungeons & Dragons–esque names for these mountains, like "The Hoary Headed Fathers" and "The Ghost Robbers." Leave it to the overimaginative and sex-starved fur trappers visiting the region in the early 1800s to have named the central trio of peaks after a part of the female anatomy: "les Trois Tétons," or "the Three Breasts." Thankfully, regional trapper Davey Jackson found his name attached to the diverse and wildlife-rich valley—or "hole," in trapper slang—before his bawdier peers claimed the naming rights.

Grand Teton National Park as it exists today didn't come into being until 1950, more than 75 years after its landmark neighbor to the north. A half-century of settlement prior to national park status has left the valley as rich in historic structures as it is in natural resources. Jackson Hole is characterized by the winding Snake River, by sagebrush steppe, and by stands of pine and aspen, but it is also dotted with turn-of-the-20th-century homesteads, ranches working and defunct, and other relics. As you drive, hike, bike, and paddle through the park, it's worth tearing your eyes every so often from the Tetons' weathered splendor in order to examine the artifacts that make Grand Teton National Park as much a living museum as an outdoor playground.

The historic Barn on
Mormon Row is beloved
by Teton photographers,
with a peaked profile that
mimics the mountaintops.

⊙ EXPLORING THE PARK

See the Grand Teton National Park and Jackson Hole maps.

When you enter Grand Teton from the north, the shoreline of **Jackson Lake** is a constant companion along the 10-mile drive to **Colter Bay Village,** where a full range of visitor facilities attracts mobs of tourists throughout the summer. The newly renovated **Colter Bay Visitor Center** (off U.S. 89/191/287, 5 miles north of Jackson Lake Junction, 307/739–3594) has a great viewing deck out back and a small auditorium showing films about Native American history. There's a bookstore and a small gallery displaying items from the park's vast collection of indigenous weapons, crafts, and other artifacts. Permits are available for boating and the backcountry.

Even when compared to the monuments behind it, Jackson Lake is an impressive sight, a huge swath of blue separating the remote northern Tetons from the roads and services on the eastern shore. A flotilla of boats takes to its still waters in high season. A spur road at Jackson Lake Junction heads east toward Moran Junction and U.S. 26/89/191, what's frequently referred to as the Jackson Highway or Outer Park Road. West of Jackson Lake Junction, where Teton Park Road crosses the **Jackson Lake Dam,** an interpretive display explains this fascinat-

Sleek and handsome, the Rockefeller Preserve Center is one of the most energy-efficient buildings in the national park system.

ing and sometimes controversial feature. Though Jackson Lake is a natural glacial lake, the dam—which predates the park by several decades—regulates the flow of water to the **Snake River.** Since Idaho farmers downstream own much of the regional water rights, irrigation demands in dry summers can drain the lake to unsightly levels. Consider it a glimpse into the messy drama of water-rights policy in the West.

South of the dam and Colter Bay, the **Signal Mountain Summit Road** (off Teton Park Rd., 4 miles south of Jackson Lake Junction) presents that rare opportunity to top out on a mountain peak without having to turn off the a/c, though the paved, five-mile route to this isolated 7,720-foot summit is no picnic for your engine (RVs and trailers are prohibited). Two overlooks—one at the summit, the other about three-quarters of the way up—show off the Teton skyline as well the valley's pastiche of forests, grasslands, and buttes. Get an alpine start (that means before dawn) to watch the sun spill into the valley over the mellow Gros Ventre Range to the east.

Continue following Teton Park Road south to reach the glacial blue **Jenny Lake.** Smaller than Jackson Lake and used by far fewer boaters, the lake nonetheless sees a lot of foot traffic on its shoreline. Next to the general store at the crowded visitor area off South Jenny Lake Junction is a modest log cabin that once served as a studio for early park photographer Hank Crandall. It now houses the **Jenny Lake Visitor Center** (Jenny Lake; 307/739–3392), consisting of a small bookstore, a few illustrated geology displays, and a 3-D relief map. It's worth stopping by the humble visitor center to sign up for the 2.5-hour interpretive hike to **Inspiration Point,** a popular daily ranger-guided trek that's limited to 25 participants (*see* Best Hiking Trails, *below*). Mountaineers and those planning backcountry trips can see an even more detailed relief map at the **Jenny Lake Ranger Station** (307/739–3343) just a few yards up the path.

**JENNY LAKE
VISITOR CENTER**

TEL:
307/739–3392

Where Teton Park Road joins back up with the Jackson Highway is the villagelike hub of **Moose,** where the Snake River separates concessionaire-run gas stations, shops, and places to eat from a small post office and the **Craig Thomas Discovery and Visitor Center** (Teton Park Rd. at Moose; 307/739–3399). The facility flashes a cool, modern architectural style, including 30-foot windows, a sweeping copper roof, and a courtyard surrounded by a timber-beam colonnade. Inside the airy museum space, wall-sized photo murals and conventional exhibit panels compete for attention with sexier multimedia elements like floor-embedded video screens that stream,

GRAND TETON NATIONAL PARK AND JACKSON HOLE

0   3   6 Miles
0   3   6   9 Kilometers

JOHN D. ROCKEFELLER JR. MEMORIAL PARKWAY

▲ Lizard Creek

GRAND TETON NATIONAL PARK

Jackson Lake

Ranger Peak 11,355 ft.

Eagles Rest Peak 11,258 ft.

Colter Bay Village

Two Ocean Lake

Jackson Lake Lodge

Emma Matilda Lake

Traverse Peak 11,051 ft.

Jackson Lake Dam

Mount Moran 12,605 ft.

Signal Mountain Lodge

Signal Mountain
Signal Mountain Summit Rd.

Moran Entrance

Leigh Lake Trail

Leigh Lake

Paintbrush Canyon Trail

Jenny Lake Rd.

Teton Park Rd.

The Potholes

TETON RANGE

Grand Targhee Ski Resort

Mount St. John 11,430 ft.

Cunningham Cabin

Jenny Lake Trail

Jenny Lake Lodge

Inspiration Pt

Cascade Canyon Trail

Jenny Lake

Triangle X Ranch

JACKSON HOLE

Snake River

River Rd.

Mount Owen
Grand Teton 13,770 ft.

Teewinot Mountain

Jenny Lake Visitor Center

Garnet Canyon Trail

Middle Teton 12,804 ft.

South Teton 12,514 ft.

Bradley Lake

Mount Wister

Taggart Lake

Manges Cabin

Buck Mountain

ANTELOPE FLATS

Chapel of the Transfiguration

Menor's Ferry

Teton Park Rd.

Moose Entrance

Phelps Lake

Mount Hunt

Mormon Row

Atherton Creek

Blacktail Butte

Laurance S. Rockefeller Preserve

Gros Ventre Slide

Kelly

River

Gros Ventre

Jackson Hole Ski Area

Jackson Hole Airport

Teton Village

National Elk Refuge

Moose-Wilson Rd.

Snake River

Phillips Ridge

W. Gros Ventre Butte

E. Gros Ventre Butte

Teton Pass

Wilson

Jackson

N
S
E
W

👥 Ranger / Information
🍴 Food Service
🧺 Picnic Area
🛏 Lodging
▲ Campground
⛽ Gas Station
🚻 Restrooms
🅿 Parking Area
⋯⋯ Trails

among other things, close-up images of a rolling Snake River. A gargantuan relief model is the best way to visualize the wide scope of the park's topography short of flying over it, and the map lights up to illustrate glacial pathways and wildlife migrations. These arcade-like elements and a smattering of touchable artifacts make the center particularly kid-friendly. Of course there's a staffed information desk and a bookstore. New in 2011, a 154-seat high-definition theater screens periodic films about the park and hosts the occasional film festival. Check with rangers for a schedule of events.

The **Laurance S. Rockefeller Preserve Interpretive Center** (Moose–Wilson Rd., 4 miles south of Moose; 307/739-3654) is a modern, wood-and-steel structure that feels more like an art gallery than an interpretive facility. The LEED-certified building is a starting point for a number of short wooded trails around nearby Phelps Lake.

Technically, the ★GROS VENTRE SLIDE (Gros Ventre Rd., 2.5 miles east of the park boundary) lies just outside the park's southwest corner, a 20-minute drive from Moose along Teton Park and Gros Ventre roads. The effects of this cataclysmic rockslide, however, were felt throughout Jackson Hole. In 1920 a homesteader named "Uncle Billy" Bierer got nervous about the face of Sheep Mountain overlooking his ranch. "Give it a wet enough year," he predicted, "and all that rock strata will fall down…like a beaver's slickery slide." Uncle Billy sold out, and on June 23, 1925, 50 million cubic yards of rock careened down the mountainside, creating a 200-foot natural dam on the Gros Ventre River inside of a jaw-dropping three minutes. Lower Slide Lake formed behind it within days. Two years later, during a wet spring, the lake burst the top portion of the dam, flooding the river, virtually destroying the town of Kelly downstream and killing six people and countless livestock inside of 15 minutes.

Twilight at Jenny Lake, a tents-only campground.

HISTORIC SIGHTS

See the Grand Teton National Park and Jackson map.

Cunningham Cabin (U.S. 26/89/191, 6 miles south of Moran Junction) lies on the sagebrush prairie like a coffin, long and low against the horizon. Pierce Cunningham, a former fur trapper who transitioned to ranching in 1888, evidently lived a spartan existence. You can step inside his two-room, sod-roofed cabin and imagine what life was like in this dark, low-ceiling space. Take advantage of the great photo op and a mile-long trail network that wanders across the surrounding prairie.

The classic postcard shot: Moulton
Barn on Mormon Row.

YELLOWSTONE AND GRAND TETON NATIONAL PARKS

Built in 1911, the **Manges Cabin** (off Teton Park Rd., 3 miles north of Moose) was isolated, the soil around it poor. When pioneering Jackson Hole homesteader Joseph Manges left to hunt or fish, he hung a sign on the door reading, "If I don't come back, try to make a living off the place." The Park Service has converted the cabin into a barn, but looking west from the Cottonwood Creek Turnout, you can spot the tiny structure looking romantically frail against its mountain backdrop. For a closer look, walk a half-mile north from the signed Taggart Lake trailhead just south of the turnout on Teton Park Road. You'll see the cabin through some trees on your right.

The thick white noise of the rushing Snake River grows louder as you approach **Menor's Ferry** (off Teton Park Rd., 1 mile north of Moose Junction), suggesting what a treacherous ford this would have been before Bill Menor established his ferry service here in 1894.

When pioneering Jackson Hole homesteader Joseph Manges left to hunt or fish, he hung a sign on the door reading, "If I don't come back, try to make a living off the place."

Rangers operate a replica that takes visitors halfway across the river (as conditions permit). It's a pretty ingenious system, where a platform attached to a river-spanning rope simply aligns itself diagonally against the current, allowing the force of the water to nudge it across.

Up a short path from the ferry, the preserved early-20th-century **Maude Noble Cabin** has a small, fascinating display of historical photographs, dating way back to the bad old days when what's now the glitzy ski paradise of Teton Village was known as "Poverty Flats." It was at the Noble cabin that a small group of locals first convened to discuss pursuing national park status in 1923. Rounding out the historic campus is a stable area with pioneer-era vehicles, a working general store carrying period merchandise, and a preserved homestead, where a chair made entirely from antlers (with points!) hints at a peculiar sort of frontier sadism.

Also found along the short road leading to Menor's Ferry is the ★**CHAPEL OF THE TRANSFIGURATION,** an architectural expression of faith that's both poetic and austere. Locals felled the logs and built the tiny cabin in 1925. An aspen stump serves as a pulpit, and behind the altar an unadorned picture window frames the mountains once known as the Hoary Headed Fathers. Only a few muted cam-

That's not a painting behind the altar at the Chapel of the Transfiguration— it's a window with a stunning Teton view.

ROCKEFELLER PARKWAY

Named for the philanthropist who helped bring Grand Teton National Park into being, the John D. Rockefeller Jr. Memorial Parkway is a corridor of land between Yellowstone and Grand Teton, adding up to 24,000 acres. Two roads go through this parkway, and 7 miles of U.S. 89/191/287 act as a sort of "grandeur buffer zone," a not-always-scenic stretch where southern Yellowstone's lava flows give way to the granite rocks of the Tetons.

The only concession in the Parkway is **Headwaters Lodge & Cabins at Flagg Ranch** (off U.S. 89/191/287, 2 miles south of Yellowstone; 800/443-2311). The historic dude ranch is newly renovated and offers camping, cabins, a restaurant, gas, and groceries.

Grassy Lake Road runs between Highway 89 and Ashton, Idaho, a narrow gravel route providing access to Yellowstone's Bechler region. The sparsely traveled **Glade Creek Trail** heads south at mile 5 through acres of wildflower meadows, providing access to miles of additional trail in the northern Tetons. **Grassy Lake Reservoir** is just west of the Parkway, a crystal lake popular for stocked cutthroat and shoreline campsites. Note that Grassy Lake Road is lousy for RVs, and it's closed to vehicles from November through May.

era clicks break the silence of the sanctuary. The Episcopal Church of Jackson Hole (307/733-2603 for services) still hosts regular services here in the summer.

As you drive, bike, or stroll down **Mormon Row** in the park's southeast corner (between Gros Ventre and Antelope Flats Rds.), it's hard to imagine how a handful of Latter-day Saints families settled this remote sagebrush wasteland in the early 1900s. You'll probably recognize the **Moulton Barn** from all the postcards—it's the charmingly dilapidated one with the pointy roofline that mimics the Teton peaks behind it. If you have trouble picking it out, just look where the hordes of photographers are pointing their cameras. The other ramshackle ranch buildings are equally photogenic. A new half-mile interpretive trail begins at the intersection with Antelope Flat and tells the settlers' story. Antelope Flats Road and Mormon Row are closed to vehicles November through April, but open to skiers and snowshoers.

☞ BEST HIKING TRAILS

Grand Teton is a hiker's park in a way that Yellowstone is not. More of its summer visitors plan backcountry trips, and there's considerably less backcountry for them to share. The downside of this situation is that absolute solitude is a little harder to come by; the upside is that trails tend to be well traveled and well marked. You're less likely to encounter an unsigned trail junction than in Yellowstone, and marked distances tend to be reliable. Major trailheads into the Teton canyons are clearly marked, mostly along Teton Park and Moose–Wilson roads. Of course, no amount of signage is a substitute for preparation. Always carry a topographic map and a compass in the Teton backcountry, and be prepared for all weather in all seasons in the mountains—snow in mid-August is not at all rare at high elevations.

The smooth surface of **Jenny Lake** gleams with the sort of perfect sapphire blue that makes other blues look plain. You can take it in from every angle along the seven-mile **Jenny Lake Loop.** Head out from the east shore boat docks or String Lake trailhead to encircle this glacial gem, spotting ospreys, grebes, and seasonal wildflowers along the way. Keep an ear cocked for the high, mad yodel of the common loon, often found on Jenny Lake's open water. The trail is flat regardless of which direction you travel, but you'll climb a very steep 250 feet if you opt to take the popular half-mile side trip to the **Inspiration Point overlook** near the mouth of Cascade Canyon. An easier-to-reach highlight, Hidden Falls, is at the start of the same spur trail but before the steep climb.

The trail into **Garnet Canyon** from the Lupine Meadows trailhead is a popular alpine access route for climbers and backcountry junkies, so you won't be alone on a day hike or overnight trip there. Still, there are plenty of wildflower meadows and sculpted rock walls to go around. Begin a steady and challenging climb along the Lupine Meadows Trail, reaching a spur trail after three miles that leads to Surprise and Amphitheater lakes, two deep blue pools shrouded in mountain shadows (another 1.6 miles). The trail becomes the Garnet Canyon Trail after the spur, and Middle Teton looms before you for the next 1.5 miles, past the end of the maintained trail and through a quarter-mile of a chunky boulder field leading to ★THE MEADOWS CAMPING AREA. This is the end of the road unless you're planning to summit Grand, Middle, or South Teton. Hemmed in by all three mountains and messy with colossal boulders and snowmelt streams, the Meadows is one of the prettiest backcountry places to pitch a tent in all the West.

Although most of the Teton canyons are oriented west-to-east, Paintbrush Canyon runs southwest-to-northeast, so the sun falls on you in unique ways as you navigate the ★PAINTBRUSH DIVIDE TRAIL. The 20-mile loop is one of the park's most popular backpacking trips, a two- or three-day excursion that begins at the Leigh Lake trailhead at the String Lake Picnic Area, off the North Jenny Lake Loop. The initial ascent leads through fields of the bright red wildflower that give the canyon its name. But the flowers are nowhere

Bull elk bugling during the fall rut; several species of blue gentians grow throughout the park.

In autumn, aspens and willows transform the landscape into a study of colorful contrasts.

PEOPLE IN THE PARKS: "BLACK GEORGE" SIMMONS, VOLUNTEER RANGER

During a 40-year career with the U.S. Geological Survey, "Black George" Simmons led mapping expeditions everywhere from Utah to Liberia. In his 60s he embarked on a second career as a volunteer ranger with the National Park Service. He retired in 2011 after 25 years, many of them spent distributing root-beer floats to surprised and grateful hikers from a small cabin at the Death Canyon trailhead in Grand Teton National Park.

Brian Kevin: Sounds like you run into a lot of people coming on and off the trail.

Black George Simmons: I meet interesting people every year—interesting because of their backgrounds, places they have been, what they do. Perhaps the most fascinating last year was a concessioner restoring the [nearby historic] White Grass Ranch. He and his wife once spent an entire year crossing the Indian Ocean in their small sailboat.

BK: As a geologist, do you approach Grand Teton differently compared with other places you've worked?

BGS: Not having done extensive study here, my interest is chiefly in being able to respond to visitor questions. It's a terrible thing to have somebody pick up a rock and ask, "What's this?" and then find

yourself unable to identify it! Geologists are never bored when they travel, since they get to try and interpret geologic history from all the passing scenery.

BK: Given all your park experience, do you ever see us making decisions about public lands that we might come to regret?

BGS: Pressure on our wild and undisturbed places is always under progressive increase. Most of the tourists I see are campers, climbers, and hikers—conservationists who are pro-wilderness. Unfortunately, not enough of them are activists who challenge development in Congress and in the courts. If you want to see appreciation for our parks, talk with visitors from Europe, where no wilderness exists.

BK: Let's pretend next week will be another cataclysmic eruption of the Yellowstone volcano. What do you do with your last week in the parks? Where do you go?

BGS: That's an easy one. I'd go nowhere. I'd stay until the last person in the vicinity had been accounted for and was out of the area, and then I'd hang on in case somebody unknown was still there. To fill in the time toward the end, I'd take many, many pictures, which I'd hope could be used later to illustrate the changes that occurred.

to be seen at the 10,700-foot Paintbrush Divide, a rocky and wind-swept ridge where snowdrifts persist throughout the summer. Before descending to Jenny Lake via Cascade Canyon to the south, you'll drop in on two crystal-blue alpine lakes.

ON AND IN THE WATER

The glacial lakes strung like beads along the Teton Fault are as inte-gral to the park's mystique as its conspicuous summits. Sliding across these waters in a **canoe or kayak** is a classic Grand Teton experi-ence. Canoes and kayaks from **Signal Mountain Marina** (off Teton Park Rd., 3 miles south of Jackson Lake Junction; 307/543–2831) or **Colter Bay Marina** (off U.S. 89/191/287, 5 miles north of Jackson Lake Junction; 307/543–2811) have to stay near shore, but Dornan's in Moose lets you take their watercraft farther afield.

Jackson Lake provides, by far, the most surface area to explore, with a number of island-hopping routes in its southern reaches and a handful of paddle-in campsites on its rugged, roadless western shore. The cliffside lake views at the Wilcox Point campsite below Moose Mountain are worth a long day of rowing from Colter Bay. Another great paddle is **Leigh Lake,** accessed via a short portage from **String Lake** along the North Jenny Lake Loop. Named for "Beaver Dick" Leigh, one of the Hole's earliest trappers and a Hayden party guide, the lake entices campers with five isolated campsites and day-trip-pers with stunning views of the pearl-white glaciers on Mount Moran's east face.

In summer a flotilla of sailboats, pontoons, and motorboats takes to the water at Jackson Lake. It can be crowded near the four boat launches at Colter Bay, Signal Mountain, **Leek's Marina** (off U.S. 89/191/287, 1 mile north of Colter Bay Junction; 307/543–2546), and **Spalding Bay** (Spalding Bay Rd., 9 miles southwest of Jackson Lake Junction), but if you're looking to escape the crowds, head over to the lake's brambled western side, where elk and black bears patrol the shoreline and 11,000-foot crags loom. The smaller Jenny Lake is similarly scenic, though motors exceeding 10 horsepower are prohibited. Find the boat ramp on the lake's south shore, off the unpaved road to Lupine Meadows. Signal Mountain has the

★ Cook Your Catch ★

If you bring in a lunker lake trout from Jackson Lake, call the dining rooms at Signal Mountain or Jackson Lodge—they'll usually prepare it for you for a small charge.

Worth getting up early for:
sunrise at Oxbow Bend floods
Mount Moran in lavender light.

It can be hard to keep your eyes
on the water of Jackson Lake,
with the peaks rising above you.

broadest selection of rental craft, including pontoons, runabouts, and deck cruisers, though you can rent motorboats at Colter Bay as well. Thankfully, Jet Skis are banned throughout the park.

If you're more Gilligan than Skipper, you can still hit the lakes at Grand Teton on several guided trips. Hour-and-a-half-long **interpretive cruises on Jackson Lake** depart daily from the Colter Bay Marina, hooking around small, sylvan **Elk Island** to peek up the canyons on the far shore. Sign on for a breakfast or dinner cruise to lay over on the island for a buffet-style picnic. The park's most popular boat rides are the **Jenny Lake Boating Company's shuttles and cruises** (307/734–9227). Named by the Hayden party for "Beaver Dick" Leigh's Shoshone wife, Jenny Lake reflects the 12,000-foot spires of the Cathedral Group. The shuttle runs every 15 minutes or so in summer, a 20-minute glide from the dock near the visitor center to the Inspiration Point trailhead on the western shore. The company also runs hourlong scenic cruises in the morning, afternoon, and early evening. Call ahead to reserve seats.

Though white water fans revere many of the Snake River's thousand-plus miles for their paddle-friendly froth, the stretch running through Grand Teton is more popular for wildlife-watching joyrides than adrenaline-fueled runs. Most visitors ride the Snake with one of the dozen or so licensed **rafting** outfitters. Most of these—including both park lodging companies—float a speedy but whitewater-free stretch between Deadman's Bar and Moose, a two-hour trip on which the Tetons loom large and moose sightings are probable. To feel a bit of the river spray, sign on for a three-hour

NOT YOUR AVERAGE PARK

If you flew into Jackson Hole, you probably noticed that you landed directly inside Grand Teton National Park—a truly unique experience because no other national park contains a commercial airport. But then, not many allow hunting and grazing, contain pockets of private land, or allow a massive dam to control the flow of their primary river, either.

Most of Grand Teton's quirks stem from Jackson Hole's having already hosted a small but thriving community when park boundaries were expanded in 1950. The airport and Jackson Lake Dam, for example, predate the current park's boundaries. Strictly regulated hunting and grazing rights were a concession to skeptical locals, guaranteed in the expansion. Today, only a handful of families still have grazing permits, and many people feel the park should phase the permits out altogether.

A few tracts remain privately owned, "grandfathered" in after 1950. The state and county claim roughly 1,400 acres here and there. As if land rights in Jackson Hole weren't complicated enough, there are seven acres near Gros Ventre Junction whose ownership is a mystery.

TETON SCIENCE SCHOOLS

The cluster of pioneer-era buildings squatting northeast of Kelly belongs to **Teton Science Schools** (1 Ditch Creek Rd.; 307/733–1313). Just inside the park's eastern border, the campus was a homestead, a dude ranch, and a hunting camp before the conservation-minded nonprofit took over in 1974. The school runs an always-evolving curriculum of youth and adult education programs, everything from half-day wildlife expeditions ($130) to weeklong backpacking adventures ($1,895). Students stay in rustic cabins with postcard-worthy Teton views or in the stylish, eco-friendly dorms on the Jackson campus.

trip with **Dornan's Scenic Float Trips** (Moose; 307/733–3699), one of only a few outfitters to run the equally scenic but faster currents between Moose and the town of Wilson. Expect higher water and faster flows in the spring. For a float that's a little more genteel, sign on with **Grand Teton Lodge Company** (307/543–2811) for lunch or dinner trips, scenic floats with breaks for smoked trout, and steaks at a private riverside campsite. The calmest Snake waters for do-it-yourself canoeists, kayakers, and rafters are just downstream from Jackson Lake.

As if the Snake River weren't unique enough, it also has its own indigenous trout species, the Snake River fine-spotted cutthroat. The speckly subspecies is prey for crowds of anglers who **float-fish** the Snake after the spring run-off. You can't swing a fly rod in the neighborhood of Jackson without hitting a fishing guide, but **Snake River Angler** (Moose; 307/733–3699) and the **Triangle X Ranch** (off U.S. 26/89/191, 6 miles south of Moran Junction; 307/733–2183) both lead trips from inside the park. Most of the park's lakes are open to fishing year-round. Jackson Lake is off-limits to fishermen during October, but holds some lunker lake trout for deep-water fishermen. Seasons and regulations in the park are complex at best, so be sure to pick up a Park Service fishing bulletin when you go for your license (*see* the Practical Information chapter).

For swimmers and soakers, the shock of the chilly water in a high-altitude lake is pretty quickly replaced by the weightless calm of floating beneath a mountain skyline. The park's lakes are open to **swimming,** though you'll definitely want to stick a toe in first. Shallow waters and sandy bottoms lure families into the water at the **String Lake Picnic Area** (off the North Jenny Lake Loop). And though it's only truly warm during the hot summer months, the large, gravel-lined pool at **Kelly Warm Spring** (Gros Ventre Rd., 2 miles west of the park boundary) draws a mixed crowd of frolicking kids, tired hikers, and laid-back kayakers practicing their rolls.

OTHER ACTIVITIES

The winged residents of Jackson Hole are far more numerous and varied than their terrestrial counterparts, and birders flock to Grand Teton in all seasons to spot a few of the 300-plus species that have been identified in the area. To get in on the **bird-watching** action, grab a checklist from one of the visitor centers, then head to **Oxbow Bend** (1 mile east of Jackson Lake Junction), a marshy meander where the Snake River turns south out of Jackson Lake. Great blue herons preen in the shallows, hungry eagles dive-bomb the water, and white pelicans visit during spring migration (some even stick around for summer). Other hot spots include **Two Ocean Lake** for waterfowl and **Antelope Flats** for rodent-hunting raptors. Local birding authority Bert Raynes's weekly column in the *Jackson Hole News & Guide* is a must-read for visiting birders. You can find copies of the free paper all over Jackson.

The comparatively flat roads in Grand Teton make the park better for **cycling** than Yellowstone. In 2012, the park completed a cycling and multi-use trail paralleling Teton Park Road, Moose–Wilson Road, and U.S. 26/89/191 south of Moose. The route runs all the way from Jackson to Jenny Lake, and a new spur in 2016 reaches Antelope Flats Road from Moose Junction. Pedal the quiet, mostly paved roads around Kelly and Antelope Flats to hear the elk bugling. And though the park's hiking trails are off-limits to pedal pushers, the network of unimproved dirt roads is a boon to **mountain biking.** Fifteen gravel miles along the scenic ★RIVER ROAD are flat enough for beginners, with a few small hills for the adventurous. The dusty two- to three-hour ride begins at the Cottonwood Creek turnout and follows the Snake River, showing off the moonlike, kettle-pocked flats known as the Potholes along the way. You'll get excellent Teton views from beginning to end, and the route is refreshingly quiet, as few visitors make their way here. Just east of Antelope Flats, steep climbs and a few singletrack routes on Shadow Mountain attract more experienced riders—follow Shadow Mountain Road north from Antelope Flats Road. The bronzed hard-core riders at **Dornan's Adventure Sports** (Moose; 307/733–3307) rent bikes and dish on other nearby trails.

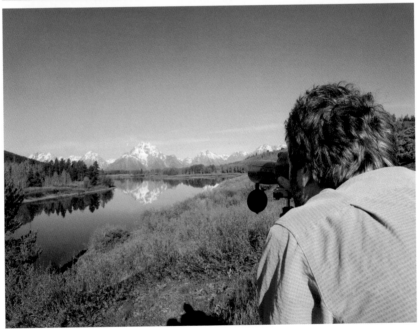

Yellowstone and Grand Teton National Parks

(previous page, top) Photographers line up before a bull and cow moose; (previous page, bottom) Oxbow Bend is a great birding location; (this page) a climber hones his chops on Blacktail Butte.

AMERICA'S ALPS

The Tetons might rightly be called the birthplace of American mountaineering. The range was considered holy ground by the fledgling mountaineers of the early 1900s, and today the names of the innumerable climbing routes read like a roll call of famous American alpinists.

Grand Teton presented an iconic challenge from the start. Yellowstone's first superintendent, Nathaniel Langford, claimed to have reached the summit with a partner during a USGS expedition in 1872. His sketches and descriptions, though, match a lower side-summit known as "The Enclosure." It's a controversial call, but first-ascent credit generally goes to mountaineer William Owen, who summitted twice in 1898 and launched an aggressive PR campaign promoting his feat.

Exum Mountain Guides (Jenny Lake; 307/733–2297) is the premier guide ser-

vice in the Tetons. The group was founded in 1946 by pioneering climbers Glenn Exum and Paul Petzoldt. Petzoldt first climbed the Grand in 1924 at the age of 16 (while wearing cowboy boots!), and he later founded the National Outdoor Leadership School. Unless you're an experienced mountaineer, a trip with Exum or **Jackson Hole Mountain Guides** (1325 S. Hwy. 89, Ste. 104, Jackson; 307/733–4979) is the best way to look down from the Teton summits.

Rock climbing is equally popular in the park, and both outfitters lead day trips to granite spires and big walls. Beginning climbers might try bouldering in the area known as **Boulder City,** a half-mile northwest of the Cathedral Group Overlook on North Jenny Lake Road.

A climber heading up Grand Teton. Intrepid climbers pioneer new routes up this peak every couple of years.

There are fewer **horseback-riding** options in Grand Teton than in Yellowstone, but many Jackson-area ranches and outfitters lead longer pack trips into the surrounding national forests. The **Jackson Lake Lodge Corral** (off U.S. 89/191/287, 1 mile north of Jackson Lake Junction; 307/543–2811) leads one- and two-hour rides along trails surrounding pine-rimmed Emma Matilda Lake. The **Colter Bay Corral** (off U.S. 89/191/287, 5 miles north of Jackson Lake Junction; 307/543–2811) takes riders on one- and two-hour outings around waterfowl-rich Hermitage Point.

⌖ WHERE TO EAT

Blue Heron Bar. This is easily the nicest bar in the park, and it holds its own against a host of Jackson hot spots as well. Local microbrews dominate the taps, including the stalwart Snake River Lager that's been racking up beer awards for years. The chatty bartenders mix a mean cocktail, too, including a handful of sweet huckleberry concoctions. Tapas-style small plates include game-meat charcuterie and tiny lobster rolls. Chatter hangs thick in the bar, but you can find some peace and quiet in a deck chair on the spacious patio. *Jackson Lodge; 307/543–3463.* **$–$$**

Dornan's has been a Grand Teton institution ever since Jack Dornan started serving burly ranch-hand fare to tourists in 1948. So the old-timey cowboy look and menu are genuine.

★DORNAN'S CHUCKWAGON. Dornan's has been a Grand Teton institution ever since Jack Dornan, the son of a Jackson Hole homesteader, started serving burly ranch-hand fare to tourists in 1948. So the old-timey cowboy look and menu are genuine. The dinner ticket loads your plate with all-you-can-eat short ribs, baked beans, mashed potatoes, and more. Breakfasts of thick sourdough pancakes and mountains of bacon are glorious; lunch covers burgers and sandwiches. Kids' menus offer scaled-down portions, and the young 'uns tend to get a kick out of eating in the on-site tepees, weeknights only. *Moose; 307/733–2415.* **$$$**

Dornan's Pizza & Pasta Company. This brewpub's dining room (requisite stone fireplace and rustic pine detailing) opens up to two pretty exceptional decks. The rooftop space has a fine Teton view, and the lower deck looks across the Snake River to Menor's Ferry. Sandwiches and salads complement the eponymous entrées for lunch and dinner; many visitors come just to enjoy the bar. The neighboring wineshop is a must-visit, a seemingly incongruous market with 1,600 wines, more than a hundred cheeses, and a wall full of plaques and awards. Get advance tickets for occasional wine tastings at the restaurant. *Moose; 307/733–2415.* $$

★JENNY LAKE LODGE DINING ROOM. Without peer in the national parks. Think Gruyère-and-duck-confit croque monsieur as a first course, tender elk medallions as an entrée, and an apricot Bavarian cream dessert. The five-course, prix-fixe dinner menu focuses on wild game and seasonal produce, and changes nightly. Decadent breakfasts follow the same prix-fixe formula, though lunch is an à la carte selection of sandwiches and salads. The space is a terrific contrast between white tablecloths and crystal wine glasses and log-cabin architecture. Dinner jackets are suggested for men, everyone needs reservations, and nonguests need high limits on their credit cards (meals are included for guests at the lodge). *Jenny Lake Lodge; 307/733–3351.* $$$$

John Colter Café Court. Under the same roof as the Ranch House, Colter Village's cheaper, counter-service option appeals to anyone looking for variety. Lunch and dinner run the gamut from burgers, deli sandwiches, pizza, and fish to a few Mexican entrées. The cafeteria gets pretty crowded at mealtimes, but the whole menu is available for takeout. *Colter Village; 307/543–2811.* $

Leek's Pizzeria. There's a relaxed cabin feel to this pizza parlor at Jackson Lake's tiny northern marina, where you can dine on the deck when it's nice out and in front of a stone fireplace when it's not. The pizzas and calzones hold their own against anything in Jackson, with largely organic ingredients and creative specialty pies like the Thai chicken with peanut sauce and sprouts. Reasonably priced draft beers add to the place's vibe, and keep things here relaxed and fun. *Off U.S. 89/191/287, 1 mile north of Colter Bay Junction; 307/543–2494.* $$–$$$

Mural Room. A moose-shaped butter pat might seem tacky elsewhere, but there's a regal tearoom feel to Jackson Lake Lodge's flagship dining room. Floor-to-ceiling windows frame the northern Tetons; the other eye-grabbers are two massive, stately murals. John D. Rockefeller Jr. commissioned the panels in the late 1950s, and artist Carl Roters delivered the 80-foot-long painting of fur trappers at a Jackson Hole rendezvous. The Mural Room serves all three meals, but the best reason to reserve a table is for a dinner of elegantly plated seafood and wild game. *Jackson Lake Lodge; 307/543-3463.* **$$$$**

The Peaks Restaurant. Granted, the Peaks dining room looks a little too industrial for its polished menu and high-end prices, but the hot seats are out on the patio, overlooking Jackson Lake and gilded Teton sunsets. This lodge is the park's standard-bearer for organic and sustainable cuisine; the feel-good choices here include sustainably raised beef from local ranches. The efficient servers even hand out little cards explaining the criteria behind their seafood selection. *Signal Mountain Lodge; 307/543-2831.* **$$$–$$$$**

Pioneer Grill. What you see is what you get at this 1950s-style, counter-service soda fountain and burger joint. It scores points with families for affordability, a children's menu, and a kid-pleasing, swivel-chair decor. If you're not impressed with the grease scent or luncheonette layout, grab a bison burger from the takeout window, then mosey out to the cathedral-like lobby or patio for better views and fresh air. *Jackson Lake Lodge; 307/543-3463.* **$$–$$$**

Ranch House at Colter Bay. With a chain restaurant decor that's gussied up with a few spurs and wagon wheels, the Ranch House fills with families for breakfast, lunch, and dinner. Entrées skew toward Western comfort food, like bacon-wrapped meatloaf and whiskey-barbecued pork ribs. It opens earlier than the adjacent (and cheaper) Colter Café Court, so it's a good option for coffee and a bite off the breakfast buffet for those looking to get an alpine start. *Colter Village; 307/543-2811.* **$$$**

The Trapper Grill. Anyone who's decidedly not an early bird should take note that the Trapper Grill serves breakfast until noon. You'll find organic veggies, free-range bison burgers, fair-trade coffee, and a vast gluten-free menu for both adults and kids. A mountainous nacho platter with beef and chicken is a longtime favorite of people seeking adventure fuel on the cheap. If you'd rather stare at a fireplace or a flat-screen TV, you can order off the same menu (except at breakfast) in the neighboring Deadman's Bar. *Signal Mountain Lodge; 307/543-2831.* **$–$$**

Gateway Towns

Sleigh rides at the National Elk Refuge bring you face-to-face with the herd.

FAMOUS NAMES

JACKSON:
Vacation home
of actor Harrison
Ford

CODY: Birthplace
of painter Jack-
son Pollock

☞ JACKSON *See the Jackson map.*

Walking past the Old West storefront facades in downtown Jackson, your shoes clopping against the wooden sidewalk, you can almost picture the dusty frontier settlement that began with a post office in 1897. Look east of Town Square, toward Center Street, and you can still pick out the wide, hip-roofed building that served as the pioneer community's first courtroom, school, and dance hall.

Then you pass the windows at Sotheby's International Realty, your eye catching on a photo ad for a $14 million home: *seven fireplaces, log construction, Teton views.* In just over a century, Jackson has gone from Old West outpost to the New West's swankiest destination town, its whirligig growth spurred almost entirely by the tourist trade. And though the locals joke a bit ruefully about the billionaires displacing the millionaires, Jackson is also a friendly micropolis catering to travelers and adventurers, a seasonal haven with plenty of room for ski bums, dirtbaggers, and family tourists alike.

Because it's enveloped by public-use land and because it's so chock-full of guides and outfitters, there's no place like Jackson to try all sorts of outdoor pursuits. It's a particularly good place for beginners to try sports that are usually the domain of specialists, like paragliding. You can get around gratis on the Southern Teton Area Rapid Transit, or **START Bus,** that runs throughout town on a seasonally variable schedule.

EXPLORING AROUND TOWN

Jackson loves its wildlife art, and a big bronze statue of two elk and a grizzly bear welcomes you to the **Jackson Hole & Greater Yellowstone Visitor Center** (532 N. Cache Dr.; 307/733–3316). Inside is a smallish wildlife exhibit, an info desk with park passes and permits, a bookstore, and about a zillion pamphlets for Jackson Hole events and activities. The center is useful from a one-stop-shopping standpoint, as it serves as a headquarters for the town's chamber of commerce as well as the Forest Service, the National Elk Refuge, the Grand Teton Natural History Association, and a few other local organizations.

Just up the road, a block of green space in the midst of bustling downtown is technically called George Washington Memorial Park, but you're more likely to hear it referred to simply as **Town Square** (Cache Dr. and Broadway Ave.). At each corner of the block stands one of Jackson's landmark elk-antler arches. The original arches were built sometime between 1953 and 1960 (no one's quite sure, though park signs go with the later date). If the antlers look bright and shiny, it's thanks to a nine-year effort to replace each of the old, increasingly brittle arches, which wrapped up in the summer of 2015. Each arch is built from around 2,000 shed antlers.

Heading into Jackson from Grand Teton, you'll notice a great stone fortress rising on a butte alongside the highway. The multicolored quartzite walls of the architecturally striking ★**NATIONAL MUSEUM OF WILDLIFE ART** (2820 Rungius Rd.; 307/733–5771) seem to shimmer in the sunlight. Inside, 12 galleries of stunning paintings and sculptures remind you that for every tacky "howling wolf" dream catcher in Western gift shops, somewhere there's an oil or stone rendering of the animal kingdom worthy of its subject. In Robert Bateman's *Chief,* for instance, a lone bison bull, mid-charge, stares out from a gargantuan canvas with a gaze that's as arresting as any roadside specimen in Yellowstone. The museum's emphasis is on Realist and Romantic works from the American West, but its past exhibits

JACKSON HOLE VISITOR CENTER

LOCATION: 532 N. Cache Dr.

TEL: 307/733–3316

An antler arch gleams with holiday lights at Jackson's Town Square.

Thousands of elk winter at the National Elk Refuge, just outside of Jackson.

To
National Museum
of Wildlife Art

have included provocative artists like Andy Warhol and Georgia O'Keeffe. In fall 2012, the museum added an outdoor sculpture trail with more than two dozen impressive installations.

Northeast of town, the 25,000-acre **National Elk Refuge** provides a winter home for around 7,500 elk from Jackson Hole and southern Yellowstone. Cut off from historical southern wintering ranges when Jackson began to swell in the early 1900s, the elk are fed alfalfa pellets during their winter stay. Their life is far from cushy, though. Not only is the refuge open to regulated hunting in the fall, but nearby wolf packs are known to cruise the area. Horse-drawn **sleigh rides** through the refuge leave from the Jackson Hole Visitor Center between mid-December and late March. In summer, megafauna are sparse, but you can drive into the refuge to tour the **Miller Ranch,** a historic homestead with a century-old, two-story log manor at its heart that's sometimes billed as Jackson Hole's first trophy home.

Underhyped attractions in Jackson include the **River Runners' Museum** (1255 S. U.S. 89/191/26; 800/458–7238 or 307/733–6203), part of Mad River Boat Trips' architecturally intriguing headquarters on the south end of town. Inside a

★ Stick 'Em Up ★

In summer, tourists crowd the Town Square Monday through Saturday evenings to watch a costumed cast salute Jackson's proud history of vigilantism with an elaborate reenacted shootout.

BULL MARKET

While gazing at the elk-antler arches in Town Square, the occasional aghast Jackson visitor asks, "How many elk did they have to kill to get all those antlers?" In fact, none. Elk shed their antlers naturally every year in the late winter. By April the antlers litter the ground at the National Elk Refuge like giant, pointy twigs. That's when the Boy Scouts sweep through, per a 1957 agreement with the U.S. Fish & Wildlife Service. They gather, bundle, and weigh some 10,000 pounds of antlers each year.

The fruits of the Scouts' labor go on display annually the weekend before Memorial Day, lining the walkways and stacked six feet high on pallets in Town Square. The bundles are auctioned off as part of Jackson's lively **Elkfest,** during which artists and other antler aficionados place bids while the other townsfolk chow on picnic food, take in outdoor concerts, and resist the temptation to make "nice rack" jokes.

Bundles of elk antlers line Jackson's streets during the annual Elkfest celebration.

giant right-angle triangle with a reflective facade, this small museum pairs some of the improbable early dinghies and rafts used to tackle white water with photo collections selling the romantic life of the river guide.

The rare playground catering to both children and adults, **Phil Baux Park** (King St. & E. Snow King Ave.) has bouldering walls for the kiddos and adept grown-up climbers, plus traditional playground equipment, horseshoe pits, and a front-row view of Snow King Mountain.

SKI RESORTS

Jackson Hole Mountain Resort (888/333–7766 general info; 307/733–2291 snow conditions) entices globe-trotting powderhounds with two steep mountains, some 450 inches of snow per year, and awesome backcountry runs. Headquarters is the chi-chi hospitality circus of **Teton Village,** a bustling cluster of Swiss chalets along Moose-Wilson Road that specializes in all things *après*.

The ★JACKSON HOLE AERIAL TRAM (Village Dr.; 888/333–7766) sails the void between "the Vill" and the 10,450-foot summit of **Rendezvous Mountain,** the largest vertical rise for a lift in North America. The Hole's iconic "Big Red Box" got a little bigger and a little redder in 2006, when the original 1960s tram was retired in favor of an upgrade. The new tram hauls up to 100 skiers, hikers, and sightseers on a nine-minute ride through the very thin Teton air. The whir of the cable is often the only sound while awed passengers drink in mountain views usually reserved for the eagles. Tram-only tickets are available at the ticket center next to the terminal. The cozier **Bridger Gondola** (behind the Bridger Center) takes you "only" to 9,095 feet, but it's free in the evening, and it drops you off at a sexy contemporary bistro (*see* Couloir, *below*).

"Big Red Box," the aerial tram at Jackson Hole Mountain Resort, ascends 4,139 vertical feet in about 15 minutes.

In summer the tram and the gondola offer equally astounding views, plus sweat-free trail access for hikers and backpackers hitting the high country. A lift-accessed mountain bike park has six specially designed single-track trails for everyone from first-timers to gearhead experts. If you've ever wanted to hurl your child into the air with a giant slingshot, you can do that, too, on the **bungee trampoline.** Get the full menu of summer activities from the **Mountain Sports School** (Bridger Center; 307/739–2779), which also runs a Nordic ski program in the winter (307/739–2629), offering lessons and half- and full-day trips into Grand Teton National Park. **Jackson Hole Sports** (Bridger Center; 307/739–2687) rents ski gear in the winter and bikes in the summer. You can also get the logo gear without even visiting

A powderhound hits the Jackson
Hole Mountain Resort ski runs.

Teton Village Ski Resort.

PEOPLE IN THE PARKS:
SHANE MOORE, WILDLIFE FILMMAKER

A lifelong Jacksonian and an accomplished cinematographer, Shane Moore has been making films in Greater Yellowstone for more than 25 years. Among his credits is the already classic *Christmas in Yellowstone*, produced for PBS's *Nature*.

Brian Kevin: How have you seen Jackson change over the years?

Shane Moore: When I grew up here, Jackson was just transitioning from a ranching/tourist community into very much a resort community, but there's been a lot of good with that. The wildlife around here keeps getting better and better—it turns out people are actually using the backcountry less than they did 20 years ago. The real wonderful opportunities for solitude are still there. And it's a very interesting and vibrant and lively community.

BK: So what do the experts know about wildlife-watching that the rest of us don't?

SM: It's the little, subtle things that lead to the wonderful events we occasionally get to film. For a lot of people, the experience is quite rushed. You can never experience all of the park in one trip anyway, so don't even try is my advice. Take a little slice and get in tune to it. You start to learn little things about a place— who's doing what? What coyote tends to

be stealing fish from the otters? Then by watching that coyote, I know where to find the otters, even if they've been in the den for hours.

BK: When you have folks in town who want to experience the parks, where do you take them?

SM: With youngsters especially, I think it's really important to interact with nature, so fishing is a wonderful experience. You know, if it becomes too much of a boardwalk experience, there's something that's lost. So I really encourage people to just get off the road and listen to a place, feel it, and smell it. Those are the things that television never does, and there's no substitute.

BK: Is there a sense in which it feels less "wild" to film in a national park, where there are buildings and roads, than in, say, Alaska?

SM: For some people, seeing something in Yellowstone from the road seems to diminish the experience. I think that view is completely wrong. It's a very authentic experience, and I don't think there's any place in the world where you can see the equivalent of the types of things that you can see in Yellowstone these days from the road.

the hill in downtown Jackson at the **Jackson Hole Resort Store** (50 N. Center St.; 307/739–2767).

While JHMR tends to get all the glory and most of the out-of-town visitors, **Snow King Resort** (400 E. Snow King Ave.; 800/522–5464 or 307/734–3194), Jackson's "other" hill, swarms with in-the-know townies on powder days. You won't find a lot of beginners' runs on this übersteep "racers'" mountain, but you can take a lesson with a legend. The ski school was founded by Bill Briggs, who made first ski descents on all three Tetons, including the Grand in 1971.

The crowd on the slopes tends to be a thriftier, down-to-earth bunch of diehards, prone to take advantage of the hill's three-hour morning lift tickets and make a few after-dark runs. Visible from almost anywhere else in Jackson, the illuminated hill glows like a big, white beacon on winter nights. In 2015, a round of upgrades at Snow King saw the mountain add a new lift and a base lodge, plus the new **Treetop Adventure Park** (zip lines, ropes courses, etc.) and a thrilling downhill **mountain coaster** for summertime visitors craving an adrenaline rush.

Crossing Teton Pass to reach **Grand Targhee Resort** (3300 E. Ski Hill Rd., Alta; 800/827–4433 or 307/353–2300), you abandon the glitz of Jackson altogether, swapping resort-town ambience for piles upon piles of the white stuff. Targhee has seen its star rise in recent years but remains relatively unspoiled, a family-style resort that benefits from being on the west side of the Teton Range, about an hour's drive from Jackson and in the path of storms moving west across Idaho and Wyoming. When these pressure systems hit the wall-like ridge of the mountains, they tend to hover, depositing some 50 feet of snow on Targhee in a good year.

(above) Snow-mobiling through fresh powder at Togwotte Pass; (bottom) a freestyle stunt at the Jackson Hole Mountain Festival.

The breadth of wide-open runs at Targhee favors intermediate skiers. There's a terrain park with jumps, rails, and boxes, and the pristine nearby backcountry has enticed the likes of the extreme athletes and filmmakers from Teton Gravity Research. Targhee's summertime mountain-bike park has recently been recognized as one of the nation's best, and expanded lodging, dining, and shopping are on the way, so visit now while the hill is still a mostly locals kind of place.

Other Winter Activities

Love them or hate them, snowmobiles are a popular and efficient way to explore the vast network of national forest trails surrounding Jackson. Outfitters like **Togwotee Adventures** (1050 S. Hwy. 89; 877/

864–9683 or 307/733–8800) leads trips along some of the more popular routes, including to Granite Hot Springs and up into Yellowstone. The **Togwotee Pass** area (off U.S. 26/287, 20 miles east of Grand Teton National Park) is holy ground for sledders, 70 miles of groomed, forested corridors through the Absarokas.

If you prefer snowmobiling as a spectator sport, consider the annual **World Championship Snowmobile Hill Climb** at Snow King Resort, where thousands gather to see a horde of snowmobilers— some of them sober—try to ascend a 1,300-foot, nearly vertical slope. It's a winter spectacle of Darwinian proportions.

Jackson Hole Iditarod Sled Dog Tours (800/554–7388 or 307/733–7388) is run by multiple-Iditarod veteran Frank Teasley. On a half-day trip an eager team of huskies pants as they pull you through Granite Creek Canyon south of town. The full-day trip reaches a natural hot spring at the end of the trail, and the cold wind loses its sting after a dip in the quiet pool.

Summer Activities

On the west side of the Elk Refuge, the Flat Creek drainage near the **Jackson National Fish Hatchery** (1500 Fish Hatchery Rd.; 307/733–2510) is near-sacred ground for local anglers, a busy fly-only river with copious hatches throughout the late summer and fall. The experts come out to stalk the creek's notoriously wily cutthroat, while first-time anglers head up the road to the fishery's stocked, half-acre **Sleeping Indian Pond,** a popular place to fish with kids.

The Snake River roars to life south of Jackson, earning its reputation for classic white water in an eight-mile stretch known as the Grand Canyon of the Snake River. **Rendezvous River Sports** (945 W. Broadway; 307/733–2471) can lead you down in bobbing raft-kayak hybrids called "duckies." **Mad River Boat Trips** (1255 S. U.S. 89/191/26; 800/458–7238) uses rafts and feeds you a top-notch picnic meal to boot. If you can tear your eyes from the rocks and waves, watch for osprey and bald eagles in the surrounding firs and pines.

Canoeing in the shadow of Mount Moran.

Hang gliding and paragliding are enormously popular around Jackson. The abrupt nature of the Tetons' east face allows aerialists to launch from breathtaking heights and watch the green-and-blue floor of Jackson Hole tumble away below. **Jackson Hole Paragliding** (307/739–2626) and **Cowboy Up Hang Gliding** (307/413–4164) both offer lessons and tandem flights. **Wyoming Balloon Company** (307/739–0900) can take you into the sky with even less effort on your part, and they do it beneath a huge nylon envelope with a psychedelic wild-life scene on it.

Within galloping distance of Jackson are more than a dozen ranches and lodges offering horseback rides. The visitor center in town can help you find the right one for your party and skill level. **Mill Iron Ranch** (3495 E. Horse Creek Rd.; 888/808–6390 or 307/733–6390) stands out for its scenery. This fourth-generation ranch 10 miles south of town is surrounded by rolling green hills and almost hoodoo-like rock formations.

THE ARTS

A cluster of modern, angular buildings makes up the **Jackson Hole Center for the Arts** campus (240 S. Glenwood St.; 307/734–8956 general info, 307/733–4900 box office). Four art galleries cultivate a vibe of experimentation, so you're as likely to see found-object trash sculpture as you are alpine photography. There's also a 525-seat theater that has pretty eclectic programming; on my last visit, the schedule included a klezmer band, a fashion show, and ballet.

In summer and fall, the center is a popular starting point for the city's open-studio **ARTwalks** on the third Thursday of each month, especially since the best contemporary galleries are found in the surrounding "SoBo" (south of Broadway) neighborhood. **Taylor Piggott Gallery** (62 S. Glenwood St.; 307/733–0555) and **Heather James Fine Art** (172 Center St.; 307/200–6090) display the sort of avant-garde apples that fall farthest from Jackson's landscapes-and-wildlife-art tree.

From rows of dangling spurs to some of Jackson's creepiest taxidermy, anything with a bit of cowboy cachet gets nailed to the wall of the Million Dollar Cowboy Bar.

NIGHTLIFE

The **Million Dollar Cowboy Bar** (25 N. Cache Dr.; 307/733–2207) is an Old West saloon gone self-aware. The landmark bar with the garish neon cowboy sign predates Prohibition, and they've evidently never thrown anything out. From rows of dangling spurs to some of Jackson's creepiest taxidermy, anything with a bit of cowboy cachet gets nailed to the wall here. The unabashedly kitschy room reverberates with live music six nights a week in summer (both kinds, country and western), and the dance floor is packed wall-to-wall on weekends with both locals and tourists.

There's a giant stuffed moose dangling over the dance floor at the **Mangy Moose** (Teton Village; 307/733–4913), but it has never stopped sweaty hordes from packing in before the small wooden stage. The concert calendar at the Moose is always a litany of top-notch touring bands, oscillating freely between hip-hop, blues, jam-band, and bluegrass acts. The crowd is young and the microbrews are local inside the pine-beamed pub. The party sometimes spills out onto a large outdoor deck.

WHERE TO EAT

Bar J Chuckwagon. It's more of a dinner theater than actual restaurant, but the Bar J is something of an institution in the Hole. Tucked away off the Moose-Wilson Road south of Teton Village, the Chuckwagon is a bastion of old timey Cowboy West—or at least the Gene Autrified movie version. A talented in-house cowboy band serenades a 700-person indoor dining room as guests slog through heaping plates of barbecued meats and cowboy fixings. Vegetarians might want to pack a bag of carrot sticks or just come to enjoy the music. *4200 W. Bar J Chuckwagon Rd., Wilson; 307/733–3370.* **$$$$**

The Bunnery. The Bunnery is your classic bakery and diner with a sort of mountain-town, cruchy-granola bent. Lines form in the early morning for first crack at sweet, wholesome cinnamon rolls and sticky buns. The breakfast menu runs the gamut from Benedicts to breakfast burritos, and many items rely on the Bunnery's "OSM flour," a trademark blend of oats, sunflower, and millet. Dinner is served only in the summer and includes juicy burgers on soft OSM buns. It's a shame to leave without a slice of the house specialty, Very Berry Pie. *130 N. Cache St.; 307/733–5474.* **$**

Couloir. Dinner at Couloir begins with a complimentary ride on the Bridger Gondola from Teton Village to the restaurant's 9,095-foot perch. In summer you'll want to sprint to the patio, where large glass panes offer a sweeping view of the valley. (But if it's too cold to eat outdoors, don't fret; the dining room has floor-to-ceiling windows.) The prix-fixe dinner menus revolve around organic produce, fish, and game; all get innovative treatment—think cornmeal-dusted oysters and wild-boar gnocchi. The chef's table in

★ *Special Souvenir* ★

At Jedediah's at the Airport you can buy sourdough starter that comes from a mother sponge reportedly older than Jackson itself. A tasty last-minute souvenir!

the kitchen is a sought-after reservation, and the vast wine and cocktail lists make it worth a trip to Couloir just for drinks. *On Rendezvous Mountain; 307/739–2675.* **$$$$**

Lift. A pubby joint that's as welcoming to families as to the exuberant skiers coming off the slopes, Lift's menu is full of comforting safe bets like beef stew, wings, and creative burgers. The real selling points are the wide deck and the cool rooftop tables, though, with killer views of Snow King mountain and the rest of town. Drink specials abound, and happy hours are busy with young locals shaking dice at the bar. *645 S. Cache St.; 307/733–5438.* **$$-$$$**

Snake River Brewing Company. The emphasis at Jackson's signature brewery is rightly on beer; the food is tailored to the suds. The brewpub's high-ceilinged room smells pleasantly of hops and yeast. The menu is loaded with sandwiches, pastas, and wood-fired pizzas, plus a couple of standouts like the veal brat with spicy beer mustard. Happy hour from 4 to 6 pm is taken seriously by many locals, but the place can become abruptly festive at all hours of the day. A hefty roster of seasonal beers complements SRB's classic pale ale and rich Zonker stout. A self-guided brewery tour allows for a glimpse behind the scene. *265 S. Millward St.; 307/739–2337.* **$$**

Snake River Grill. Since it opened in 1993, Snake River Grill has been *the* place in Jackson for contemporary, white-tablecloth dining. A new bar area in 2011 gave the "rustic-luxe" dining room a shot of vitality, and a list of top-shelf cocktails is as clever and sophisticated as the dinner-only menu. Entrées like wild game bolognese and elk chops with sweet potato couscous are characteristic of the kitchen's cutting-edge spin on Western favorites. The wine list at "SRG" is also consistently recognized as one of the region's best. *84 E. Broadway Ave.; 307/733–0557.* **$$$$**

★**TETON THAI.** A local institution beloved by longtime Jacksonites and visitors alike, Teton Thai made the move from Jackson proper to Teton Village in 2010. The airy new space is a big step up from the restaurant's humble former digs, and the menu's no worse for wear. Authentic family recipes for Pad Kee Mao, Tom Yum Gai, and others could go toe-to-toe with most any Thai joint in the country. The new Teton Thai also has a full bar that its BYOB predecessor lacked. On the other side of Teton Pass, a second location in Driggs, Idaho, serves up an identical menu, but beware of the far inferior "Teton Thai Plate," an unaffiliated imposter that's moved into the old space in downtown Jackson. *Teton Village: 7342 Granite Loop Rd.; 307/733–0022. Driggs: 18 N. Main St.; 208/787–8424.* **$$-$$$**

★TRIO. Local foodies and out-of-towners tired of lodge decor make up the smartly dressed crowd at this chef-driven bistro. The room's modern, minimalist feel benefits from an open floor plan, an exposed kitchen, and a sexy marble bar. The seasonal entrées rely heavily on fish and game, such as pan-seared Idaho trout or grilled bison. A side dish of waffle fries with blue-cheese fondue is as luscious as anything on the dessert menu. This isn't really a spot for kids, but the wood-fired pizzas might work for their palates and your wallet. *45 S. Glenwood Dr.; 307/734–8038.* **$$$–$$$$**

⤳ WEST YELLOWSTONE

See the West Yellowstone map.

It was tourism that spawned this little town at the end of the Union Pacific rail line in 1908, and it's tourism that sustains it today. In summer the strip in "West" is a lively faux-Western promenade of souvenir stands, fly shops, hotels, and cafés. In winter the high bumblebee whine of snowmobiles is omnipresent, and the machines seem to outnumber cars on city streets two to one. That said, the town is idyllically set at the foot of the skyscraping Madison Range, just south of the point where the Gallatin River cuts dramatically through the cliffs of Gallatin Canyon. If you do manage to find some locals, they're likely to be laid-back folks with a passion for the outdoors.

EXPLORING AROUND TOWN

There is something weirdly postmodern about visiting Yellowstone as a tourist and, while there, going to a museum dedicated to the history of tourism in Yellowstone. It's still worth a visit, though, to the **Yellowstone Historic Center** (104 Yellowstone Ave.; 406/646–1100), where weathered iron railroad equipment, several generations of yellowed photographs, and early visitors' journals document the human experience in the park. The collection fills the restored 1909 Union Pacific train depot, a great stone-columned building with a short, symbolic stretch of rail behind.

Observing the "product-testing" of new bear-proof storage technologies at the Grizzly & Wolf Discovery Center is a voyeuristic thrill, particularly since the determined grizzlies usually emerge triumphant.

The nonprofit **Grizzly & Wolf Discovery Center** (201 South Canyon Rd.; 800/257–2570) is a well-managed education and research facility that takes in animals otherwise likely to be euthanized. The center is a good stop for young children who lack the patience for wildlife-watching in the park. In summer naturalists lead programs twice daily, during which kids learn about bears' scavenging habits by hiding food and watching the bears seek it out. Observing the "product-testing" of new bear-proof storage technologies is another voyeuristic thrill, particularly since the determined grizzlies usually emerge triumphant, leaving twisted metal and plastic shards in their wake. A fascinating eagle aviary allows a chance to observe and learn about these normally elusive raptors.

Twenty-seven miles northwest of town, the **Earthquake Lake Visitor Center** (U.S. 287; 406/682–7620) sits atop the 80 million tons of rock that slid into the Madison River during the 1959 Hebgen Lake Earthquake (*see right*). Interpretive displays and a 15-minute movie retell the story of the night the earth bucked. A short walking trail leads to vistas of the scarred Sheep Mountain and Quake Lake itself, a six-mile lake that used to be a green river valley dotted with campsites and cabins. Among the haunting sites at Quake Lake is the **ghost village,** visible from a dirt road that turns south five miles east of the visitor center. There, on the far side of the river, a scatter of decrepit wooden cabins looks eerily untouched, each one tilting drunkenly in the position left to it by receding floodwaters.

OTHER ACTIVITIES

A few miles northeast of town, **Hebgen Lake** sloshes in the shadow of the Madisons, a 12,500-acre playground for fisherman and boaters behind the man-made Hebgen Lake Dam. You can put in on the south side of the lake at **Lonesomehurst Campground** (on Hebgen Lake Rd., 8 miles west of West Yellowstone off U.S. 20) or on the east side at **Rainbow Point Campground** (on Rainbow Point Rd., 5 miles north of West Yellowstone off U.S. 191), and several resort marinas offer rentals. The often choppy waters yield a healthy supply of brown and rainbow trout. Ice shanties belonging to truly dedicated fisherman pepper the lake's north end during the winter.

THE HEBGEN LAKE EARTHQUAKE

It prompted evacuations at Old Faithful, caused rock slides in California, and dropped water tables as far away as Puerto Rico. The 7.5-magnitude earthquake that struck on August 17, 1959, was the strongest and deadliest in Montana's history. Though the shaking lasted less than a minute, the Sheep Mountain landslide poured into the Madison River Canyon at 100 miles per hour, destroying a campground and a mile-long stretch of highway and sending 30-foot waves in both directions. In Yellowstone, some 160 geysers broke into a chorus of simultaneous eruption, and many were permanently altered.

Twenty-eight people were killed by falling rocks or drowned as the river rapidly pooled behind the debris to form Quake Lake. Fearing a flood, the U.S. Army Corps of Engineers worked around the clock for weeks to dig a slough through the debris. Fault scarps from the quake reach 21 feet high, and the implausible walls of dirt can be explored in spots like the **Cabin Creek Scarp Area** (off U.S. 287, 4 miles west of Earthquake Lake Visitor Center).

North of West Yellowstone, the gray walls of Gallatin Canyon close in around the Gallatin River, transforming it into a frothy, roaring white-water mecca. The Shoshone called this river "Cut-tuh-o-gwa" or "swift water." Local paddlers call its toughest section "the Mad Mile," a stretch of continuous white water north of Big Sky that drenches bold rafters and kayakers as they navigate rapids with names like "Screaming Left Turn" and "Rodeo Hole." An hour north of town at Gallatin Gateway, **Montana Whitewater** (63960 Gallatin Rd., 406/

763–4465) leads full- and half-day rafting trips that are likely to soak you. They run mellower stretches, too, in case you'd rather not, you know, wet yourself.

The tiny **Bear's Den Cinema** (15 N. Electric St.; 406/646–7777) shows first-run movies throughout the year, but if you're going to catch a flick in Yellowstone, wouldn't you rather see one that's six stories tall? In the summer the **Yellowstone Giant Screen Theatre** (101 S. Canyon St.; 888/854–5862) runs the 40-minute park documentary *Yellowstone* repeatedly between 9 am and 7 pm. The film is a decent intro to the park, with some memorable historical quotes and cute bear hijinks. The theater mixes it up with a few other nature-themed films throughout the year, plus blockbusters, on its towering screen.

NIGHTLIFE

Generally speaking, you'll find more excitement stargazing on a Saturday night in West Yellowstone than you will in any of the town's no-frills bars and pubs. The Stagecoach Inn's **Coachman Lounge** (406/646–7381) keeps busy on weekends, though, with live rock music loud enough to make your teeth rattle. The bar draws a lively crowd of snowmobilers and other winter adventurers when the powder flies, possibly on account of the big fireplace but more likely for the strong drinks. This being Montana, you'll also find the ubiquitous video gambling machines.

WHERE TO EAT

Mocha Mamma's. It's not a meal exactly, but the best espresso in West Yellowstone comes from this tiny, five-stool coffee bar tucked into the corner of the outdoor apparel store Freeheel & Wheel. The espresso is locally roasted, and the baristas get it right every time. The bar's big selling point is the young staff, an active and enthusiastic crew that can relate as much about local skiing and mountain biking as any guide in town, all over a blueberry bagel and a cup of joe. *40 Yellowstone Ave.; 406/646–7744.* **$**

Serenity Bistro. Tiny, 10-table Serenity Bistro could hold its own in a much larger city on the strength of its kitchen and stylish food presentation. The short menu hypes local and fresh ingredients in surprisingly sophisticated dishes like luscious squash ravioli and cilantro-lime Thai calamari. The room itself is pretty guileless, cozy with simple wood trim and some art deco posters on the walls, but no other menu in West Yellowstone aims this high. *38 Canyon St.; 406/646–7660.* **$$$**

CODY *See the Downtown Cody map.*

The tourism industry in Cody has done more to preserve the rugged myth of the cowboy than country music and truck commercials combined. At once more authentically Western than other Yellowstone gateway towns (it's the "Rodeo Capital of the World") and more pedestrian (it has a Walmart), Cody is in large part what you make of it. "Buffalo Bill" Cody knew this when he and a group of developers essentially willed the town into existence in the 1890s. Cody personally courted settlers, brought the railroad to town, and convinced President Roosevelt to dam the Shoshone River to provide power.

Today the Shoshone flows through a town filled with century-old structures, Old West museums, Western-furniture galleries, and one giant rodeo arena. Though it's an hour's drive along the Buffalo Bill Scenic Byway to reach Yellowstone's east entrance, the river vistas and rock formations along the way make it one of the most scenic routes into the park.

Ready, aim, fire: art and guns share top billing at Cody's Buffalo Bill Center of the West.

Yellowstone and Grand Teton National Parks

EXPLORING AROUND TOWN

The **Buffalo Bill Center of the West** (720 Sheridan Ave.; 307/587–4771) is Cody's answer to the Smithsonian, five themed museums in one seven-acre facility, each as elaborate as the Wild West shows promoted by the center's namesake. The **Whitney Western Art Museum** includes stunning early paintings and photos of Yellowstone by Thomas Moran and William Henry Jackson, plus a gallery of splashy contemporary work. Four other museums focus on Plains Indian art, Yellowstone natural history, and old Buffalo Bill himself. The **Cody Firearms Museum** is by a long shot the least conventional, a maze of glass cases so full of antique pistols and rifles it would have made even Charlton Heston a little nervous.

A bright red-and-green trolley rolls up to the historical center three times a day during summer to load passengers for the **Cody Trolley Tours** (kiosk at the Irma Hotel, 1192 Sheridan Ave.; 307/527–7043). An ebullient tour guide in Western garb narrates a one-hour trip aboard the air-conditioned car, dropping tidbits of local history along with a few well-timed groaners. The trolley passes by (but does not stop at) **Old Trail Town** (1831 DeMaris Dr.; 307/587–5302), an atmospheric street of log cabins, clapboard stables, and swinging-door storefronts. The architectural relics were collected from across western Wyoming and reassembled museum-style on the original Cody townsite. The trolley also heads west through the striped sedimentary cliffs of Shoshone Canyon—literally through them, via a series of arching tunnels—to visit the **Buffalo Bill Dam and Reservoir.** At 325 feet tall, the dam was once the world's largest, and it remains impressive for its unlikely positioning, wedged tightly between the sheer walls of a plummeting granite canyon.

(opposite top) Bonanza *meets the baroque at the Buffalo Bill Center of the West; (bottom) the stagecoach used in Buffalo Bill's Wild West Show.*

Cheers echo off the roof of the grandstand as another bronc and dusty rider burst from the chute at the ★**CODY NITE RODEO** (on the west edge of town on U.S. 14/16/20; 307/587–5155). Every night in June, July, and August, you'll find amateur and pro cow-people clinging to jerking broncos, wrestling 300-pound steers to the ground, and casting lassos at sprinting calves. If you've never experienced a rodeo, there is really no better place to do it, with the high brown Wyoming desert as a backdrop, the pungent smell of stock in the air, and more dudes in chaps than at a Harley-Davidson rally. Aside from some ribald humor from the announcers' booth, the events are kid-friendly. Young rodeo fans are invited into the arena before each show for a "calf scramble," where packs of screaming children terrorize a baby cow by trying to pluck a ribbon off of it. The

There's nothing ironic about this cowboy finery—in Cody, it's a lifestyle.

week of July 4th, the big-purse **Cody Stampede Rodeo** attracts the world's best riders and a Stetson-clad crowd of diehard fans.

OTHER ACTIVITIES

Between Cody and Yellowstone, some dozen guest ranches tuck in among the river vistas and rock formations of the **Buffalo Bill Scenic Byway,** and they all have stables. Most offer a slate of horseback trips ranging from afternoon trots to weeklong wilderness trips in the surrounding Shoshone National Forest. **Bill Cody Ranch** (2604 Yellowstone Hwy.; 307/587–2097) is among those offering day rides for nonguests, including beginners. Twenty-five miles east of town, they lead afternoon trips that top out above 7,000 feet, with limitless Absaroka views and trail-prepared cowboy lunches.

If you need to pick up any last-minute gear for your exploits in the parks, hit the **Sierra Trading Post Outlet Store** (1402 8th St.; 307/578–5802), a crucial and budget-friendly adventure headquarters.

The **Heart Mountain Interpretive Center** (14 miles northeast of Cody, just off U.S. 14 on Rd. 19; 307/754–8000) features replicated barracks and other exhibits detailing the experience of more than 14,000 Japanese Americans who were interned there during World War II. Gazing out across the spare desert landscape from the windowed Reflection Room, visitors get a sense of how internees must have imagined themselves at the far end of the earth.

NIGHTLIFE

On Thursday nights in July and August, a forest of lawn chairs sprouts in front of the park bandshell for **summer concerts at City Park** (908 Sheridan Ave.; 307/587–0400). The acts are mostly local, ranging from jazz combos to—surprise!—cowboy balladeers. The 6 pm curtain time, along with the park's playground and mini-golf course, make this a popular night out for families with younger children.

When Cody locals feel like kicking their spurs in the air and waving them like they just don't care, they head to **Cassie's Supper Club & Dance Hall** (214 Yellowstone Ave.; 307/527–5500), which the proprietors will tell you has been entertaining Cody-ites since 1922. Until the 1930s it was entertaining them with prostitutes, and artifacts from this era of ill repute decorate the massive wooden dining, drinking, and dancing space, including a robe worn by the bar's namesake madam. The atmosphere is twangy roadhouse, with live country music most nights in summer.

BUFFALO BILL WRANGLING

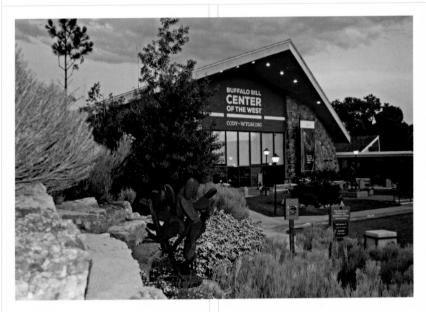

To pay your respects to the impresario of the Wild West, you may have to look outside of his namesake town. Buffalo Bill Cody died after falling on hard times. A bad debt to a pair of shyster promoters in Denver kept him performing in circuses almost into his 70s. He died there in 1917, and folks back in Wyoming blanched when Mrs. Cody proclaimed that Bill, in a last-minute change of heart, decided to be buried in Colorado rather than at his presumed gravesite in Cody. Controversy still rages as to whether the same Denver shysters bribed or harassed Cody's wife into the arrangement.

He was buried on Lookout Mountain near present-day Golden, Colorado, and a niece declared afterwards that she would "fight every person in Colorado" to bring him "back" to Cody. The Cody American Legion felt similarly. They posted a $100,000 reward in 1948 for anyone who could steal and "return" the body. In response, Denver's Legion put up guards until the city could deepen the grave and cover it with 30 tons of concrete. Today, though, rumors persist that some Cody-ite pulled it off, that Buffalo Bill lies in an unmarked grave somewhere in Shoshone country.

Cody's Buffalo Bill Center of the West

WHERE TO EAT

The Irma. Although he probably didn't have anything to do with the 1950s-diner-style sign outside, Buffalo Bill Cody himself built the showy Irma Hotel and Restaurant in 1902. In one of the restaurant's two dining rooms stretches an ornate cherrywood backbar presented to Cody by Queen Victoria in 1900. The antique cash register and archival photos on the wall also contribute to the room's museum feel. The menu is eclectic, ranging from omelets to Mexican entrées and an occasional wild card like whiskey bread pudding. Children under six eat free from the breakfast and lunch buffets. *1192 Sheridan Ave.; 307/587–4221.* **$$-$$$**

Wyoming's Rib & Chop House. So you spent the evening watching people in chaps ride and wrestle giant steers, and now you want to eat one. This Montana and Wyoming chain has a reputation for turning out some of the region's best red meat, like the tender, hand-cut rib eye. Tangy, slow-cooked baby back ribs are another carnivore favorite. The smallish dining room in this squat, brick building fills quickly in summer, so reservations are a must. Grab a table near the giant front windows for excellent people-watching. *1367 Sheridan Ave.; 307/527–7731.* **$$$**

☞ GARDINER

Yellowstone's first "gateway town" may have been created as a form of revenge. Its founder, James McCartney, has the dubious distinction of having been one of the park's first profiteers. He and a partner informally claimed land and set up a shabby hotel at Mammoth Hot Springs in 1871. When the Feds finally gave an angry McCartney the boot in 1879, he went out and founded Gardiner, right up against the park's northern boundary. Now the community is Yellowstone's only year-round entry point.

Gardiner boomed with the arrival of the Northern Pacific in 1902, and by the time the railroad shuttered almost 50 years later, it was a well-established tourism hotspot. The town is still a micro-mecca for lodging and other visitor facilities, but it comes off as a quieter, more genuine place than other entrance communities. The Yellowstone River flows right through, augmented south of town by the Gardner. Note the different spelling between the river and the town—both are named for mountain man Johnson Gardner, but the village adopted a phonetic rendering based on renowned trapper and storyteller Jim Bridger's southern accent.

Exploring Around Town

The regal **Roosevelt Arch** (park entrance on North Entrance Rd.) was built to wow the early waves of Yellowstone visitors, who were awed by the landscape around the park's north entrance. As the park's chief engineer, Hiram Chittenden, noted sourly in one annual report, "The first impression of visitors entering the park was very unfavorable." President Theodore Roosevelt himself laid the cornerstone for the arch in 1903. At 50 feet high, the basalt structure goes a long way toward compensating for the (arguably) dull scenery. The arch's surroundings were spruced up for the NPS centennial in 2016, with a new park and visitor center at the gateway (along with a bypass for those who'd rather skip the landmark altogether). Construction along the entrance road will likely continue beyond 2016 as nearby roads and the town's historic rail depot get a similar face-lift.

The **Yellowstone National Park Heritage & Research Center** (20 Old Yellowstone Trail; 307/344-2662), while not exactly a tourist attraction, is an astounding depository of all things Yellowstone, from crates of historical documents to early staff uniforms to preserved plant specimens. Parts of the research library are open to the public, and there's a small history exhibit in the lobby, but the best way to glimpse the recesses is to join one of the biweekly summer tours, open to a mere 10 visitors at a time. This will give you a truly unique glimpse at a low-key Yellowstone treasure.

Where to Eat

Iron Horse Bar & Grille. Gardiner is not an epicure's town, but this cavernous burgers-and-beers joint mixes it up with tasty elk tacos, bison meatloaf, elk nachos. Even the burgers are game meat all the way. The real selling point is the immense deck overlooking the Yellowstone River. It gets crowded and festive out there in peak season. *212 Spring St.; 406/848-7666.* **$$-$$$**

Where to Stay

The stars look incredibly bright and close out here.

Fireworks over Teton Village during the Jackson Hole Mountain Festival.

Whether you're stepping out of your room into the pine-pillared lobby of a historic park hotel or nestling deeper into your sleeping bag while gray jays whistle at the dawn, waking up inside a national park is a singular experience. Lodging in the gateway communities can be equally adventuresome, as the parks' peripheries attract a funky collection of sexy resorts, quilt-and-teacup B&Bs, and offbeat roadhouse motels.

Park lodging terminology can be a little tricky. It's useful to remember that, more often than not, a "lodge" in Yellowstone and Grand Teton refers to a campus made up of cabins, cottages, and one or more "main lodge" buildings with dining rooms, lounges, and other public spaces. Public spaces in all of the park accommodations are open to nonguests for sightseeing or hanging out.

ARE YOU IN OR ARE YOU OUT?

Your biggest choice is whether to stay inside or outside the park. Park lodging tends to be a little pricier than a night's stay in the gateway towns, but many visitors find the cost is offset by the obvious perks of scenery and proximity to park attractions. Then you have to weigh the intangibles. Cabins, inns, and hotels inside Yellowstone and Grand Teton usually date back a few decades or more. If you're after a historic vibe, then you're likely also signing on for a smaller room and a more casual attitude toward upkeep than you'd find outside the park.

You won't find in-room televisions inside Yellowstone, and they're rare in Grand Teton. Coffeemakers, telephones, and private bathrooms aren't always givens; neither is heat or air-conditioning. The best rule of thumb for booking a room inside the parks is not to take anything for granted. If a particular amenity is important to you, ask about it upon reservation. (*See* the Practical Information chapter for more information about phone and Internet access in and near the parks.)

Maintaining cabins and hotel rooms in Yellowstone and Grand Teton is a constant battle for park concessionaires, and creaky hinges, leaky faucets, or torn or missing window screens are not at all unusual. Concessionaire staff members are helpful and sympathetic, though, and they'll deal swiftly with serious problems.

GET A ROOM

June through August is peak season in Greater Yellowstone, when rooms fill fast and prices are at their highest. It's wise to make reservations a year or more in advance for the more sought-after park accommodations (Old Faithful Inn, Lake Hotel, and Jenny Lake Lodge). You can get away with six months' advance reservation for most cabins, and even less if you're not picky about location or amenities. The reservation timeline varies greatly outside the park. Generally speaking, the more unusual your chosen accommodation, the earlier you ought to book. Chains have more last-minute options.

You can often save money on lodging by visiting in the "bumper seasons" of April and May or September and October. Winter deals are most prevalent in January, when extreme temperatures put a damper on tourism.

In the listings below, frequently repeated phone numbers and websites are due to the fact that **Xanterra Parks & Resorts** manages all lodging in Yellowstone, and **Grand Teton Lodge Company** manages most properties in Grand Teton. These concessionaires and others also manage many of the campgrounds, though some are administered by the NPS. This divvied-up arrangement means that there's no single clearinghouse for campground information. Around

The Old Faithful Inn is one of the crown jewels of the national park system.

Jackson, **Jackson Hole Central Reservations** (888/838–6606; www. jacksonholewy.com) is useful for "one-stop shopping."

LODGING AND CAMPING
(a single night's peak-season rate for a standard double room)

$=under $50	$$=$50–$100	$$$=$101–$175	$$$$=over $175

⊕ LODGES, HOTELS, AND INNS

Yellowstone's Lower Loop

OLD FAITHFUL

★OLD FAITHFUL INN. The steep and many-gabled roof of the Old Faithful Inn cuts a regal profile across the Yellowstone sky, flags waving from its widow's walk. Once inside the iron-studded front doors, you're engulfed by the seven-story space. The inn's awesome main hall has a 90-foot ceiling, a gargantuan stone fireplace, and a spiraling series of intricately hand-wrought wooden balconies. Known as the Old House, this portion was completed in 1903, and is one of the most photographed destinations in the park. Room choices vary from wood-framed quarters with claw-foot tubs to more modern units in the east and west additions. Those with the best geyser basin views are in the Old House and the west wing. For a view that only a handful of park visitors ever see, ask a bellman to put you on the list to follow inn staff onto the roof for the flag-raising and -lowering. *Old Faithful; 307/ 344–7311 or 866/439–7375; www.yellowstonenationalparklodges.com.* **$$$-$$$$**

Old Faithful Lodge Cabins. Though this complex's 1928 lodge is a magnificent stone-and-wood structure looking out over the glistening jet of Old Faithful, the cabins themselves are more dated than historic. Budget cabins look like tiny wooden utility sheds from the outside, share a bathroom complex, and sleep three in a double and single bed. Frontier cabins are a slight step up, with one or two doubles and private bathrooms. Cabins are packed pretty tight, but a handful are within earshot of the Firehole River, and you can't really beat the proximity to Old Faithful. *Old Faithful; 307/344–7311 or 866/ 439–7375; www.yellowstonenationalparklodges.com.* **$$-$$$**

Old Faithful Snow Lodge. Clean and contemporary, the Snow Lodge is the newest lodging option in the park, completed in 1999. While the timber and wrought-iron interior can't compare to that of the neighboring Old Faithful Inn, its fireplace lobby and plush, airy sitting room are still ideal for lounging. The guest rooms are standard modern, each with a full bathroom and wildlife-themed bedspreads. True to its name, the Snow Lodge is one of just two in-park hotels open in winter, accessible by snowcoach or snowmobile. *Old Faithful; 307/344–7311 or 866/439–7375; www.yellowstonenationalparklodges. com.* **$$$$**

Old Faithful Snow Lodge Cabins. Both varieties of Snow Lodge cabins have a clean, motel-style look, with plain wood furniture and some nonthreatening landscape art hanging on the walls. The four-plex Western cabins are a little larger and brighter, with wood-and-shingle exteriors and very small porches. The duplex Frontier cabins are a bit plainer. The cabin cluster is tucked behind the developed area around the Snow Lodge, with a less-than-inspiring view of the village access road. Expect to walk a quarter-mile or so to shopping and dining at the lodge or general store. *Old Faithful; 307/344–7311 or 866/439–7375; www.yellowstonenationalparklodges.com.* **$$$**

LAKE VILLAGE

Lake Lodge Cabins. The Lake Lodge itself, a five-minute walk from the most distant cabin, is a pine-log masterpiece with a lounge and a porch that might be the two best places to unwind in all of Yellowstone. Like the lounge, the cabins date back to the 1920s, but they lack its rustic charm. Furnishings in the cheaper Pioneer

Lake Yellowstone Hotel was built plain and boxy in 1891; architect Robert Reamer spruced it up with columns in 1904.

cabins are quite dated, all wood paneling and aged carpeting. The multi-unit Western cabins are similarly out of date, and light sleepers should beware the thin walls. Still, all the cabins have private bathrooms, plus a quiet, wooded setting with dining, laundry, and a gift shop just up the road in the lodge. *Lake Village; 307/344-7311 or 866/439-7375; www. yellowstonenationalparklodges.com.* $$-$$$

Lake Yellowstone Cabins. These garish yellow shacks clustered on an exposed lot behind the Lake Yellowstone Hotel were built in the 1920s, and they look their age from the outside. All were remodeled around 2004, though, and the interiors are actually spacious, clean, and modern, if bland. Each has a private bathroom and two double beds; the common areas of the Lake Yellowstone Hotel are a short walk away. Don't be surprised to open your front door and find a bison browsing nonchalantly on your lawn. *Lake Village; 307/344-7311 or 866/439-7375; www. yellowstonenationalparklodges.com.* $$$

★**LAKE YELLOWSTONE HOTEL.** Lake Yellowstone Hotel is the oldest Yellowstone structure still in use, though the photogenic front portico was added later. Dramatic renovations have left the place bright and fresh, without diminishing the historical character—plus, now every room has a private bathroom. Forty-five of the renovated rooms are set up for wired Internet, a rarity in the park. The grand, colonnaded common area is filled with sunlight and plush loungers, the nicest place in Yellowstone to relax with a cocktail (the bar in the corner was recently expanded, too). The hotel gift shop specializes in fine crystal, and the dining room is

THE FATHER OF PARKITECHTURE

Robert Reamer was just 29 when Yellowstone's first major concessionaire commissioned him for a new inn near the geyser basin at Old Faithful. Though a tremendous talent, the self-taught, transplanted Easterner was also a drinking man, and as one biographer wrote, he was rumored to have "sketched the plans while coming shakily out of a monumental submersion in malt." Reamer was also incredibly dedicated, often neglecting to eat or change clothes during the 1903–04 construction of the Old Faithful Inn.

The Arts and Crafts–style detailing in Reamer's inn, the use of materials to mimic the natural surroundings, and the building's scale all helped solidify a notion of national park architecture in the public consciousness. His approach handily bridged the gap between rustic and elegant. Reamer became Yellowstone's go-to architect for the next 35 years, renovating the hotels at Lake and Mammoth and building the Lake Lodge and the Prairie-style (and now demolished) Canyon Hotel. He also added the asymmetrical wings to his masterwork at Old Faithful and designed the Roosevelt Arch in the gateway town of Gardiner. We have his influential style to thank for every gaudy stone fireplace and faux-pine chandelier that finds its way into a motel in Greater Yellowstone.

arguably the park's best. *Lake Village; 307/344–7311 or 866/439–7375; www.yellowstonenationalparklodges.com.* **$$$$**

GRANT VILLAGE

Grant Village Lodge. The six generic gray rectangles that make up the lodge at Grant aren't much to look at, inside or out, but they're clean and modern. The "front desk" is a small office building a short distance from the motel complex. Guest rooms have two double beds and private, albeit small, bathrooms. You might score a lake view if you book very early—the alternative is a parking lot. It's a two-minute walk through lodgepole forest to reach either of the village's restaurants. *Grant Village; 307/344–7311 or 866/439–7375; www. yellowstonenationalparklodges.com.* **$$$**

YELLOWSTONE'S UPPER LOOP

MAMMOTH

★**MAMMOTH CABINS.** Though far from luxurious, Mammoth's clean, well-situated cabins are the best in the park. Take your average comfy-but-no-frills hotel room. Put it under its own roof, within sauntering distance of village amenities. Tack on a small, shaded porch. Add elk wandering by. Staying in the Mammoth cabins puts you a short distance from the Mammoth Hot Springs Hotel, but what you lose in front-desk service and decorous common areas, you gain in that most underrated of amenities, the great outdoors. The simple units are virtually identical to the hotel's (right down to the option of private bathrooms versus shared), but you can spend an evening on your porch making eyes with a she-elk—and in four of the cabins you can do this from a hot tub. *Mammoth Hot Springs; 307/344–7311 or 866/439–7375; www.yellowstonenationalparklodges. com.* **$$-$$$**

Mammoth Hot Springs Hotel. The public spaces outshine the rooms at the site of Yellowstone's first tourist accommodation. In the stately Map Room, dirt-stained hikers and bejeweled dowagers sit side by side, gazing out floor-to-ceiling windows at the antics of elk herds. Off the lobby, the For Future Generations gift shop is an eco-friendly building, with a number of green souvenirs, all rated for their social and environmental footprint. Guest rooms come with or without bathrooms, and while both varieties are spartan, wood headboards and vanities keep them from being austere. In two available suites you'll find that rarest of all Yellowstone species,

Horseback trail-riders from the Roosevelt Lodge, Yellowstone National Park.

YELLOWSTONE AND GRAND TETON NATIONAL PARKS

the cable television. *Mammoth Hot Springs; 307/344-7311 or 866/ 439-7375; www.yellowstonenationalparklodges.com.* **$$-$$$**

ROOSEVELT

Roosevelt Lodge. A dude ranch vibe dominates Roosevelt, where lanes between cabin rows have names like "Bronco Trail" and "Stampede Trail." The more economical Roughrider cabins have one to three double beds, shared bathrooms, and cast-iron wood-burning stoves. The ostensibly nicer Frontier cabins are similarly decorated in plain wood and plaid but have two double beds, private

Stagecoach rides are part of the cowboy vibe at Yellowstone's Roosevelt Lodge.

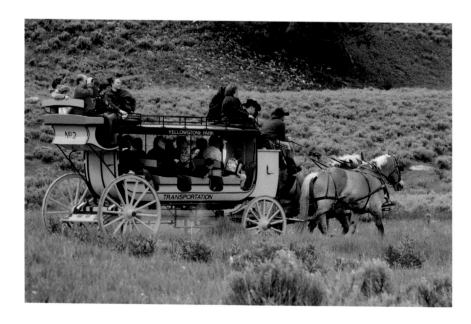

bathrooms, and electric heat instead of stoves. The lodge itself is a giant, cozy cabin of rough-hewn timber and stone, with petrified wood incorporated into the foundation. Though the fireplace lobby works for a card game, the place to unwind is in a wooden rocking chair on the covered porch. Don't buy the myth that President Roosevelt camped here during his 1903 visit—Teddy's actual tent pad was up the road near Calcite Springs. *Roosevelt; 307/344-7311 or 866/439-7375; www.yellowstonenationalparklodges.com.* **$$-$$$**

CANYON

Canyon Cabins. Set in a wooded area behind the village square, the cabins at Canyon are roomy if rather no-frills, with shaded porches and a bit of Western atmosphere in their pine headboards, benches, and light fixtures. All have private bathrooms and tubs, and they're grouped in clusters of four to six, so expect to say hi to the neighbors from time to time. *Canyon Village; 307/344–7311 or 866/439–7375; www.yellowstonenationalparklodges. com.* **$$$$**

Canyon Lodge. Following a $70 million construction project, Canyon replaced much of its cabin fleet with a set of five modern, wood-and-stone lodges designed to mimic Yellowstone's more historic "parkitechture." Canyon's standard rooms (with one queen and a shower), superior rooms (with two queens and shower with tub), and suites (one king and one queen in separate rooms, plus a wet bar and other perks) are all in these new buildings. Premium rooms are found in the two older lodges, called Cascade and Dunraven, which have the atmosphere and comforts of a typical American budget chain (and have full baths and one or two double beds). Cascade lacks both an elevator and a lobby, while Dunraven has both. It's a 10- or 15-minute walk from any of the lodges to the front-desk building in the village square. Dining is similarly distant, but in a bustling location like Canyon, the relative isolation feels like a blessing. Bison and elk often loiter around the lodges. *Canyon Village; 307/344–7311 or 866/439–7375; www.yellowstonenationalparklodges. com.* **$$$$**

MISSION ACCOMPLISHED?

As visitors streamed into the park following World War II, NPS officials launched a broad plan to upgrade Yellowstone's roads and guest facilities by 1966. The park's carrying capacity definitely grew under "Mission 66," but people have been known to decry the project's two biggest results, Canyon and Grant villages.

The boxy, modernist structures at Canyon opened in 1957, but the cabins and shops turned off a lot of park lodging diehards. Fans of the old Robert Reamer-designed Canyon Hotel continued to flock to it while the new rooms undersold. The grand hotel suffered from structural problems, but when it was demolished in 1959, some accused the NPS of a hidden agenda to make good on the Mission 66 cabin investment.

Grant Village represented a trade: a new development in exchange for removal of facilities at Fishing Bridge, a site that threatened critical grizzly habitat. But folks in Cody protested losing Fishing Bridge, which was their nearest village, and although park officials went forward with Grant, they drastically scaled back the Fishing Bridge removals. Then they further angered environmentalists by building Grant in a trout-spawning area about as important to grizzlies as the habitat they were trying to save. Tack on the village's maligned, nonrustic atmosphere and you see why Grant, for all its perks, is one of Yellowstone's most politically unpopular sites.

Grand Teton is even more
imposing in winter.

GRAND TETON NATIONAL PARK

Colter Bay Cabins. With some 200 cabins spread out across a mostly forested tract, the lodging complex at Colter Bay is like a bustling village. Not the place to contemplate nature in silence, but it's ideal if you want a bit of rusticity alongside cafés, shopping, and a launderette. The log structures have an authentic feel, with old-fashioned furniture and simple, patterned linens. Floor plans change from cabin to cabin; some have multiple rooms and most have a full bath. The cheaper, canvas-sided tent cabins are a cozy way to quasi-rough it, with bunked cots and shared bathrooms. *Off U.S. 89/191/287, 5 miles north of Jackson Lake Junction; 307/543–2811 or 800/628–9988; www.gtlc.com.* **Cabins $$-$$$$; tent cabins $$**

Dornan's Spur Ranch Cabins. The Dornan's complex is like a miniature city, its sometimes frenzied set of shops and places to eat sitting just across the Snake River from park headquarters. Still, the pretty little cabins at Dornan's are set a few steps away from all that, gathered in a quiet cluster on the bank of the river, so you're more likely to spot a moose than a tourist with an antler hat. The cabins blend modern and rustic styles, with lodgepole furnishings and humble-looking wood exteriors but also carpeting, full refrigerators, and stoves. *Moose; 307/733–2522; www.dornans.com.* **$$$$**

Headwaters Lodge & Cabins at Flagg Ranch. During the early 1900s, Flagg Ranch evolved from a military station to a successful dude ranch, and a few of the log structures here are relics from those early days. But you wouldn't know it from the cabin interiors, which were renovated in 2012 and have the clean, modern feel of a midscale hotel. The wooded Rockefeller Parkway location makes for easy access to both Yellowstone and the Tetons. You can glimpse the Tetons from wooden rocking chairs on the small porches. *John D. Rockefeller Memorial Pkwy., 2 miles south of Yellowstone park boundary; 307/543–2861 or 800/443–2311; www.gtlc.com.* **Cabins $$$$; camper cabins $$**

Jackson Lake Lodge. This flat-roofed modernist castle centers around an expansive main hall, where guests unwind or plink on their laptops before a 60-foot viewing window overlooking Jackson Lake and Mount Moran. Surrounding the hall are multiple dining options, a lively bar, a gift shop, and an adventure desk that can set up lake cruises, horseback riding, and other activities. A few hundred cottage rooms laid out within walking distance are roomy with comfy furnishings and Native American–themed art on the walls. Rooms inside the lodge are mostly identical, but some have balconies and Teton views that will take your breath away. *Off U.S. 89/191/287, .5*

The patio of
Jenny Lake Lodge
in Grand Teton.

mile north of Jackson Lake Junction; 307/543–2811 or 800/628–9988; www.gtlc.com. $$$$

★JENNY LAKE LODGE. These small log cabins may be the handsomest lodging in all the national park system. From the luxe down comforters and handmade pine furnishings in the one-room cabins to the ornate hooked rugs and authentic wood-burning stoves in the suites, the trappings at Jenny Lake Lodge show a resortlike attention to detail. Also resortlike are the perks: free access to a fleet of shiny cruiser bikes, complimentary horseback rides, and meals in the knockout dining room. You can admire the Cathedral Group of peaks from the main lodge's pine-log porch. *North Jenny Lake Loop; 307/ 733–4647 or 800/628–9988; www.gtlc.com.* $$$$

★MOULTON RANCH CABINS. From the porch of a century-old Jackson Hole homestead you can look across to arguably the park's finest view of the Teton Range. Photographers have been patronizing the old Moulton property for decades, in part to capture picturesque old farm structures like the nearby Moulton Barn, but also for the magnificent and unmarred view of the mountains. Five varied accommodations on this sunflower-dotted spread include the homestead's original bunkhouse as well as newer cabins. None is luxurious or particularly large, but the romance of country quilts and old barnwood is hard to resist. *Mormon Row, .5 mile south of Antelope Flats Rd.; 307/ 733–3749; www.moultonranchcabins.com.* $$$-$$$$

Signal Mountain Cabins. Although these rustic cabins lack a view, they're within a couple of minutes' walk of the Jackson Lake shoreline. Handmade pine chairs, tables, and bedposts add to the cabins' woodsy ambience. Blander, motel-style units are available, too. The varied floor plans sleep anywhere from two to six. Also a short walk away, the lodge itself is an unassuming stone and wood building with a lively television lounge always full of ebullient Europeans watching soccer matches. Search the lodge for the awesome full-size moose made entirely of scrap metal fragments, the work of a talented former employee. *Off Teton Park Rd., 3 miles south of Jackson Lake Junction; 307/543–2831 or 800/672–6012; www.signalmountainlodge.com.* **$$$-$$$$**

Signal Mountain Retreats. The mess of lodging choices at the bustling, lakefront Signal Mountain Lodge includes roomy bungalows, suite-style "lakeside retreats," and a monster, fully furnished log home. All three are a step up in comfort from the cabin options, with plush couches and small kitchens stocked with cookware. The log home sleeps up to six, and its gas fireplace and log interior give it a bit more ambience than the other options. The retreat rooms are the only units to take advantage of Signal Mountain's signature Teton views—Mount Moran practically invades your living room through a wide picture window. *Off Teton Park Rd., 3 miles south of Jackson Lake Junction; 307/543–2831 or 800/672–6012; www.signalmountainlodge.com.* **$$$$**

Triangle X Ranch. The last of the old dude ranches that once characterized Jackson Hole, Triangle X is a working stock ranch with a row of no-frills log cabins and a famously welcoming family atmosphere. The same family has been shoeing horses here since 1926, and though any stay revolves around the equestrian experience, ranch pursuits also include rafting and guided fly-fishing trips. Activities are included in the nightly rates, as are meals (thick steaks and other gut-busting Western fare served family style in the "big house"). On each cabin's open porch, Adirondack chairs face the mountains, perfect places to rest saddlesore backsides. *Triangle Ranch Road, off U.S. 89/26/191, 6 miles south of Moran Junction; 307/733–2183; www.trianglex.com.* **$$$$**

Jackson Area

Alpine House. Are all the innkeepers in Jackson rock-star outdoorspeople? An Exum mountain guide and an Olympic biathlete are the gracious proprietors of Alpine House, a small inn with an eco-country flair near Town Square. Repurposed and recycled products are among the inn's building materials; local ingredients fill the menu; and energy use is wholly offset with purchased wind-power credits. In summer you can ride one of the inn's complimentary bikes. As you'd guess, the owners are great sources of advice on the outdoors. *285 North Glenwood St.; 307/739–1570; www.alpinehouse.com.* **$$$$**

Amangani. Perched atop East Gros Ventre Butte, the templelike Amangani looks like it was built by some advanced but ancient civilization, all minimalist redwood walls, sandstone columns, and the scent of burning money. Floor-to-ceiling windows are everywhere, and it might be hard to tell whether you're indoors or out if it weren't for the bazillion thread-count linens, woven cowhide chairs, and plasmascreen TVs. Spa treatments and a heated outdoor infinity pool with a gobsmacking view round out the perks at Jackson's cushiest resort. *1535 N. East Butte Rd.; 307/734–7333; www.amanresorts.com.* **$$$$**

Antler Inn. Budget lodging in Jackson is largely the domain of the chains, and often pushed out to the city's commercial hinterlands. Not so at the Antler, which offers motel-style lodging and a smattering of Western charm just a block from Town Square. From the building's old-timey wood facade and dated neon sign you might expect something a little chintzier, but the clean, simple rooms have nice touches like wood headboards and wireless access. *43 W. Pearl St.; 307/733–2535; www.townsquareinns.com/antler-inn.* **$$$**

Hotel Terra. Other properties talk the eco-talk, but Hotel Terra takes green hospitality to the next level. From café seat backs made of recycled seat belts to custom-made, non-chemical mattresses, and from bottle-free water stations to the building's abundance of natural light, there's a true conservation mindset at the heart of this hotel. It's luxe to the core, with a hip, urban feel and all the amenities the price tag suggests. The on-site restaurant, Il Villaggio Osteria, has a reputation as one of the best in Jackson Hole. The rooftop infinity pool is stunning (and filled with saltwater instead of chlorine, naturally). *3335 W. Village Dr., Teton Village; 307/201–6065 or 855/318–8707; hotelterrajacksonhole.com.* **$$$$**

★SNAKE RIVER LODGE AND SPA. A person sitting in the right spot in the Snake River Lodge lobby can count no fewer than six carved grizzly bear tchotchkes, plus one stuffed mountain lion. Don't let the Western bric-a-brac fool you, though—Snake River is all luxury. The stylish, contemporary rooms benefit from plush bedding, iPod docks in every room, and solid granite countertops; suites have views of slopes. Renovations in 2012 brought new carpeting in every room and new headboards and mattresses in the double queens. It's a three-minute walk to the lifts, and beyond ski season you can entertain yourself with a whopping menu of spa treatments, concierge-planned activities of every type, and an indoor-outdoor pool area that looks like something from *The Blue Lagoon. 7710 Granite Loop Rd., Teton Village; 307/732–6000 or 855/342–4712.* **$$$$**

A Teton Treehouse. Your hosts at this funky bed-and-breakfast are old Jackson Hole hands who can boast of a first ascent or two and are known around town for founding one of Jackson's first commercial rafting outfitters. You'll hear their stories around a breakfast table overflowing with homemade granola, freshly made breads, and other treats. The wooden bungalow isn't actually a treehouse, but it's atop a high hill, its wings winding among tree trunks. A lofty common area centers around an immense fireplace and a grand, wooden spiral staircase. Each room is unique, with a warm, lived-in feel. Some have decks and balconies that sprout at unpredictable angles. *6175 Heck of a Hill Rd., Wilson; 307/733–3233; www.atetontreehouse-jacksonhole.com.* **$$$$**

West Yellowstone

The Historic Madison Hotel. The knotty-pine pillars and railings at the Madison are remnants of West Yellowstone's first days as a tourist town. The hotel itself was founded in 1912, and most rooms retain the historic feel with hand-carved headboards, pioneer-style quilts, and clawfoot tubs. There's a block of (less interesting) cabin-style motel rooms as well. Shared, dorm-style rooms upstairs make up West Yellowstone's only hostel. The on-site gift shop is so packed with tchotchkes you have to duck to avoid the dream catchers. *139 Yellowstone Ave.; 800/838–7745 or 406/646–7745; www.madisonhotel motel.com.* **$-$$$**

Three Bear Lodge. A log-and-stone exterior gives this sprawling motel complex a country look, but inside, the rooms are standard modern. Unlike most West Yellowstone accommodations, Three Bears stays open through the off-season, catering to winter adventurers with snowcoach tours and snowmobile packages. Sled traffic on the nearby streets can be intense. The lobby has a cool collection of historic Yellowstone photos and a self-guided exhibit showing how materials from the lodge's 80-year history have been repurposed. *217 Yellowstone Ave.; 800/646–7353 or 406/646–7353; www.threebearlodge.com.* **$$$-$$$$**

Gardiner

Riverside Cottages. Fourteen simple cottages cluster in a small semicircle, making the most of a gravel parking lot in the middle of town. The property overlooks the Yellowstone River, and several of the units have private decks with views out over the water. The last five years have seen rolling renovations, including new fixtures and an expanded (shared) deck and a new, roomier hot tub along the riverbank. *521 W.*

Scott St.; 877/774–2836 or 406/848–7719; www.riversidecottages.com. **$$$-$$$$**

Yellowstone Village Inn. Wolf comforters, bison wallpaper, framed elk paintings . . . if you can print a tacky wildlife image on it, then they've got it at the Yellowstone Village Inn. The decorating may be over the top, but the rooms at this large, modern hotel are very clean and the staff appreciably sociable. Because the inn is on the northern outskirts of Gardiner, bison and elk have a tendency to loiter on the front lawn. *1102 Scott St.; 800/228–8158 or 406/848–7417; www.yellowstonevinn.com.* **$$$-$$$$**

CAMPGROUNDS

YELLOWSTONE'S LOWER LOOP

Madison Campground. Proximity is the major selling point at Madison. It's a short drive to West Yellowstone, a short drive to the geyser basins, and just a quick stroll to the wildlife-rich spread on the banks of the Madison River. A trail network winds from the campground down to the river meadow, where herds of elk and bison lounge year-round. Sites at Madison are tucked within thick pine stands and spread out enough that the area feels less congested than it is. There are flush toilets but no hookups or showers. *West Entrance Rd. at Madison Junction; 307/344–7311 or 866/439–7375; www.yellowstonenationalparklodges.com.* **$**

YELLOWSTONE'S UPPER LOOP

Canyon Campground. Where a lot of campgrounds in Yellowstone could be taken at first glance for RV parks, Canyon is truly a camper's campground. About a third of the 272 sites are set aside for tents, and most are heavily wooded—great not just for shade, but for a semblance of privacy. Canyon's 7,700-foot elevation makes for chilly nights in early and late season. All sites are within a few minutes' walk of pay showers and laundry. Generators are permitted during the day at the RV sites. *Canyon Village; 307/344–7311 or 866/439–7375; www.yellowstonenationalparklodges.com.* **$**

Indian Creek Campground. At just 70 sites, this comparatively small location is among a handful of Yellowstone frontcountry campgrounds with a decidedly backcountry feel. The sites themselves are clustered within a lodgepole forest, and it's just a quarter-mile walk up the adjacent Big Horn Pass Trail to reach meadows frequented by moose and elk. Two fairly mellow creeks flank the campground; Obsidian Creek to the east is a good place to fish for small brook trout. Adding to the wilderness ambience are vault toilets and the quiet that comes from banning generators. *Mammoth-Norris Rd., 8 miles south of Mammoth; 307/344–7381; www.nps.gov/yell.* **$**

Pebble Creek Campground. Primitive, remote Pebble Creek is appealing for the ecological confrontations happening all around it, the transition zones where forest meets rock and rock meets water. The namesake creek runs through the wooded camp, and a half-mile walk upstream leads to a small, peaceful limestone canyon. Tent sites sit close enough for neighbors to hear each other, though they're set off from the smallish motorized sites. Big rigs should look elsewhere. This is grizzly country, so tent campers should utilize the food storage poles or risk an ecological confrontation of their own. *Northeast Entrance Rd., 8 miles southwest of Northeast Entrance; 307/344–7381; www.nps.gov/yell.* **$**

Slough Creek Campground. You're in wild country at Slough Creek, where mule deer and bison wander right through camp and hordes of anglers relax after working the blue-ribbon trout stream. The first come, first served sites are decidedly primitive, providing only a picnic table, fire pit, and a few shared bear-proof storage containers. Half of the 23 sites can accommodate 30-foot RVs, while the rest are best suited to tents and smaller trailers. A few coveted sites sit directly on the creek. Listen at night for not-so-distant cries from the region's four wolf packs. *Slough Creek Rd., 6 miles east of Tower Junction; 307/344–7381; www.nps.gov/yell.* **$**

Pull back the tent flaps for an unparalleled view at Grand Teton's Jenny Lake Campground.

GRAND TETON

Gros Ventre Campground. Gros Ventre Road sees a lot less traffic than the park's main thoroughfares, so you can still grab some peace and quiet at this campground, even though it's the park's largest. Though Gros Ventre tends not to fill up until late in the day, you should pull in early for your pick of sites. Some are on relatively exposed sagebrush prairie, others shaded by cottonwoods. Nightly ranger programs at the nearby amphitheater might focus on the bison you're almost guaranteed to see browsing the flats nearby. *Gros Ventre Rd., 5 miles northeast of U.S. 89/26/191; 307/543-2811 or 800/ 628-9988; www.gtlc.com.* $

★JENNY LAKE CAMPGROUND. Quite simply, some of the best views of any campground in the National Park system. Jenny Lake's cozy, tents-only campground sits right at the base of the range, and at many sites, Teewinot Mountain seems to loom so close that you'd think it was going to topple onto your tent. Arrive early if you want a spot—Jenny Lake is a first-come, first-served campground, and it's a rare day when there are open sites after 11 am. *South Jenny Lake Junction; 307/543-2811 or 800/628-9988; www.gtlc.com.* $

Lizard Creek Campground. More secluded and less developed than some of the monster campgrounds in Grand Teton, the sites at Lizard Creek are heavily wooded and right on the shore of Jackson Lake, making for killer views of the mountains. There are no showers, hookups, or staffed amenities at the first come, first served campground, but the toilets flush and there's drinking water on-site. Swimming and paddling are big here, except when low water occasionally turns the lakeside campsites into mud flats. It's worth calling to check on lake levels. *Off U.S. 89/191/287, 3 miles south of park boundary; 307/543-2831 or 800/672-6012; www.signalmountainlodge. com.* $

GRAND TETON NATIONAL PARK CAMPGROUNDS AT A GLANCE CHART

NAME	AREA	OPEN*	RESERVATIONS	# OF SITES	FEE	RVs	FACILITIES
Colter Bay	Colter Bay Village	Late May–early Sept.	No	350	$24	Yes at most sites, generators permitted	Flush toilets, showers, laundry, marina, amphitheater, dump station
Colter Bay RV Park	Colter Bay Village	Late May–late Sept.	Yes (800/628–9988)	112	$58–$68	All, most sites pull-through, generators permitted	Flush toilets; water, sewer, and electrical hookups; amphitheater; showers; laundry; marina
Headwaters at Flagg Ranch	Rockefeller Parkway	Early Jun.–late Sept.	Yes (800/443–2311)	175	$35/tent; $69/RV	97 sites, generators permitted	Flush toilets; showers; laundry; water, sewer, and electrical hookups
Gros Ventre	5 miles northeast of U.S. 89/26/191 on Gros Ventre Rd.	Early May–mid Oct.	No	350	$24	Yes at most sites, generators permitted at some sites	Flush toilets, amphitheater, dump station
Jenny Lake	South Jenny Lake Junction	Mid-May–early Oct.	No	60	$24	No	Flush toilets, tents only
Lizard Creek	3 miles south of park boundary	Early Jun.–early Sept.	No	60	$22	30 sites, generators permitted	Flush toilets
Signal Mountain	Signal Mountain Village	Early May–mid-Oct.	No	86	$22	75 sites, generators permitted	Flush toilets, boat launch, dump station, amphitheater, some electrical hookups

*Open dates are weather-permitting and subject to change. Call ahead to confirm.

Yellowstone National Park Campgrounds at a Glance

NAME	AREA	OPEN	RESERVATIONS	# OF SITES	FEE	RVs	FACILITIES
Bridge Bay	2 miles southwest of Lake Village	Late May– early Sept.	Yes (800/439-7375)	431	$22.50	262 sites, generators permitted	Flush toilets, dump station, amphitheater, marina
Canyon	Canyon Village	Early Jun.– early Sept.	Yes (800/439-7375)	273	$27	188 sites, generators permitted	Flush toilets, showers, laundry, dump station, amphitheater
Fishing Bridge RV Park	1.5 miles northeast of Lake Village	Mid-May– late Sept.	Yes (800/439-7375)	346	$47.75	All, generators permitted	Flush toilets; dumping station; amphitheater; showers; laundry; water, sewer, and electrical hookups
Grant	Grant Village	Late Jun.– late Sept.	Yes (800/439-7375)	430	$27	256 sites, generators permitted	Flush toilets, dumping station, amphitheater, showers, laundry
Indian Creek	8 miles south of Mammoth	Mid-Jun.– mid-Sept.	No	75	$15	All, 45 sites pull-through	Pit toilets
Lewis Lake	8 miles south of Grant Village	Mid-Jun.– early Nov.	No	85	$15	All	Pit toilets, boat launch
Madison	Madison Junction	Early May– late Oct.	Yes (866/439-7375)	280	$22.50	149 sites, generators permitted	Flush toilets, dump station, amphitheater

Mammoth	Mammoth Village	Year-round	No	85	$20	All sites pull-through, generators permitted	Flush toilets, amphitheater, showers
Norris	Norris Junction	Late May–early Sept.	No	116	$20	All, generators permitted	Flush toilets, amphitheater
Pebble Creek	8 miles southwest of Northeast Entrance	Mid-May–late Sept.	No	27	$15	All	Pit toilets
Slough Creek	6 miles east of Tower Junction	Mid-May–late Oct.	No	23	$15	All	Pit toilets
Tower Fall	Tower–Roosevelt	Late May–late Sept.	No	31	$15	All	Pit toilets; amphitheater

Geology, Flora, and Fauna

Indian paintbrush is also called "prairie fire" for its bright, flamelike scarlet tufts.

An elk with antlers "in velvet." This fuzzy, skin-like layer circulates nutrients to growing antlers.

A close-up look at heat-loving thermophiles in Yellowstone's Upper Geyser Basin.

Such thermophiles create the namesake streaks of color at Orange Mound Spring in Yellowstone's Mammoth Hot Springs.

⌖ GEOLOGY

YELLOWSTONE'S HOTSPOT

The first thing to remember is that we're all floating—all of us, all the time. We're adrift on huge continental islands or "plates" that comprise the planet's uppermost 50 to 80 miles, known to geologists as the lithosphere. These lithospheric plates drift around on a gurgling sea of plasticized rock called the asthenosphere, bumping and grinding and occasionally sliding beneath one another at a rate of an inch or two every year.

Another 1,500 miles below the asthenosphere, much deeper into the layer known as the lower mantle, the rock goes from plasticized to out-and-out molten. Gobs of this molten rock occasionally get so hot that they have to ascend—like the lava in a lava lamp—and they do so in long, narrow plumes running upward through the mantle. When these molten plumes hit the bottom of a solid lithospheric plate, they flatten out into the wide molten pools we call hotspots.

Gobs of this molten rock occasionally get so hot that they have to ascend, like the lava in a lava lamp.

Yellowstone's hotspot formed between 20 and 70 million years ago, and many scientists believe its plume originates closer to the surface than those of other hotspots. What's certain is that the Yellowstone hotspot was originally farther west, in a way. As the continental plate crept slowly southwest over the plume, the hotspot left a traceable path through Oregon and Idaho in the remnants of magma chambers, places where molten rock from the hotspot rose up to the Earth's crust, pooled there, then erupted onto the surface.

ERUPTIONS

The hotspot "arrived" beneath Yellowstone just over two million years ago, and wasted no time announcing its presence. A magma chamber just a few miles beneath the Earth's surface melted parts of the silica-rich crust, further filling itself with molten rhyolite and volcanic gases, amping up its own pressure. A little magma broke through the crust, triggering pressure-relieving earthquakes that caused the underground gases to instantaneously expand. The expansion of these gases forced magma, rock, and water vapor out from the chamber. This explosion, called the Huckleberry Ridge event, was so powerful that it left behind a 2,000-square-mile crater. Known as a caldera, the sinking crater swallowed up entire mountain ranges.

Similar volcanic blasts rocked the Yellowstone area twice since then. About 1.3 million years ago the Mesa Falls eruption left a smaller caldera just west of the current park, and 640,000 years ago the Lava Creek event created the 1,400-square-mile Yellowstone caldera we know today. This last explosion was roughly a thousand times bigger than the Mount St. Helens eruption in 1980; it created a cloud of ash that stretched from the Pacific Ocean to the Gulf of Mexico. Yellowstone's Mount Washburn and the cliffs at Gibbon Falls are both remnants of this caldera's rim.

There's still a magma chamber simmering beneath Yellowstone. Since the Lava Creek eruption, volcanic vents have released smaller rhyolite flows here and there, filling in parts of the caldera and smoothing it out to create the Yellowstone Plateau. The heat from the magma chamber powers the park's hydrothermal features (*see* Spotlight On: Geothermal Features), and two "resurgent domes" have emerged at Sour Creek and Mallard Lake, where underground magma is rising to reinflate old, emptied chambers.

An eruption today on the scale of Lava Creek would cover half the country in ash, prompting catastrophic climate changes. But you shouldn't lose sleep over this disaster-movie scenario. The Yellowstone Volcano Observatory monitors what doomsday documentaries have dubbed the "Yellowstone Supervolcano," and they're not expecting another eruption anytime soon.

EARTHQUAKES AND THE TETON FAULT

The Absaroka Mountains were formed by intense volcanic activity some 45 to 55 million years ago, and afterward residual heat in the Earth's crust caused the North American Plate to stretch out, like pavement does during a hot summer. This stretching of the plates created faults in the Yellowstone area and these periodically act up, altering the park's hydrothermal plumbing (*see* the Gateway Towns chapter for more on the 1959 Hebgen Lake Earthquake).

The Teton Fault formed this way about 13 million years ago, as a crack running north to south along what's now the eastern front of the Teton Range. During millions of years of tremendous earthquakes—some prompted by energy from the hotspot—chunks of the eastern plate sank into the fault, sliding beneath and displacing chunks of the western plate. In essence, Jackson Hole has given rise to the mountains by pouring itself into the fault, thrusting rock upward from deep within the earth. As a result, the Tetons are the youngest mountains in the Rockies, but they're comprised of some of the oldest rocks. We have these seismic origins to thank for great views of the Tetons' sharp eastern face.

GLACIATION

Glaciers put the finishing touches on the modern Yellowstone and Grand Teton landscapes. During the last two million years, periods of cooling global temperatures sometimes caused great fields of snow and ice to build up in the Yellowstone high country, forming glaciers. In a process that repeated itself maybe a dozen times, these ice sheets advanced from the plateau into the surrounding country, then receded again as temperatures warmed. The most recent cycle, known as the Pinedale Glaciation, ended only 14,000 years ago. At its peak, the Pinedale ice sheet covered entire mountain ranges, smothering 10,000-foot peaks like a lead blanket over an X-ray patient.

As glaciers advanced and receded, they left evidence of their progress on the landscape. They broadened river valleys like the Madison and the Firehole, depositing debris swept down from higher elevations. Where glaciers melted rapidly, they dropped debris in great clumps, creating mounds like the Twin Buttes west of Midway Geyser Basin. In the Tetons, glaciers formed in the mountains, scooping out U-shaped canyons like huge, alpine half-pipes as they descended into Jackson Hole. As the glaciers reached into the valley, they pushed before them huge heaps of till (silt, clay, and gravel), piles that got left behind when the glaciers eventually receded. Known as moraines, these ridgelike piles trapped glacial meltwaters, forming Jenny Lake, Leigh Lake, and the other mirrored pools that sit at the foot of the Tetons.

FLORA

LODGEPOLE PINE

Lodgepole pine is the crabgrass of the arboreal world—it can grow anywhere, and it's impossible to get rid of. Yellowstone's ubiquitous stands of lofty, slender lodgepoles are superbly suited to the area's dry, inhospitable volcanic soil. What's more, some lodgepole cones require extreme temperatures to release their copious seeds, meaning lodgepoles actually benefit from the forest fires for which they provide fuel. The name derives from the Native Americans' use of the thin trunks to construct tepee frames.

WHERE THERE'S SMOKE

By the time the Yellowstone fires of 1988 were igniting, the NPS had spent roughly 15 years changing its fire-suppression policy in the park. But the resultant overabundance of fuel conspired with that summer's dry, windy conditions to scorch more than a third of the park. The gargantuan fires brought into public consciousness for the first time questions about fire's role in our dwindling natural heritage sites. Luckily, neighboring Grand Teton National Park escaped with minimal damage.

Fire is an essential component of the Yellowstone ecosystem. Among other things, it allows for plant succession, creates habitat, and restores soil nutrients. Purposefully set prescribed burns are more common in Grand Teton National Park than in Yellowstone, where high fuel loads near developed areas are usually cleared by hand, but the park does allow most natural fires to burn within preestablished limits. A fire set by a less-than-careful backpacker is suppressed, but fire from a lightning strike is likely only to be monitored, so long as weather conditions don't spell trouble and it doesn't threaten human life or property.

Current fire reports are posted in visitor centers and on each park's website.

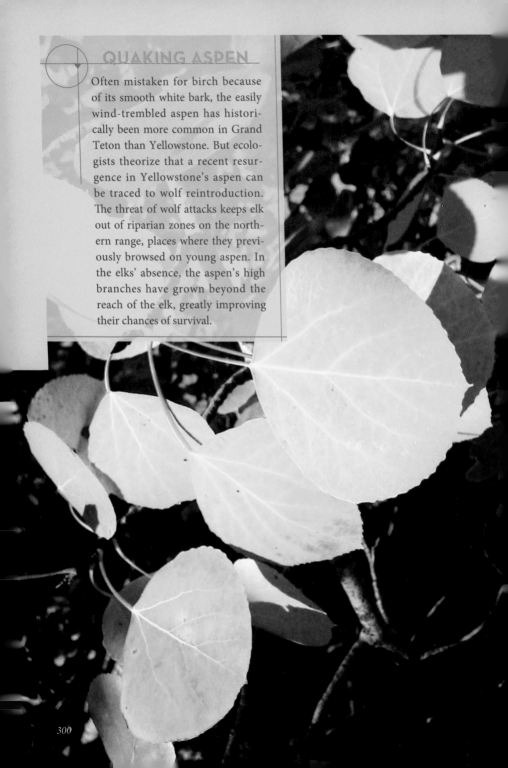

QUAKING ASPEN

Often mistaken for birch because of its smooth white bark, the easily wind-trembled aspen has historically been more common in Grand Teton than Yellowstone. But ecologists theorize that a recent resurgence in Yellowstone's aspen can be traced to wolf reintroduction. The threat of wolf attacks keeps elk out of riparian zones on the northern range, places where they previously browsed on young aspen. In the elks' absence, the aspen's high branches have grown beyond the reach of the elk, greatly improving their chances of survival.

ENGELMANN SPRUCE

Engelmann spruce populates the Teton canyons above 6,800 feet, plus a few damp, high-elevation gullies throughout Yellowstone. Shallow, lateral roots allow the tree to get by on the thin alpine soils. The evergreen is one of the taller alpine trees, reaching between 40 and 130 feet at a mature age of 300 years. The spruce's blue-green needles are surprisingly sharp, so be careful brushing by.

GENTIAN

A number of different gentian species appear above 10,000 feet, all very small with thin, cup-like flowers. The prettiest is the fringed gentian, the official flower of Yellowstone National Park, which has lobes atop its ruffled, lavender cups. Arctic gentians have paler white cups spotted with purple. Both thrive in damp alpine bogs. The flowers are named for an ancient Balkan king who "discovered" their healing properties—not a discovery borne out by science, so please don't eat the gentians.

LUPINE

Bright blue thickets of this prolific wildflower pop up all summer among lodgepole stands and in sagebrush prairie. Lupine flowers are legumes, and the seeds are sometimes used in cooking, but since parts of the plant are poisonous, it's best not to taste.

INDIAN PAINTBRUSH

Wyoming's state flower has eye-catching, scarlet brushlike bracts surrounding a small, yellowish flower. Its other nickname is "prairie fire," and when Indian paintbrush blooms from mid-June to September, the flowers light up the meadows along the Teton canyon trails. More than a dozen different paintbrush species occupy the parks. Each filches water and nutrients from the roots of surrounding plants.

FAUNA

TRUMPETER SWANS

Isolated trumpeter swan populations in Yellowstone helped save this elegant water-fowl from extinction in the early 1900s. Today, the continent's largest wild fowl has bounced back nationwide, but populations in Greater Yellowstone are declining. Migratory trumpeters are still a presence in winter, though, and they show off a six- to eight-foot wingspan when they land in the unfrozen thermal-fed waters.

BISON

The nappy, dispassionate American bison may not be the park's most charismatic ungulate, but it's certainly the most iconic. Yellowstone's bison population dwindled to a mere 23 animals in 1902, but today, the country's only continuously wild herd numbers hovers around 4,000. A hefty bull can reach six feet at the shoulder and weigh a ton. Bulls and cows alike sport short, curved horns, which they'll use to gore tourists who invade their personal space—keep your distance! In winter, a bison's light-brown coat darkens and the animals grow noticeably wan as their diet of grasses and sedges becomes scarce. You'll hear "bison" and "buffalo" used interchangeably, but technically the latter refers to distant Asian and African relatives. The Lamar, Hayden, and Pelican valleys are among the most reliable places to spot bison herds throughout the year.

Bison and the Brucellosis Debate

Like many Yellowstone controversies, the current challenge facing bison involves balancing the needs of wildlife with the needs of ranchers. The ranching industry is on guard against brucellosis, a cattle-infecting disease that causes spontaneous abortion in cows. Yellowstone bison have been known to carry the bacteria since 1917, and they regularly migrate out of the park and into Montana in winter. Montana is currently certified as brucellosis-free, and it wants to stay that way.

Bison have never spread brucellosis to cattle, but the ranching industry isn't taking any chances. Because private cattle herds graze immediately outside Yellowstone in Montana, bison migrating out of the park are seen as a threat. A 2000 NPS management plan sought to establish a corridor of the park where bison could travel in the winter, when many head to lower elevations. In 2011 managers began allowing small numbers of bison to wander a protected area in the Gardiner basin. In 2014, some 100 Yellowstone bison were transferred to the Fort Peck Indian Reservation in northwest Montana, establishing the first wild herd outside of the park.

Bison roaming outside the designated zones are sometimes hazed back into Yellowstone, though most simply turn and walk out again. More often, they're sent to slaughterhouses by the NPS and Montana state agents. Opponents like the Buffalo Field Campaign protest both the killings and the damage to the bison herd's genetic diversity.

WOLVES

Reintroduced in 1995, wolf packs now occupy every corner of Yellowstone and have extended into Grand Teton. At 70 to 120 pounds, grey wolves are larger than Yellowstone's coyotes and darker in color. They travel and hunt—mostly elk—in territorial, highly stratified packs led by an alpha male and female. Lamar Valley is typically a wolf-watching hotspot, especially in winter.

WOLF REINTRODUCTION: AN ECOLOGICAL CHAIN REACTION

The West's most maligned predator was a victim of systematic eradication from the moment settlers began showing up with livestock. By 1940, Yellowstone's wolves had been hunted, trapped, and poisoned out of existence. Reintroduction was first seriously proposed in the early 1970s, prompted by out-of-control elk populations and the passage of the Endangered Species Act.

After 20 years of intense back-and-forth with ranchers who feared livestock predation, the NPS transplanted 41 Canadian wolves into Yellowstone between 1995 and 1997. Ecologically, the process has largely been a smash. Today's wolf population in the greater Yellowstone ecosystem is around 400 animals, with additional packs outside the park. Wolves helped cut elk numbers in half and subdued an unwieldy coyote population. Their presence is indirectly credited for the willow resurgence, which itself has been a boon to struggling beavers. Fewer coyotes, in turn, has meant higher survival rates among red foxes.

Controversy hasn't faded, though. Some critics insist wolves are now depleting elk herds on the northern range, though park biologists disagree. Other debates have flared since Montana, Wyoming, and Idaho removed the wolves' Endangered Species Act protections, opening hunting seasons for wolves outside the park. In 2012, 10 Yellowstone wolves were legally shot and killed, five of which wore radio collars for research purposes.

BIGHORN SHEEP

Clambering along rocky ledges, bighorns fascinate with their ability to travel so easily where the rest of us can't. The docile herd animals, once central to Sheepeater diet and culture, were decimated by hunting and livestock diseases before 1900. They rebounded once protected from poachers. Rams have heavy, curled horns, while ewes' horns are short and slightly bent. You can often spot summering bighorns in the Gardner River Canyon, and during the early winter rut, listen for the thunder-crack of the 300-pound rams locking horns echoing in the canyons of the northern range.

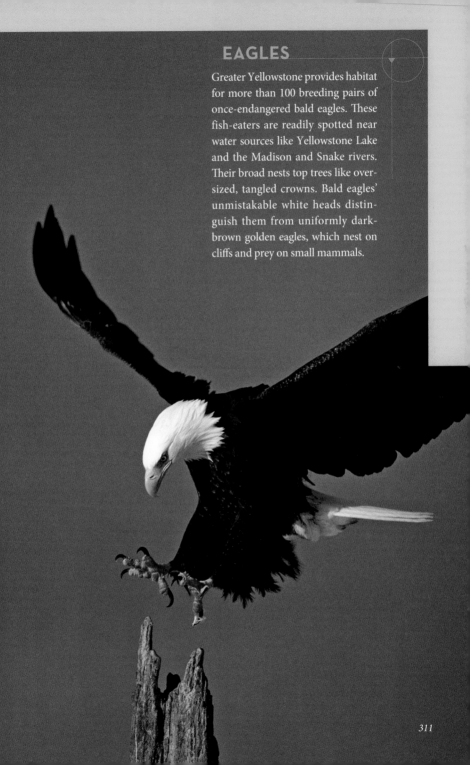

EAGLES

Greater Yellowstone provides habitat for more than 100 breeding pairs of once-endangered bald eagles. These fish-eaters are readily spotted near water sources like Yellowstone Lake and the Madison and Snake rivers. Their broad nests top trees like oversized, tangled crowns. Bald eagles' unmistakable white heads distinguish them from uniformly darkbrown golden eagles, which nest on cliffs and prey on small mammals.

BLACK BEARS

Black bears are sometimes cast as grizzlies' drowsy, likable cousins, but make no mistake: although the smaller foragers are largely vegetarians and more tolerant of humans, they can still be aggressive, especially if they're after food or protecting a cub. And they can still smell your freeze-dried dinner from a mile away. Black bears lack the grizzly's prominent shoulder hump, their ears are bigger, and their forehead-to-nose profile is straight. Most are indeed black, though tan or cinnamon-colored bears are not uncommon. Look for them in both parks' subalpine forests.

GRIZZLY BEARS

These furry bogeymen alternately fascinate and frighten. A mature male grizzly can weigh 700 pounds and stand 8 feet tall. Whitish shoulder hairs give grizzlies their name and help distinguish them from black bears, as do a distinctive muscle mass on their back and the concave curve of their snout. High meadows are their prime habitat, especially at dawn and dusk. Grand Teton has seen rising populations in recent decades, as Yellowstone bears migrate south. Hibernation generally lasts from around November to March, after which bears emerge hungry, prompting trail and campground closures.

ELK

Elk are the parks' most plentiful large mammals. Though populations vary (controversially!) each year, Greater Yellowstone supports around 40,000 of these regal herd animals. A bull's antlers can weigh 40 pounds and, in summer, shed a soft fur known as antler velvet. Elk congregate where forests meet meadows, summering at high elevations before migrating lower in winter—many to Jackson's National Elk Refuge. In September and October, bulls attract a "harem" of mating partners by bugling, a loud and surreal whistling.

MOUNTAIN LION

Chances are you won't see a mountain lion while visiting the parks, but that doesn't mean they're not out there. The stealthy, solitary cats, also called "cougars," establish territory in remote, rocky regions, though they may move to lower elevations in winter. They resemble tawny house cats, only 8 feet long and 150 pounds, able to take down a mule deer or elk. Attacks on humans are quite rare.

FLORA

ALPINE FORGET-ME-NOT

On these flower heads just a few millimeters across, a bright yellow center shines out from among five perfect sky-blue petals. These dainty-looking flowers are actually very hardy, adapted to the wind and poor soils of their high-elevation habitat by growing in low, broad mats. (They're only found above 10,000 feet.) They're Grand Teton National Park's official flower.

SUBALPINE FIR

The tops of subalpine firs point upward like evergreen dunce caps, narrow among the more blunted crowns of pines, Douglas firs, and spruces. Up close, you can identify a subalpine by the way its cones point upward on its higher branches. The trees love shade, so they can get a toehold in thick stands of lodgepoles and spruce. Crush a few of the flat, curved needles in your palm for a classic "Christmas-tree smell."

HUCKLEBERRY

Huckleberries are to Montana and Yellowstone what peaches are to Georgia. The tart little berries start as tiny white flowers, then grow purple and juicy on short shrubs in forested areas of south Yellowstone and Grand Teton. The berries ripen in mid-August. The lower reaches of the Teton are good places to hunt (but be sure of your identification before eating anything).

SAGEBRUSH

The ubiquitous gray-green shrubs found throughout the parks are the quintessential Western vegetation. Mule deer, sage grouse, and pronghorn browse the sagebrush's tiny, wedge-shaped leaves, although you'd find the taste bitter compared to conventional kitchen sage. The smell is similar, though, and after a rain, the sagebrush prairies of Lamar Valley and Jackson Hole are filled with the thick, sweet fragrance.

FAUNA

COYOTES

Imagine having food on your mind all the time. That's life for Yellowstone and Grand Teton's sniffing, fretting, foraging omnivore. Coyotes' indiscriminate diets include carrion, small mammals, insects, and grasses. Yellowstone's coyotes are husky, often 30 pounds or more, but their smaller size and distinctive, sulky trot distinguish them from much larger wolves. The gray-tan canines travel alone or in small packs and, with rare exceptions, pose little threat to humans.

MOOSE

Because the solitary moose feeds on fir, willows, and aspens, you're more likely to spot one in Grand Teton, where these trees are more abundant. Distinctive characteristics include the moose's antlers, flat like palmate satellite dishes. As tall as seven feet at the shoulder and pushing 1,000 pounds, moose are formidable opponents with few natural predators. Spot them in marshy areas like Oxbow Bend around dawn and dusk.

CUTTHROAT TROUT

This native trout with a spotted tail is unique to the drainages of the Yellowstone and upper Snake rivers. The fish have lately faced stiff competition from lake trout introduced illegally. Lake trout devour the smaller cutthroats, sending cutthroat populations into freefall. (Yellowstone has a catch-and-release-only policy for cutthroats.) You can still watch leaping cutthroats at Fishing Bridge and LeHardy Rapids.

PIKA

These endangered, big-eared furballs are the size of small guinea pigs. Sometimes called rock rabbits, pikas (pronounced "pie-kas") live and graze on mountain-slope talus fields where rocks protect them from raptors and other predators.

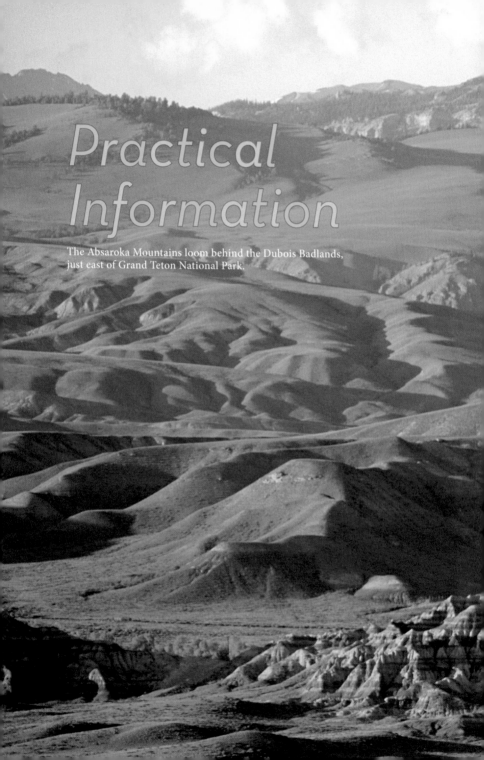

Practical Information

The Absaroka Mountains loom behind the Dubois Badlands, just east of Grand Teton National Park.

⊕ BEST TIMES TO VISIT

A visit between mid-June and early September will give you the fullest access to both Yellowstone and Grand Teton national parks, and in general this is when you'll encounter the warmest, driest weather. These are the parks' busiest months by far. I think the best time to visit, though, is during the "shoulder seasons" of May through mid-June and mid-September through October. You'll brave colder temperatures, fewer concessionaire facilities, and maybe the occasional snowed-in road, but the rewards include relative solitude, better wildlife sightings, and the natural beauty of the transitional seasons. Ultimately, there is no "bad time" to visit, as every season in Greater Yellowstone does have something genuinely unique to offer.

Like grizzlies, the roads and facilities in Yellowstone begin to emerge from winter slumber in late April, and a **spring** visit reveals an ecosystem in renewal. You can feel nearly alone in the park this time of year, watching bison calves find their legs in early May or spotting antlerless elk returning from the winter ranges. The remains of animals that didn't make it through the winter and elk-calving in late May attract wolves and grizzlies to lower elevations, so wildlife-viewing is superb. Mountain runoff swells the waterfalls and rivers. You'll encounter snow here and there into June, so leave the sandals at home and expect occasional road closures.

Summer sees the peak number of visitors. Virtually all facilities open by mid-June and some 900,000 visitors appear in July alone, the park's busiest month. Sure, there are traffic jams, but there are also long days and warm nights made for hiking and camping. Carpets of wildflowers reach their vivid prime by July—earlier in the month at lower elevations, later as you ascend. The transformation of the sleepy gateway towns into bombastic tourism carnivals lasts until about September.

Seeking better forage, wildlife converges on the low country in **autumn,** so elk, bison, and moose seem as ubiquitous as lodgepoles throughout September and October. With a more diverse palette of trees, Grand Teton is especially scenic in early October, and squadrons of migrating waterfowl make pit stops on the many lakes. During the elk rut in September, their spine-tingling bugle calls echo across Jackson Hole and the Northern Range. The number of visitors in both parks tapers off in September and drops steeply in October.

Old Faithful gets more visitors in a single summer day than all of Yellowstone gets in January. And while year-round road access in

Grand Teton brings slightly more skiers and snowshoers into Jackson Hole, visiting either park in **winter** feels like stepping through the looking glass. Only the northernmost route through Yellowstone stays open to cars year-round, and hospitality concessions are sparse. (*See* the Spotlight On: Winter in Greater Yellowstone for a detailed description of the parks' "quiet season.")

COMMUNICATIONS

PHONES

In both parks, pay phones are found in every developed area.

Cellular service with the nationwide carriers tends to be reliable in the gateway towns of Yellowstone and Grand Teton. Yellowstone has been cautiously and controversially installing cellular towers since 2001. Towers are up at Mammoth, Old Faithful, Grant, Lake, and on Mt. Washburn.

Verizon Wireless and AT&T customers have strong voice and intermittent data reception in and around Mammoth, Old Faithful, Canyon, Lake, and Grant, with spotty reception reported around Roosevelt. Users on other networks may occasionally encounter roaming access. Service in the backcountry is basically nil, and it's spotty on the park roads between the hospitality villages. Smartphone users should not expect to download or send large amounts of data due to limited bandwidth.

Cell towers at Signal Mountain and the Jackson Hole Airport—combined with the valley's relative flatness—make cellular coverage quite thorough in Grand Teton National Park. Sprint, Verizon, and AT&T users will have luck at each of the lodges and campgrounds. There's also reliable reception along the two major roads and even occasionally along trails (useful for emergencies, not for gabbing while hiking). Roaming access on other networks is reliable, though again, data coverage is limited.

INTERNET ACCESS

Wireless Internet access is readily available and usually free in all the gateway towns, where most hotels offer it and cafés cater to digital junkies ready for their fix.

No lodges or cabins offer guest computers in Yellowstone, but wireless access has been on the increase since the park altered its digital communications policy in 2009. On recent visits, third-party Internet was available for a fee and reliable in the Canyon Lodge public area, Old Faithful Snow Lodge, Mammoth lounge, Grant Lodge buildings, and the Lake Lodge cafeteria. Laptop users with cellular data cards should expect weak-to-no reception and slow speeds. Some rooms at the Lake Hotel are equipped for wired Internet access, if you're traveling with an Ethernet cable.

Grand Teton is another story. Wireless Internet signals are free, strong, and reliable in the lobbies and cabins at the Jackson Lake and Jenny Lake lodges, as well as in the lounge area at Signal Mountain and the bar at Dornan's Pizza & Pasta Company.

⌖ FESTIVALS AND SEASONAL EVENTS

(top) Pickin' and grinnin' at the Mountain Man rendezvous during Elkfest in Jackson; (bottom) a mess of antlers ready for auction at Elkfest.

SPRING AND SUMMER

"Christmas" in Yellowstone, Yellowstone National Park. This longtime park employee tradition has become a favorite with guests, who drive north from Old Faithful to see Christmas Tree Rock, an island in the Firehole River with one spindly, garlanded lodgepole. Holiday meals and treats are served at Lake and Old Faithful, and if the staff has had their eggnog, you may even hear carolers. *Aug. 25*

Cody Stampede Rodeo, Cody. More than just burly cowpokes getting tossed off angry steers, the Stampede is one of the country's largest rodeo events: four days of parades, horse-and-rider acts, and raucous country rock. *July 1–4, www.codystampederodeo.com*

Elkfest, Jackson. Come for the supermarketlike rows of thousands of elk antlers; stay for the live music, food, and historical reenactments. Jackson's most unique fest draws crowds to the Town Square to participate in the spectacle of the annual elk-antler auction (*see*

Dog-sledding in the
Absaroka Mountains.

The annual torchlight parade at Snow King Resort lights up New Year's Eve.

"Bull Market" in the Gateway Towns chapter). *The weekend before Memorial Day Weekend; www.elkfest.org*

Gardiner Brewfest, Gardiner. Plenty of suds and a stage of rock and roots music attract a multigenerational crowd near the scenic Roosevelt Arch at the park's north entrance. After 14 years, the fest went on hiatus during the Arch construction project in 2015; expect its return in the years to come. *Third Sat. in Aug.; www.gardinerbrewfest.weebly.com*

Spring into Yellowstone Birding & Wildlife Festival, Cody. Bird nerds unite for five days of guided nature walks, film screenings, raptor demonstrations, and more feathered fun. After a day of field trips and workshops, Cody's galleries open up for wildlife-themed art crawls. *Mid-May; www.springintoyellowstone.com*

FALL AND WINTER

Jackson Hole Wildlife Film Festival, Jackson. Some of the world's most accomplished wildlife filmmakers gather for a week of workshops and screenings. Venues include Jackson's Center for the Arts and the high-definition theater in the park's Craig Thomas Discovery and Visitor Center. *Biennial in late Sept.; www.jhfestival.org*

Jackson Hole WinterFest, Jackson. Bundle up for snow sculptures and fat-tire snow-bike races at this multiweek celebration of all things snow. The festival's highlight is the Wyoming tradition of cutter races, where teams of horses pull drivers on chariots across the frozen ground. *Late Feb.; jacksonholechamber.com*

Yellowstone Ski Festival, West Yellowstone. A few weeks before snowmobiles take over the streets in West Yellowstone, thousands of cross-country skiers congregate for a week of races, clinics, and gear demonstrations. The carnival atmosphere carries into the town's bars and restaurants, many of which reopen for the occasion. *Thanksgiving week; www.yellowstoneskifestival.com*

 GETTING THERE

BY AIR

Most major airlines serve Bozeman, Montana, and Jackson, Wyoming. **Bozeman Yellowstone International Airport** (406/388–8321) is 80 miles north of Gardiner via Paradise Valley and U.S. 89, or 90 miles north of West Yellowstone via Gallatin Canyon and U.S. 191. **Jackson Hole Airport** (307/733–7682) is inside Grand Teton National Park, 10 miles north of Jackson and about 50 miles south of Yellowstone's south entrance. Delta and United serve Cody's **Yellowstone Regional Airport** (307/587–5096), 50 miles east of the park's east entrance along U.S. 20/40/16. From June through September, Delta affiliate SkyWest flies from Salt Lake City to the adorably small **Yellowstone Airport** in West Yellowstone, immediately outside the park. All four airports offer car rentals.

By Car

FROM BOZEMAN, MONTANA

The two-lane highways leading into Yellowstone from Bozeman are as scenic as anything inside the park. The Gallatin Canyon route, U.S. 191, to West Yellowstone is an occasionally cliff-hugging road following the Gallatin River—you may recognize the rugged Montana splendor from the film *A River Runs Through It*. On the other side of the Gallatins, U.S. 89 follows the Yellowstone River through Paradise Valley. Both routes can hug their respective rivers a little too close for comfort. Roadside wildlife is both a perk and a hazard. Despite Montana's reputation for lax speed limits, it is a pity and a peril to drive faster than what's posted (as low as 50 on U.S. 191, 70 on U.S. 89, both of which some locals consider too high). Lurching and speeding semis are also a danger, particularly in Gallatin Canyon. Best to avoid driving either route at night.

FROM CODY, WYOMING

Budget a good hour and a half for the stunning drive between Cody and Yellowstone's east entrance on U.S. 14/16/20, a two-lane road with the occasional passing lane. The last 28 miles before Yellowstone are designated as the **Buffalo Bill Cody Scenic Byway.** Steep cliffs and surreal rock formations overlook the road, which follows the thick blue braid of the North Fork of the Shoshone River. Still, this route tends to be less perilous than the highways from Bozeman, because it's not hugging the cliff faces, it's less steep, and it has fewer abrupt corners.

FROM SALT LAKE CITY, UTAH

It's a five-hour, 300-mile trip from the closest "big city," Salt Lake City, to either West Yellowstone or Jackson. The route follows Interstate 15 north for 170 miles to Pocatello, Idaho, where it enters the Snake River Plain. From Pocatello, the interstate swooshes northeast to Idaho Falls, where a series of U.S. highways leads either northeast to West Yellowstone or through Idaho's Big Hole Mountains and over the Teton Pass. Either route will put an RV's transmission to the test.

FROM BILLINGS, MONTANA

From the eastern Montana industrial center of Billings, it's 125 miles to tiny Cooke City and Yellowstone's northeast entrance. The route mostly follows U.S. 212, which becomes the astounding **Beartooth Scenic Highway** south of Red Lodge, Montana. The Northern Rockies' highest-elevation highway is breathtaking in summer and completely impassable the rest of the year—it's usually open only from Memorial Day until early October. The roller-coaster road leads through three national forests and past glinting glaciers in the Absaroka and Beartooth mountains. If you'd rather enter the park from the north or east, I-90 heads west from Billings to Livingston (115 miles) and Bozeman (140 miles).

⌖ GETTING INTO THE PARKS

Unless you're a dedicated cyclist or aboard a tour bus (*see* Guided Tours, *below*), a car is the only way to get into and explore Yellowstone and Grand Teton national parks. The entrance fee at either park is $30. This gives a single vehicle (and its occupants) seven-day access. Following a controversial fee hike in 2015, access to both parks requires a $50 pass (or paying the $30 entrance fee separately at each access gate). Put your admission receipt in your glove box—you'll need it for reentry. Motorcyclists save $5 on the single-park fee and $10 on the dual-park fee, and folks on foot, bike, or skis pay $15 and $20, respectively. Entrance fees remain unchanged in the winter, though a $5 day permit is available for Grand Teton only. Standard entry can only be bought at the entrance stations.

Sixty dollars gets you a year's worth of unlimited access to both Yellowstone and Grand Teton, but if you're planning to visit more than two or three parks in a given year, the best value is an $80 Interagency Pass. The wallet-sized plastic card covers entrance fees for a year at nearly every national park, plus a variety of national forests and other public lands. People over 62 get the same perks with the $10 lifetime Senior Pass, and a free lifetime Access Pass is available to those with disabilities. Active military personnel also get free annual passes. These special passes can be acquired in advance at store.usgs.gov.

Passes are purchased at any of the parks' drive-through entrance stations. There are five such stations in Yellowstone. The **north entrance** is behind the Roosevelt Arch in Gardiner, Montana; the **west entrance** is in West Yellowstone, Montana; the quiet **northeast entrance** sits four miles west of Cooke City, Montana; 50 miles west of Cody,

Wyoming, is the **east entrance;** and the **south entrance** separates Yellowstone from the Roosevelt Parkway along the South Entrance Road. Grand Teton has only two entrance stations, both several miles inside the park's boundaries. The **southern station** is at Moose, where Moose-Wilson Road meets Teton Park Road. The **northern station** is at Moran Junction, where U.S. 287 joins U.S. 89.

PETS IN THE PARKS

Pets are allowed into both parks, though they're barred from the backcountry, meaning you can have Fido with you only in the campground and around the villages. Pets in the backcountry risk spreading diseases to wildlife (or acquiring them), becoming lunch for bears or coyotes, and generally irritating visitors. Make sure your pet is leashed at all times and never left out tied—rangers have little patience with irresponsible pet owners. Every gateway town has kennels except West Yellowstone.

GETTING AROUND

DRIVING IN YELLOWSTONE

The figure-eight of Yellowstone's Grand Loop Road makes navigation in the park relatively simple. Nearly all of the most popular sights and boardwalk trails are found along this route. The five entrance roads simply meander between the entrance stations and corners of the two loop roads. On the pavement anyway, **it's hard to get lost in Yellowstone.**

Yellowstone National Park has a firm **45-mile-per-hour speed limit.** Obey it. Wildlife regularly sprints across the road, and behind every blind corner may be a herd of bison or elk nonchalantly straddling the center line. That RV in front of you will slam on its breaks without a moment's hesitation should the driver spot a bear in the neighboring meadow. Icy conditions can occur in high-elevation patches in the dead of summer. Neither Yellowstone nor Grand Teton is a place to take risks behind the wheel.

Anyone behind the wheel should make "patience is a virtue" a mantra. Traffic jams materialize and dissipate with the frequency and unpredictability of spring rains. When a herd of bison blocks your path in the road, you wait for them to move. It's their park, and **under no conditions should you attempt to disperse wildlife with your car.** Fellow drivers who neglect to use roadside pull-outs can back up traffic for miles. The most you can do is keep your cool and resolve to

A male grizzly on
Mount Washburn,
in Yellowstone.

not be one of these inconsiderate sightseers. Use pull-outs where provided, and if you must stop where there aren't any, maneuver as far to the side of the road as is prudent.

The park roads can slither up some steep grades, particularly going over Dunraven, Craig, and Sylvan passes. If you have doubts about your car or RV's ability to hack it, consult the map or talk with rangers about alternative routes. Should you find yourself in need of repairs, there are service stations at Old Faithful, Canyon, Grant, and Fishing Bridge. All have gas, as do additional stations at Mammoth and Roosevelt. In general, you'll pay a few cents more for petrol in the parks than you will in the gateway towns, which tend to have prices comparable to the those in the rest of Montana and Wyoming.

Road construction in Yellowstone is perpetual. The park bulletin issued at the entrance gate provides updates on seasonal construction. For the most current information on **road conditions,** including construction info and openings/closings, call 307/344–2117. For road conditions outside the parks in either Wyoming or Montana, dial 511.

All Yellowstone **park roads close to cars** the first week of November, except between the north and northeast entrance, which stays open year-round, and the Canyon-Tower Road over Dunraven Pass, which closes mid-October or earlier if snow makes it impassable. Snow accumulation permitting, Yellowstone's roads open to snowcoaches and snowmobiles on December 15, then close on a staggered schedule in early March.

Roads open in the spring on a complex schedule, beginning with those in the park's western half in mid-April and followed one at a time through May by the eastern routes. Park facilities open and close on an even more byzantine timetable—check the park's website or call 307/344–7381 for info.

DRIVING IN GRAND TETON

Grand Teton has a just few main roads, and all are clearly marked. The **speed limit is 45 miles per hour** in most places, although on U.S. 89/26/187 it occasionally goes up to 55 miles per hour. As in Yellowstone, **watch out for wildlife** crossing the roads—and be wary of other drivers who might brake suddenly. There are plenty of pull-outs to use if you want to get a better look at something.

Inside Grand Teton, **gas** is sold at Colter Bay, Jackson Lake Lodge, Signal Mountain Lodge, and the Dornan's complex at Moose (you can also fill up at Flagg Ranch in the Parkway). Gas is a bit more expensive inside the park than in the gateway towns.

The spring **opening schedules for roads and facilities** are complex to say the least. It's best to check the park's website or call 307/739–3300 for schedules.

From November through April, Grand Teton bans motorized vehicles from most of Teton Park Road, the southern portion of Moose-Wilson Road, and Antelope Flats Road. Highway 89 remains open from Jackson to Flagg Ranch, though conditions may be snowy and icy—chains and all-season tires are recommended.

Road construction in Grand Teton is sporadic. For the most current information on the park's **road conditions,** including construction info and openings/closings, call 307/739–3614.

GUIDED TOURS

A host of operators leads bus trips through Yellowstone and Grand Teton from the surrounding towns. Scan the pamphlets at your hotel or just ask around—finding a scenic bus tour is probably one of the easiest things to do in Greater Yellowstone.

Among the most interesting tour operators are the park concessionaires themselves. In Yellowstone, **Xanterra** (307/344–7311 or 866/439–7375) operates a fleet of restored banana-colored buses. Each is from the early automobile era and looks like a stretch Rolls-Royce (*see* the "Old Yeller Buses" sidebar in the Yellowstone's Lower Loop chapter). Half-day, full-day, and evening tours depart from every village in the park, exploring everything from the Old Faithful village roads to the rugged Beartooth Scenic Highway. Trips are priced from $25 to $110.

The **Grand Teton Lodge Company** (307/543–2811 or 800/628–9988) leads half-day or full-day Grand Teton tours with curator-guides knowledgeable of Jackson Hole history. Two-day excursions explore both parks. Tours range from $65 to $100 and leave from Jackson Lake Lodge or Colter Bay. Call for reservations or stop by the Jackson Lake Lodge activities desk or Colter Bay Marina. The company also runs a **shuttle** five times a day between both sites and downtown Jackson. It's free for guests, and others ride unlimited all day for a $15 fee.

Climbers hiking toward base camp in preparation for a Grand Teton ascent.

⊕ LICENSES AND PERMITS

BOATING

Privately owned boats require a permit purchased from either park. In Grand Teton, annual permits for motorized and non-motorized boats are $40 and $10, respectively. Get one in Grand Teton at the

Craig Thomas, Jenny Lake, or Colter Bay visitor centers. In Grand Teton, boaters also need a Wyoming invasive species decal, available at the marinas. The decal costs $10 for motorized vehicles registered in Wyoming, $30 for out-of-state watercraft. Non-motorized decals go for $5 for Wyoming residents, $15 for out-of-staters. In Yellowstone, annual permits cost $20 for motorized boats and $10 for non-motorized, with week permits available at half those costs. Permits are available at the south entrance, Bridge Bay ranger station, and Grant Village backcountry office, with nonmotorized permits also available at the Mammoth backcountry office and permits specifically for float tubes available at the Canyon and Old Faithful backcountry offices, the northeast entrance, and the Bechler ranger station. Open water is the name of the game, as the only river that allows boaters, floaters, or paddlers is the Snake. In Yellowstone, only Yellowstone Lake and Lewis Lake allow motorized boats. Consult rangers to find out where else boats are prohibited and learn the precise rules for displaying your permit sticker.

Fishing

To fish in Yellowstone you need only a park-issued fishing permit, available at all ranger stations, visitor centers, and general stores. A three-day permit costs $18, a seven-day permit goes for $25, and a season permit costs $40. Kids under 16 can get a free permit with an adult's signature.

Grand Teton anglers need a Wyoming fishing license, available at Signal Mountain and Colter Bay marinas and from Snake River Anglers in Moose. Non-resident annual licenses run $92, but day permits are available for $14 (license pricing is subject to change). Kids under 14 can fish without a license.

With some exceptions, the fishing season in Yellowstone begins the Saturday of Memorial Day weekend and runs through the first Sunday in November. And, with some exceptions, lakes in Grand Teton are open year-round. Fishing rules in both parks are rife with exceptions, so it pays to listen to the rangers, ask a lot of questions, and get a copy of each park's regulations handbook. Identifying protected and exotic species is an especially necessary skill.

Backpacking

Both parks require that you have a permit to spend one or more nights in the backcountry. The permits reserve specific campsites for specific nights, so it's important to have your trip planned in detail when requesting one. It's also smart to have backup plans should your first-choice sites be taken.

Advance Yellowstone reservations are made by mail only (Backcountry Office, P.O. Box 168, Yellowstone National Park, WY 82190), from January through October for a $25 fee. In Grand Teton, permits for summer can be reserved for a $35 processing fee between the first Wednesday in January and May 15, via recreation.gov.

Pick up reserved permits from the Jenny Lake Ranger Station or Moose and Colter Bay visitor centers in Grand Teton and from virtually any ranger station or backcountry office in Yellowstone. Hikers can also request permits on a first come, first served, walk-in basis in both parks. In Yellowstone you can't do this more than 48 hours before your trip, and backpackers pay a $3 per-person, per-night fee between Memorial Day and September 10 (or buy a $25 annual backcountry pass). In Grand Teton, walk-up permits cost $25 and are available no more than 24 hours before a trip.

All backpackers in Grand Teton are required to carry approved bear-proof canisters for food storage. Backcountry offices in the park have some for loan.

⊕ ONLINE RESOURCES

The **official NPS websites** for Yellowstone and Grand Teton are essential, if not always completely intuitive, clearinghouses for park information. *www.nps.gov/yell; www.nps.gov/grte.*

Two NPS-produced Yellowstone video podcasts make for excellent primers on park history and biology. The **Inside Yellowstone video podcasts** are two-minute overviews hosted by a ranger, usually covering specific locations and phenomena—a supplement to the park's interpretive signs. Episodes of *Yellowstone In-Depth* cover broader park topics in five- to 10-minute segments, mini-documentaries that might hold your teenager's interest on the drive in. *Available from iTunes or at www.nps.gov/yell/photosmultimedia.*

The free **Yellowstone National Park—The Official Guide smartphone app** includes embedded interpretive videos, along with a zoomable, fairly detailed map that's available offline. The **NPS Yellowstone Geysers app**, meanwhile, offers estimated eruption times. *Available in the iTunes and Google app stores and at www.yellowstonewildlife.com.*

WolfQuest is an utterly addictive online game developed by the Minnesota Zoo, an educational tool that puts the player in control of

LEAVE NO TRACE

Leave No Trace principles are the law of the land in Yellowstone and Grand Teton. The "take only photos, leave only footprints" ethic applies in the frontcountry as well as in the backcountry. Below are a few basic tenets of Leave No Trace. Talk with rangers or visit www.lnt.org for a more detailed rundown.

- Pack out **everything** that you pack in— this includes all trash, leftover food, toilet paper, and other hygiene products.
- Minimize the impact of tents and campfires. Camp close together, and if you must have a fire, keep it small, using only dead and downed wood.
- Dispose of human waste properly by digging, then covering a six- to eight-inch hole, at least 200 yards from camp, trails, and water sources.
- Remove nothing from the parks in either the frontcountry or the backcountry. Don't pocket stones, don't pick wildflowers, don't take home that nifty elk antler you found near camp. Removing artifacts from the park is illegal, and rangers are far from lenient when it comes to this sort of vandalism.
- Never, under any circumstances, throw trash, rocks, or other debris into a thermal feature.

a Yellowstone wolf, hunting, mating, and chasing coyotes across an astoundingly accurate digital representation of the park's Northern Range. *www.wolfquest.org.*

The **"Backpacking 101"** feature from *Backpacker* magazine is a useful resource for those heading into the backcountry for the first time, a briefing on everything from basic first aid to quality trail-mix recipes. *www.backpacker.com/backpacking101.*

⌖ PARK PUBLICATIONS AND OTHER VISITOR INFO

Rangers at the entrance stations hand out maps and copies of the parks' newspapers, which are published seasonally and print up-to-date lists of seasonal ranger programs, construction updates, and safety bulletins.

Short trail-guide pamphlets to Yellowstone's major boardwalk areas are available at each of the visitor centers for a 50¢ donation. You can also pick them up on the honor system at each of the trailheads. The Yellowstone Association runs impressively well-stocked bookstores at each of the park villages, plus at Madison, Norris, and West Thumb.

Worth picking up in Grand Teton are the pocket-sized guidebooks published by the Grand Teton Natural History Association. These volumes are concise but impressively researched introductions to the park's history, plant and animal life, geology, and waterways.

The chambers of commerce and tourist bureaus in the gateway towns are never short on literature of the pamphlet variety.

Cody Country Chamber of Commerce: 836 Sheridan Ave., Cody, WY; 307/587–2777; www.codychamber.org

Cooke City/Colter Pass/Silver Gate Chamber of Commerce: 206 Main St., Cooke City, MT; 406/838–2495; www.cookecitychamber.org

Gardiner Chamber of Commerce: 216 Park St., Gardiner, MT; 406/848–7971; www.gardinerchamber.com

Jackson Hole Central Reservations: 888/838–6606; www.jacksonholewy.com

Jackson Hole & Greater Yellowstone Visitor Center: 532 N. Cache St., Jackson, WY; 307/733–3316; www.jacksonholechamber.com

Park County Travel Council: 836 Sheridan Ave., Cody, WY; 307/587–2297; www.yellowstonecountry.org

West Yellowstone Chamber of Commerce: 30 Yellowstone Ave., West Yellowstone, MT; 406/646–7701; www.westyellowstonechamber.com

Yellowstone Country Regional Tourism Commission: 800/736–5276; www.yellowstonecountry.net

⌖ SAFETY

It can't be overstated: Yellowstone and Grand Teton national parks can be dangerous places, and your safety is never guaranteed. A little caution and a little education go a long way, though. **Stay cautious and alert around thermal features.** Don't leave the boardwalks in areas where they're provided, keep an eye on kids, never bring pets into thermal areas, and never try to touch or swim in a hot spring.

Rubbernecking causes car accidents in both parks. When stopping the car to snap that elk herd, be sure to use the pull-outs or, at least, signal and pull as far onto the road's shoulder as possible.

HEALTH ISSUES

Giardia is a rather awful, though rarely fatal, condition caused by a parasite occasionally found in untreated drinking water. Giardia parasites travel in the fecal matter of animals like deer, sheep, and beavers, and are most commonly passed on via tainted food and water. Symptoms include explosive diarrhea, stomach pain, and nausea that can last six weeks untreated. Avoid giardia by treating your water in the backcountry, either by boiling it or preferably with a reliable commercial water filter. If you begin showing symptoms (which can manifest themselves weeks later), seek treatment from a doctor.

Visitors to Greater Yellowstone from lower elevations should be conscious of **altitude sickness.** Mild cases are not uncommon in mountain visitors, and symptoms include headaches, dizziness, and fatigue. Avoid it by drinking plenty of water and, if possible, spending a night or two at moderate elevations (say, 6,200 feet at Mammoth) before heading to higher ones. Severe cases are generally limited to high-elevation hikers and climbers, who risk fluid in the lungs and swelling of the brain by ascending too high too fast.

Hypothermia is a danger to hikers, particularly in cold, wet weather. Shivering, slurred speech, and drowsiness are symptoms of this condition. Prevent hypothermia by dressing appropriately for the Yellowstone climate. Wear a hat, avoid cotton materials that easily soak up water, and dress in layers, preferably with a windbreak layer. Boaters and paddlers in the parks' cold lakes face a particular risk, and should consider wearing a wetsuit. Severe hypothermia, characterized by disorientation, rigid muscles, and a slow pulse, requires evacuation and medical attention. But mild to moderate hypothermia can be treated in the field by sheltering, drying, and slowly warming the victim, most effectively with hot fluids and shared body heat. A hypothermia victim needs an increase in core warmth, not surface warmth, so rubbing the skin is ineffective and can even be dangerous.

The rodent-carried **hantavirus** has been responsible for more than a dozen human deaths in Wyoming and Montana since the early 1990s. The respiratory disease is most often contracted by handling or inhaling particles of urine, feces, and saliva from infected deer mice. Store food in rodent-proof containers, and camp away from potential mouse burrows like wood piles. Absolutely avoid contact with mouse droppings, which look like black or dark brown grains of rice. Should you encounter any in a room or cabin, leave immediately and notify the staff. Should you come down with flulike symptoms following potential exposure, seek medical attention immediately.

Though **ticks** are common in Yellowstone—particularly in the high grass of the prairies—tick-borne diseases like Lyme disease are very rarely reported. Still, it's good to take precautions. Avoid loose clothing. Tuck your shirt into your pants and your pants into your boots. Wear an insect repellent containing DEET and check your clothes and skin thoroughly after hiking. Remove any ticks promptly, pulling them straight up from as close to the skin as pos-

The long, thrilling howl of wolves often echoes around parts of Yellowstone and Grand Teton.

sible, preferably with blunt tweezers or forceps. Apply antiseptic ointment to the area, and inspect to see whether any mouthparts were left in the skin. If they were, or if you begin to show a rash or run a fever, see a doctor.

WILDLIFE

Hiking and camping in bear country present unique dangers that can be minimized with some preparation. For starters, **don't hike alone.** Make noise when approaching blind corners and dense underbrush. Bear bells aren't all that effective, and, frankly, they're a little goofy. An occasional shout will do the trick. Avoid hiking after dark, and always carry a cayenne-based bear spray, available at the general stores.

Don't leave food out at camp and never store food in your tent, either in the frontcountry or the backcountry. Bears have a super powerful sense of smell, and they can smell food from literally miles away. At backcountry campsites in particular, use common sense in food preparation and storage. Store and prepare food downwind from your campsite, and don't wear to bed the same clothes you cooked in. Use a bear-proof storage container (mandatory and supplied in Grand Teton) or bundle and tie your food to the bear poles provided at most Yellowstone backcountry campsites.

Grizzly bear males are also known as boars.

Watch for signs—tracks and droppings—and be willing to turn back rather than risk a confrontation. Never approach a bear in the frontcountry or the backcountry, and never feed a bear under any circumstances. A fed bear, as they say, is a dead bear, since the park service is forced to euthanize bears that lose their fear of humans. Stephen Herrero's *Bear Attacks: Their Causes and Avoidance* is an excellent intro to bear country, and it's available in the Yellowstone Association's bookstores.

If you spot a bear, give it at least 100 yards of clearance. If you encounter a bear at a closer distance, face it and back away slowly, making some noise or speaking firmly at a moderate volume. **Don't run,** which could trigger the bear's instinct to chase. Playing dead while protecting your head and neck is a last resort should the bear charge. Also remember, though cubs may look harmless, mama is never far behind, and sows are fiercely protective of their cubs.

More park visitors are injured by bison and other animals each year than by bears. (Bison are unpredictable and not at all as docile as they look.) **Stay at least 25 yards away from other wildlife,** and at least 100 yards away from wolves.

RECOMMENDED BOOKS AND FILMS

BOOKS

Anderson, Roger, and Carol Shively, *A Ranger's Guide to Yellowstone Day Hikes*, 2000. A hiking guide you can read for pleasure, this thin volume is rich with stories about Yellowstone's human and natural history.

Black, George, *Empire of Shadows*, 2012. That rarest of sub-genres: a detailed public-lands history that's also a page-turner. Black's chronicle of the exploration and early commercialization of Yellowstone paints rich historical characters and examines what motivated them.

Burt, Struthers, *Diary of a Dude Wrangler*, 1924. Burt's surprisingly heartfelt dude-ranching memoir dishes on Jackson's then-fledgling tourist trade. It's out of print, so look for this at libraries or used-book sellers.

Cahill, Tim, *Lost in My Own Backyard: A Walk in Yellowstone National Park*, 2004. One of our savviest travel writers dozes off next to feeding grizzlies and gets spooked by stone goblins while exploring and explaining the million-plus acres out his back door.

Peacock, Doug and Andrea, *The Essential Grizzly: The Mingled Fates of Men and Bears*, 2006. Taking a broad look at human/grizzly relations—the good, the bad, and the ugly—the authors argue that mankind benefits from occasionally abdicating the top of the food chain. Yellowstone's grizzlies in particular are a central part of the book.

Smith, Douglas W., and Gary Ferguson, *Decade of the Wolf: Returning the Wild to Yellowstone*, 2005. A biologist and a nature writer recap the drama that led to wolf reintroduction, and examine the cascading effects on Yellowstone's ecosystem 10 years later.

Turner, Jack, *Teewinot*, 2000, and *Travels in Greater Yellowstone*, 2008. With the patience of a philosopher and the lyricism of a poet, climbing guide Turner examines, respectively, Teton climbing culture and the complexities of Yellowstone's ecosystems. Each is a deeply personal introduction to the area.

Whittlesey, Lee, *Death in Yellowstone: Accidents and Foolhardiness in the First National Park*, 1995. Who'd have thought we'd figure out so many ways to die inside 3,500 square miles? The park historian's morbid-but-fascinating catalog counts them down.

FILMS

Christmas in Yellowstone, 2006. Set to a lush orchestral score, this masterpiece collection of moving images captures the silent, snow-covered kingdom that is Yellowstone in winter.

In the Valley of the Wolves, 2007. This brilliantly shot documentary traces the rise and fall of Yellowstone's Druid wolf pack, with enough drama and spectacle to rival any Hollywood epic.

Index

The Teton range reflected in
a beaver pond, Grand Teton
National Park.

A

Abyss Pool *101*
admission to the parks *326–327*
aerial tram *182, 238, 239*
air travel *324–325*
Albright Visitor Center *143,
    144, 145*
alpine forget-me-not *314*
Alpine House *277*
altitude sickness *336*
Amangani *278*
Antelope Flats *223*
Antler Inn *278*
Artist Paint Pots *113*
Artist Point *172*
ARTwalks *246*
aspen trees *300–301*

B

backpacking, online
    information about *333,
    334; permits for 332–333;
    also hiking trails*
Backpacking 101 *334*
ballooning *245–246*
Bar J Chuckwagon *247*
Bear Den gift shop *85*
bears *312, 328; safety
    precautions regarding 338*
Bear's Den Cinema *252*
Beartooth Scenic Highway *326*
Beauty Pool *60–61*
Beaver Ponds Trail *152*
Bechler region *100*
Beehive Geyser *71, 120*
Beryl Spring *116*
bighorn sheep *310*
Bill Cody Ranch *258*
Billings, Montana *326*
birding, Grand Teton *223;
    Yellowstone's Upper Loop 175*

Biscuit Basin *75*
bison *90–91, 117, 157, 158,
    180, 186–187, 306–307; safety
    precautions regarding 338*
black bears *312*
Black Canyon of the
    Yellowstone *26–27, 154*
Black Growler Steam Vent *112*
Black Sand Basin *75*
Black Tail Butte *225*
Blue Funnel Spring *104–105*
Blue Heron Bar *227*
boating, Grand Teton *217,
    220, 221–223; Yellowstone's
    Lower Loop 97–98, 109;
    permits for 330, 332*
bobcats *181*
Boiling River *155*
books on Yellowstone area *339*
Bozeman, Montana *324, 325*
Bozeman Yellowstone
    International Airport *324*
Bridge Bay Marina *97*
Bridger Gondola *239*
Brink of the Lower Falls *170, 172*
Brink of the Upper Falls *172–173*
brucellosis disease *307*
Buffalo Bill Dam and
    Reservoir *257*
Buffalo Bill Center of the West
    254–255, 256, 257, 259
Buffalo Bill Scenic
    Byway *258, 325*
Bunnery, The *247*
bungee trampoline *239*
Bunsen Peak Road *152, 154*
Bunsen Peak Trail *152*

C

Cabin Creek Scarp Area *251*
Calcite Springs Overlook *161*

campgrounds *42, 213, 251, 280–281, 284–287; price categories 18, 267*

Canary Spring *136–137, 138–139, 145*

canoeing and kayaking, Grand Teton *217; Jackson 245; Yellowstone's Lower Loop 98, 106, 109*

Canyon Cabins *273*

Canyon Campground *280*

Canyon Corral *175*

Canyon Lodge *273*

Canyon Lodge Cafeteria and Deli *175*

Canyon Lodge Dining Room *175*

Canyon Soda Fountain *175*

Canyon Village *168–175, 273*

Canyon Visitor Education Center *173*

car travel, in the parks *326–327, 329–330; to the parks 325–326*

Cascade Corner *100*

Cascade Lodge *273*

Cassie's Supper Club & Dance Hall *258*

Castle Geyser *62–63, 75, 118*

chambers of commerce *335*

Chapel of the Transfiguration *210, 211–212*

Chittenden Road *174*

"Christmas" in Yellowstone *320*

Churning Cauldron *94*

Cistern Springs *112*

Clark, William *47*

Clepsydra Geyser *64–65, 81*

climate *318, 319*

Coachman Lounge *252*

Cody, Wyoming *253; dining 258, 260; drive to the parks from 325; exploring around town 257–258; festivals 320, 324; map of 253; nightlife 258; outdoor activities 258*

Cody Country Chamber of Commerce *335*

Cody Firearms Museum *257*

Cody Nite Rodeo *257–258*

Cody Stampede Rodeo *258, 320*

Cody Trolley Tours *257*

Colter, John *48*

Colter Bay Cabins *275*

Colter Bay Corral *227*

Colter Bay Marina *217*

Colter Bay Village *203*

Colter Bay Visitor Center *203*

Constant Geyser *112*

Continental Divide Dog Sled Adventures *183*

Cooke City/Colter Pass/ Silver Gate Chamber of Commerce *335*

Couloir *247–248*

Cowboy Up Hang Gliding *245*

coyotes *315*

Craig Thomas Discovery and Visitor Center *204, 207*

Crater Hills Geyser *92–93*

cross-country skiing *186–187*

cruises *221*

Crystal Falls *173*

Cunningham Cabin *207*

cutthroat trout *315*

cycling and mountain biking, Grand Teton *223; Yellowstone's Lower Loop 85; Yellowstone's Upper Loop 155, 174*

D

Daisy Geyser *123*

dining, best places to eat in the parks *43; Cody 258, 260;*

Gardiner 261; Grand Teton
227, 229; Jackson 247–249;
price categories 18; West
Yellowstone 252; Yellowstone's
Lower Loop 85–86, 99–100,
110; Yellowstone's Upper
Loop 156, 167, 175
dog sledding 183, 245, 322
Dornan's Adventure Sports 223
Dornan's Chuckwagon 43, 227
Dornan's Pizza & Pasta
Company 227–228
Dornan's Scenic Float Trips 222
Dornan's Spur Ranch Cabins
275
Doublet Pool hot spring 125
Dragon's Mouth Spring 94
Dunraven Lodge 273
Dunraven Pass 174

E

eagles 311
Earthquake Lake Visitor
Center 250–251
earthquakes 251, 295–296
Echinus Geyser 112
Elephant Back 95, 97
elk 117, 140, 180, 199, 230–231,
234–235, 236, 290–291, 313
Elkfest 237, 320, 321, 324
Elk Island 221
Emerald Pool 75
Emerald Spring 112
Engelmann spruce 302
Everts, Truman 154
Excelsior Geyser 74, 75

F

Fairy Falls Trail 82, 84
fauna see wildlife

festivals and seasonal
events 320, 324
Firehole Lake 81
Firehole Lake Drive 81
Firehole River 73, 74, 114–115
Firehole Spring 129
fir trees 314
fishing, best fishing location
43; Grand Teton 222; Jackson
245; permits for 332; West
Yellowstone 251; Yellowstone's
Lower Loop 97–98, 114–115,
117; Yellowstone's Upper
Loop 167, 175
Fishing Bridge 95
Fishing Bridge General
Store 95, 99
Fishing Bridge Visitor Center 95
Fishing Cone 101, 106
Flagg Ranch Resort 212, 275
flora 297–303, 314
Fountain Flat Drive 81
Fountain Geyser 81
Fountain Paint Pots 81, 131
foxes 181
fumaroles 132

G

Gallatin Skyline Trail 154
Gardiner, Montana 260;
dining 261; exploring
around town 261; festivals
324; lodging 279–280
Gardiner Brewfest 324
Gardiner Chamber of
Commerce 335
Garnet Canyon 213
gentian 302
geology of Yellowstone
region 294–296
George, "Digger" Jerry 107

geothermal features *118–134*
Geyser Grill *85*
Geyser Hill *71*
Geyser Kayak Tours *98, 109*
geysers *70–82, 84–85, 101,*
    112, 120–124, 133
ghost village *251*
Giant Geyser *71, 72*
Giantess Geyser *71*
giardia *335–336*
Gibbon Falls *113, 116*
Gibbon Hill Geyser Group *124*
glaciation *296*
Glade Creek Trail *212*
Grand Canyon of the
    Yellowstone *168–175*
Grand Geyser *71*
Grand Prismatic Spring
    75, 76–77, 128
Grand Targhee Resort *243*
Grand Teton Lodge
    Company *222, 265, 330*
Grand Teton National Park
    192–197; admission to
    326–327; autumn colors
    214–215; dining 227–229;
    driving in 329–330; exploring
    203–212; guided tours 226,
    330; hiking trails 212–213,
    217; historic sights 207–212;
    land-based activities
    223–227; lodging 275–277,
    284–285; maps of 19, 205;
    natural history of 198–201;
    watersports 217, 220–223
Grandview Point *170*
Grant Village *100–101, 270, 273*
Grant Village Dining Room *110*
Grant Village Grill *110*
Grant Village Lodge *270*
Grant Village Visitor Center *106*
Grassy Lake Reservoir *212*

Grassy Lake Road *212*
Great Fountain Geyser *55,*
    78–79, 81
Grizzly & Wolf Discovery
    Center *250*
grizzly bears *312, 328*
Gros Ventre Campground *284*
Gros Ventre Slide *207*
guided tours *226, 330*

H

hang gliding *245*
hantavirus *336*
Hayden, Ferdinand *49*
Hayden Valley *90–93, 94–95*
Headwaters Lodge & Cabins
    at Flagg Ranch *212, 275,*
    337–338
health issues *335–336, 338*
Heart Lake Trail *108–109*
Heart Mountain Interpretive
    Center *258*
Heather James Fine Art *246*
Hebgen Lake *251*
Hebgen Lake earthquake *251*
Hidden Falls *40, 213*
hiking trails, best trails
    24–27, 40–41; Grand Teton
    212–213, 217; Yellowstone's
    Lower Loop 82, 84–85,
    95, 97, 108–109, 116–117;
    Yellowstone's Upper Loop
    152, 154, 165–166, 173–174
Historic Fort Yellowstone *145*
Historic Madison Hotel *279*
Historic Yellow Bus Tours *42, 99*
history of Yellowstone
    region *46–59*
Hoodoos, the *148*
horseback riding, Cody
    258; Grand Teton 227;

Jackson 246; Yellowstone's
    Upper Loop 166, 175
hot springs 125–130
Hotel Terra 278
Howard Eaton Trail 174–175
huckleberry 314
Hymen Terrace 144
hypothermia 336

I

ice-skating 155–156
Imperial Geyser 84
Indian Creek Campground
    280–281
Indian paintbrush 288–289, 303
Inside Yellowstone podcasts 333
Inspiration Point (Grand
    Teton) 204, 213
Inspiration Point (Yellowstone)
    40–41, 170, 172, 213
Internet access 320
Irma, The 260
Iron Horse Bar & Grille 261

J

Jackson, Wyoming 232–233;
    the arts 246; dining 247–249;
    exploring around town
    233–239; festivals 320, 324;
    lodging 277–279; map of 236;
    nightlife 246–247; ski resorts
    239–243; summer activities
    245–246; Town Square 232,
    233; winter activities 243, 245
Jackson Hole Aerial
    Tram 238, 239
Jackson Hole Airport 324–325
Jackson Hole & Greater
    Yellowstone Visitor
    Center 233, 335

Jackson Hole Center
    for the Arts 246
Jackson Hole Central
    Reservations 267, 335
Jackson Hole Iditarod Sled
    Dog Tours 183, 245
Jackson Hole Mountain
    Resort 238, 239, 240
Jackson Hole Paragliding 245
Jackson Hole Resort Store 243
Jackson Hole Snowmobile
    Tours 243, 245
Jackson Hole Sports 239
Jackson Hole Wildlife Film
    Festival 324
Jackson Hole WinterFest 324
Jackson Lake 203, 217, 220, 221
Jackson Lake Dam 203–204
Jackson Lake Lodge 275–276
Jackson Lake Lodge Corral 227
Jackson National Fish
    Hatchery 245
Jenny Lake 204, 206, 213
Jenny Lake Boating
    Company 221
Jenny Lake Lodge 34,
    36–37, 228, 276
Jenny Lake Campground
    282–283, 284
Jenny Lake Lodge
    Dining Room 228
Jenny Lake Loop 213
Jenny Lake Ranger Station 204
Jenny Lake Visitor Center 204
John Colter Café Court 228
Junior Ranger program 82

K

kayaking see canoeing
    and kayaking
Kelly Warm Spring 222–223

Kepler Cascades *82*
Kite Hill Cemetery *145*

L

Lake General Store *99*
Lake Hotel Deli *99*
Lake Hotel Dining Room *43, 99*
Lake House Restaurant *110*
Lake Lodge Cabins *268–269*
Lake Lodge Cafeteria *99–100*
Lake Overlook *106*
Lake shuttle *98*
Lakeshore Geyser *101*
Lake Village *86–100, 268–270*
Lake Yellowstone Cabins *269*
Lake Yellowstone Hotel *269–270*
Lamar Valley *32–33, 157, 158,
   161*
Laurance S. Rockefeller Preserve
   Interpretive Center *203, 207*
Leave No Trace principle *334*
Leek's Marina *217*
Leek's Pizzeria *228*
Leigh Lake *217*
Lewis, Meriwether *47*
Lewis Falls *106*
Lewis Lake boat launch *109*
Liberty Cap *144*
license requirements *330,
   332–333*
Lizard Creek Campground *284*
lodgepole pines *298–299*
lodging, best lodging options
   *34–37, 43; campgrounds 42,
   213, 251, 280–281, 284–287;
   Gardiner 279–280; Grand
   Teton 275–277, 284–285;
   "inside or outside the park"
   issue 264–265; Jackson
   277–279; lodges, hotels, and
   inns 267–280; price categories*

*18, 267; reservations 265, 267;
   West Yellowstone 279; winter
   190; Yellowstone's Lower
   Loop 267–270, 280, 285–287;
   Yellowstone's Upper Loop 270,
   272–273, 280–281, 286–287*
Lonesomehurst Campground
   251
Lone Star Geyser *84–85, 122,
   124*
Lookout Point *170*
Lower Falls *22–23, 168, 170–172*
Lower Geyser Basin *81*
lupine *303*
Lyme disease *336, 338*
lynx *181*

M

Mad River Boat Trips *245*
Madison *110–111*
Madison Amphitheater *113*
Madison Campground *280*
Madison Information Station
   113
Madison River *43*
Mammoth Cabins *270*
Mammoth Hot Springs *130,
   140–156*
Mammoth Hot Springs Hotel
   270, 272
Mammoth Hot Springs Hotel
   Dining Room *156*
Mammoth Hot Springs Ice
   Rink *155–156*
Mammoth Terrace Grill *156*
Manges Cabin *211*
Mangy Moose *247*
Map Room *156*
Maude Noble Cabin *211*
Meadows Camping Area,
   The *213*

Menor's Ferry *211*
Middle Teton Glacier *196*
Midway Bluff *75*
Midway Geyser Basin *75*
Miller Ranch *236*
Million Dollar Cowboy Bar
  246–247
Mill Iron Ranch *246*
Minerva Terrace *145*
Mocha Mamma's *252*
Montana Whitewater *251–252*
Monument Geyser Basin *30–31,*
  116–117
Moore, Shane *242*
moose *315*
Moose, Wyoming *204*
Moose Falls *108, 110, 176*
Moran, Thomas *153*
Mormon Row *202, 208–209, 212*
Morning Glory Pool *30–31, 67,*
  72, 75
Moulton Barn *202, 208–209, 212*
Moulton Ranch Cabins *276*
mountain biking see cycling
  and mountain biking
mountain coaster *243*
mountaineering *225, 226*
mountain lions *313*
Mountain Sports School *239*
Mount Moran *192–193,*
  218–219, 244
Mount Washburn *42, 173–174*
movies on Yellowstone area
  339
movie theaters *252*
mud pots *131*
Mud Volcano *94, 96*
Mural Room *228–229*
Museum of the National
  Park Ranger *113*
Mystic Falls *40–41*
Mystic Falls Trail *84*

N

Narrows, The *161*
National Elk Refuge *230–231,*
  234–235, 236
National Museum of
  Wildlife Art *233, 236*
Natural Bridge *95*
Nez Percé Indians *50*
Nordic Center *239*
Norris Geyser Basin *110–117,*
  142
Norris Museum *112*
North Rim Trail *173*

O

O.A.R.S. *106*
Obsidian Cliff *148, 149*
Obsidian Dining Room *85–86*
Ojo Caliente Hot Springs
  81–82
Old Faithful *68, 69, 71, 80*
Old Faithful Basin Store *86*
Old Faithful Inn *34–35, 267*
Old Faithful Inn Dining
  Room *86*
Old Faithful Lodge Cabins *267*
Old Faithful Lodge Cafeteria
  and Bake Shop *86*
Old Faithful Snow Lodge *268*
Old Faithful Snow Lodge
  Cabins *268*
Old Faithful Village *66–86*
Old Faithful Visitor Education
  Center *71, 82*
Old Gardiner Road *155*
Old Trail Town *257*
Old West Dinner Cookout
  166
online resources *333–334*
Opal Terrace *144*
Osprey Falls Trail *154*

otters *181*
Oxbow Bend *192–193,*
  218–219, 223, 224

P

Paintbrush Divide Trail
  24–25, 213, 217
paragliding *245*
Park County Travel Council *335*
Peaks Restaurant, The *229*
Pebble Creek Campground *281*
Pebble Creek Trail *165*
permit requirements
  330, 332–333
Petrified Forest *165–166*
Petrified Tree *161, 163–165*
pets in the parks *327*
Phil Baux Park *239*
phones *319–320*
pikas *315*
pine trees *298–299*
Pinwheel Geyser *112*
Pioneer Grill *229*
plantlife *297–303, 314*
Pocket Basin *81*
price categories *18, 267*
publications *334–335*

R

Rabbit Creek Thermal Area *125*
rafting, Grand Teton *221–222;*
  Jackson 245; West Yellowstone
  251–252
Rainbow Point Campground *251*
Ranch House at Colter Bay *229*
Reamer, Robert *156, 269*
Red Rock Point *170*
Rendezvous Mountain *239*
Rendezvous River Sports *245*
Riddle Lake Trail *108*

River Road *223*
River Runners' Museum *236, 239*
Riverside Cottages *279–280*
Riverside Geyser *73, 75*
Roaring Mountain fumarole *132*
rock climbing *226*
Rockefeller Parkway *212*
rodeos *257–258, 320*
Roosevelt, Theodore *160*
Roosevelt Arch *261*
Roosevelt Corral *166*
Roosevelt Lodge *272*
Roosevelt Lodge Dining
  Room *167*

S

safety concerns *133,*
  190, 335–336, 338
sagebrush *314*
sailboat trips *221*
Salt Lake City, Utah *325*
Sapphire Pool *54, 75*
Sedge Bay Boat Launch *98*
Serenity Bistro *252*
Sevenmile Hole *174*
Shoshone Geyser Basin *84*
Shoshone Lake *109*
Sierra Trading Post
  Outlet Store *258*
Signal Mountain Cabins *276–277*
Signal Mountain Marina *217*
Signal Mountain Retreats *277*
Signal Mountain
  Summit Road *204*
Silver Cord Cascade *173*
Simmons, "Black George" *216*
skiing, cross-country
  186–187; Jackson Hole ski
  resorts 239–241, 243
Sleeping Indian Pond *245*
sleigh rides *230–231, 236*

Slough Creek *42, 167*
Slough Creek Campground *281*
Snake River *204*
Snake River Angler *222*
Snake River Brewing Company *248*
Snake River Grill *248*
Snake River Lodge and Spa *278*
Snow King Resort *243*
snowcoaches *182*
snowmobiling *184–185;*
   Jackson 243, 245
snowshoeing *188–189*
Sour Lake *94*
South Rim Trail *173*
Spalding Bay *217*
Sprint into Yellowstone Birding
   & Wildlife Festival, Cody *324*
spruce trees *302*
stagecoach rides *166*
Steamboat Geyser *112*
String Lake *217*
String Lake Picnic Area *222*
subalpine fir *314*
Sulfur Cauldron *128*
Surging Spring *101*
swans *305*
swimming, Grand Teton
   222–223; Yellowstone's
   Lower Loop 109–110, 117

T
Taylor Piggot Gallery *246*
Terrace Mountain *148*
Teton Fault *295–296*
Teton Park Road *38–39*
Teton Science Schools *222*
Teton Thai *248*
Teton Treehouse, A *43, 279*
Teton Village *239, 241*
thermophiles *127, 292, 293*

Thorofare Trail *97*
Three Bear Lodge *279*
Thumb Paint Pots *101*
ticks *336, 338*
Togwotee Adventures *243, 245*
Togwotee Pass *245*
Tower Fall *161, 162*
Tower-Roosevelt *156–167*
Trapper Grill, The *229*
Treetop Adventure Park *243*
Triangle X Ranch *222, 277*
Trio *249*
trout *315*
trumpeter swans *305*
Two Ocean Lake *223*

U
Uncle Tom's Trail *172*
Undine Falls *148*
Union Falls *109*
Upper Geyser Basin *28–29, 71*
Upper Falls *170, 172–173*

V
Virginia Cascade *113*
visitor information *334–335*
volcanic eruptions *294–295*

W
Wapiti Lake Trail *174*
Washburn, Henry *49*
websites *333–334*
West Thumb Geyser Basin
   101–110, 179
West Thumb Kayak Trips *106*
West Thumb Visitor
   Information Station *101*
West Yellowstone, Montana
   249–250; dining 252; exploring

around town 250–251; festivals 324; lodging 279; map of 249; nightlife 252; outdoor activities 251–252

West Yellowstone Chamber of Commerce 335

when to visit 318–319

Whirligig Geyser 112

White Dome Geyser 81

Whitney Western Art Museum 257

wildlife 290–291, 304–313, 315; best wildlife-watching areas 32–33; safety precautions regarding 338; in winter 180–181

Will Dornan's Scenic Float Trips 222

Will Dornan's Snake River Angler 222

winter in Yellowstone 176–191

WolfQuest online game 333–334

wolves 308–309, 337, 338

World Championship Snowmobile Hill Climb 245

Wraith Falls 148

Wyoming Balloon Company 245–246

Wyoming's Rib & Chop House 260

X

Xanterra Parks & Resorts 265, 330

Y

Yellowstone Airport 325

Yellowstone Country Tourism Region 335

Yellowstone Expeditions 36–37, 191

Yellowstone Geysers App 333

Yellowstone Giant Screen Cinema 252

Yellowstone Historic Center 250

Yellowstone hotspot 294–295

Yellowstone Institute 167

Yellowstone Lake 86–89, 94, 98, 109

Yellowstone National Park, admission to 326–327; driving in 327, 329; guided tours 330; map of 19; winter in 176–191; also Yellowstone's Lower Loop; Yellowstone's Upper Loop

Yellowstone National Park Heritage & Research Center 261

Yellowstone Regional Airport 325

Yellowstone River Picnic Area Trail 165

Yellowstone Ski Festival 324

Yellowstone's Lower Loop 60–65; Grant Village and West Thumb 100–110, 270; Lake Village 86–100, 269–270; lodging 267–270, 280, 286–287; Madison and Norris 110–117; map of 66–67; Old Faithful Village 66–86

Yellowstone's Upper Loop 134–139; Canyon Village 168–175; lodging 270, 272–273, 280–281, 286–287; Mammoth Hot Springs 140–156; map of 142–143; Tower-Roosevelt 156–167

Yellowstone Village Inn 280

Yellowstone Wildlife smartphone app 333

Young, Linda 172

Yurt Camp 36–37, 191

⊙ FROM THE PUBLISHER

All photographs in this book are by Jeff Vanuga unless otherwise noted below. Compass American Guides is grateful to the following individuals or organizations for the use of photographs or illustrations:

Greater Yellowstone's History: 47 (both portraits), *Independence National Historic Park, Philadelphia.* 49 (left), *National Archives and Records Administration.* 49 (right), *Public Domain.* 50, 52, and 53, *Library of Congress Prints and Photographs Division.* 54 (top), *Detroit Photographic Co./Library of Congress, Library of Congress Prints and Photographs Division.* 54 (bottom) and 55 (top), *National Park Service.* 55 (bottom), *William Henry Jackson, Library of Congress.* 56, *National Park Service.* 58-59, *Library of Congress Prints and Photographs Division.*

Yellowstone's Lower Loop: 80, *Sharon D./Shutterstock.*

Yellowstone's Upper Loop: 144, *Neal Herbert/NPS, Public Domain.* 153 (all), *Department of the Interior, Yellowstone National Park.* 160, *National Park Service.*

Grand Teton National Park: 213 (bottom) and 217, *National Park Service.*

Gateway Towns: 259, *Nancy McClure.*

Geology, Flora, and Fauna: 310, *Walter Siegmund/wikipedia.org.* 312 (left), 313 (left) and 314 (3rd from top), *National Park Service.* 315 (top), *RG Johnsson/National Park Service.* 315 (2nd from top), *Richard Lake/National Park Service.* 315 (third from top), *Keri Thorp/ National Park Service.* 315 (bottom), *Ragesoss/wikipedia.org.*

⊙ ABOUT THE AUTHOR

A transplanted Midwesterner, **Brian Kevin** first discovered Yellowstone and Grand Teton national parks as a hitchhiking college student more than 15 years ago. As an avid backpacker, Brian has since explored the parks in every season, drawn by the infinite variety of the Greater Yellowstone backcountry.

Brian is the author of *The Footloose American: Following the Hunter S. Thompson Trail across South America.* Brian's writing on travel, culture, and the outdoors has appeared in publications like *Sierra, Outside, Men's Journal, Travel + Leisure,* and others. He's the recipient of the Lowell Thomas Award from the Society of American Travel Writers. Brian lives alternately in Montana and Maine, and www.briankevin.com is his home on the Web.

⊙ ABOUT THE PHOTOGRAPHER

Jeff Vanuga lives in Dubois, Wyoming, and has photographed professionally for more than 25 years. His work has been published worldwide in magazines such as *National Geographic, National Geographic Traveler, Audubon, Field and Stream,* and *Outside.* Companies such as Ford and Patagonia have also used his photographs for advertising media. He has won several major photography awards, including first place in the BBC Wildlife Photographer of the Year and the National Wildlife competitions. He has also hosted TV shows on nature photography for the Outdoor Life channel and leads photography tours around the world for Joseph Van Os Photo Safaris and First Light Photographic Workshops.